Studying Buddhism in Practice

"This volume assembles interesting and colorful pictures of Buddhism as actually practiced by ordinary and ordained people alike. The first-person narratives by long-term specialists draw the reader into sites such as towns and villages, temples and pagodas, funeral grounds and pilgrimage treks. The informative accounts underscore the cultural diversity of Buddhist practices and the importance they hold for the practitioners."

Martin Baumann, *University of Lucerne, Switzerland*

"This text stands out with its unique dual focus on Buddhist practices and on the practices of those who study Buddhism. Readers will learn much from the contributors' descriptions of an array of Buddhist rituals and frank reflections on the scholarly methods they have deployed in their fieldwork around the world."

Christopher Ives, *Stonehill College, USA* and author of *Imperial-Way Zen*

This book introduces the rich realities of the Buddhist tradition and the academic approaches through which they are studied. Based on personal experiences of Buddhism on the ground, it provides a reflective context within which religious practices can be understood and appreciated. The engaging narratives cover a broad range of Buddhist countries and traditions, drawing on fieldwork to explore topics such as ordination, pilgrimage, funerals, gender roles, and film-making. All the entries provide valuable contextual discussion and are accompanied by photographs and suggestions for further reading.

John S. Harding is Associate Professor and Chair of the Religious Studies Department at the University of Lethbridge in Alberta, Canada. His books include *Introduction to the Study of Religion* with Hillary P. Rodrigues (2008) and *Wild Geese: Buddhism in Canada* with Victor Sōgen Hori and Alexander Soucy (2010).

Studying Buddhism in Practice

A volume in the *Studying Religions in Practice* series

Edited by
John S. Harding

Series editor
Hillary P. Rodrigues

LONDON AND NEW YORK

First published 2012
by Routledge
2 Park Square, Milton Park, Abingdon, Oxon OX14 4RN

Simultaneously published in the USA and Canada
by Routledge
711 Third Avenue, New York, NY 10017

Routledge is an imprint of the Taylor & Francis Group, an informa business

British Library Cataloguing in Publication Data
A catalogue record for this book is available from the British Library

Library of Congress Cataloging in Publication Data
Studying Buddhism in practice / edited by John S. Harding.
p. cm. -- (Religions in practice series)
Includes bibliographical references.
1. Buddhism--Customs and practices. 2. Buddhism and culture.
I. Harding, John S., 1971–
BQ4975.S78 2011 294.3'4--dc23
2011026800

ISBN: 978-0-415-46485-7 (hbk)
ISBN: 978-0-415-46486-4 (pbk)
ISBN: 978-0-203-14396-4 (ebk)

Typeset in Times New Roman and Gill Sans
by Bookcraft Ltd, Stroud Gloucestershire

Printed and bound in Great Britain by the MPG Books Group

Dedicated to William R. LaFleur
1936–2010

Contents

List of illustrations

Series preface

Studying Religions in Practice

General editor: Hillary P. Rodrigues

The intent of this new series is to assemble an assortment of texts that primarily instruct by addressing two aspects of human activity. One aspect is the practice of religion, and the other is how such practice is studied. Although these books may be profitably consulted on their own, they are ideal supplements to a comprehensive introductory textbook on each of the traditions in question. This is because introductory texts are rarely able to attend adequately to the range of activities that are integral features of most religious traditions. However, religious practice is a vast field of study, and each anthology in this series makes no claim to providing a complete picture of either the religion it addresses or its rich assortment of practices. Instead, the objective in this series is to provide the reader with vignettes of religious practices within particular traditions, as viewed through the experiences of scholars engaged in the study of these religions. As such, the series offers readers a window onto both the "doings of religion," and the scholarly study of those doings.

As scholars who study religion in its varied dimensions, and as instructors who teach about religion, we routinely scout for resources to enhance our students' learning experience. We wish to teach them about various religions, but also to teach them about the scholarly endeavor of studying religion. Introductory textbooks, however comprehensive they might be in providing necessary factual and foundational information, are typically unable to convey the richness of religious life as experienced by practitioners. By necessity, introductory textbooks tend to favor history, intellectual developments, and teachings from written sources of and about the tradition. Even when they address religious practice, the tone in these textbooks is generally distant and explanatory, rather than descriptively engaging and evocative. Additionally, since the author's persona and presence are often excised from the accounts, these books do little to get across to students what scholars who engage in research actually do and experience. This series is designed to address some of these lacunae.

Each book in this series contains an assortment of pieces written specifically for the anthology in question by established scholars in their field. Other series that focus on practice tend to be collections of translations of religious texts about religious practices, or are anthologies of classic articles previously published in scholarly journals. Texts of the former type are actually still slanted to the textual tradition, while those of the latter type do not have novice students as their intended audience. The essays in the volumes of this series are purposely crafted differently from typical articles published in scholarly journals, chapters in edited academic volumes, or papers presented at scholarly conferences. They are even different in style from what one might find in textbooks and ethnographic anthropological literature, although recent writings from the latter category are probably closest in stylistic character. The writings in these collections derive from the memories, notes, photos, videos, and suchlike of scholars who were in the process of studying, and who still continue to study, some aspect of religious practice.

The sensibilities within, and tone of, these writings are partly derived from postmodern orientations that indicate that, regardless of whether one is an insider or an outsider, one's understanding of reality is always partial. A pervasive and generally erroneous belief is that insiders to a tradition (i.e., adherents) know the *real* meaning of what is transpiring when they engage in religious activities. However, even for religious insiders, that is, believers and participants in a religious practice – such as a pilgrimage or rite of passage – the understanding of the phenomenon they are experiencing is always mediated by their own backgrounds, cultural familiarity, age, experience, degree of interest in their religion, and so on. They do not necessarily know "the" meaning of what is going on, simply because they are insiders. Each insider's understanding is partial. Nevertheless, one effective way to learn about religious practice would be to read about these activities from the perspective of insiders. But the volumes in this series are not collected writings by religious insiders about their practices, however valuable and interesting such accounts might be. Rather, these are writings by persons engaged in the academic study of religion.

Those who embark on the scholarly study of religious phenomena are often outsiders (although not exclusively so), and place themselves in an unusual position. They often seek to understand as much as they can by engaging deeply with the phenomenon studied (striving to become akin to insiders), but then also attempt to convey what they have understood to others (typically fellow outsiders). They may read the literature of the religion, study the ancient languages of its scriptural texts, learn local contemporary languages, travel to distant places, and live among the cultures where the religion is found and practiced. In certain respects, this often makes them more informed than the unschooled insider. Anthropologists refer to the process of immersing oneself within a culture, while maintaining a scholarly stance, as participant observation. Although not all of the contributors to these anthologies utilize a robust anthropological field methodology, they all utilize the approach of participation, observation, and reporting back on what they have experienced, observed, and reflected upon.

The final category of reflection is particularly significant when distinguishing the insider's experience from that of the scholar. Religious practitioners need not report on their experiences to anyone. Their religious activities typically emerge within the framework of their cultures. Their lives are affected in particular ways during the course of their activities, and these effects influence and orchestrate the practitioners' subsequent thoughts and actions. These processes work to sustain and transform the cultural matrix of the practitioners. In contrast to this, scholars immerse themselves into the practitioners' religious culture and patterns of activity, seek to inform themselves about the traditions that they are studying, and strive to extricate themselves from those contexts to report back to their own milieu on what they have learned. Unlike the conventional scholarly formats in which they report their findings, which may include reading papers at academic conferences, publishing articles in peer-reviewed journals, writing book-length monographs, or contributing chapters to edited scholarly volumes, the contributions in these collections are perhaps unique in character. The authors are expected to reveal something about their process of engagement with the activities they study. The discipline of religious studies is often misunderstood. Some people think it is religious education, others that it is akin to theology. Neither view is true, for the study of religion is not conducted to inculcate the values or beliefs of a particular religious tradition, and it does not have the objective of developing the religious content of a particular religion. The study of religion takes religion in all of its manifestations, including religious education and theology, as its object of study. Scholars of religion attempt to understand, with a vigorous blend of objectivity and empathetic curiosity, all facets of the human religious response. The methodological tools for such study may be drawn from other disciplines such as anthropology, sociology, literary criticism, history, psychology, and so on, often selected because they are well suited to the religious phenomenon under consideration. As previously mentioned, since the focus of the contributions in these anthologies is on contemporary practices, the methods of participant observation central to the discipline of anthropology are highlighted here. This does not mean that all the scholars featured in these volumes are anthropologists, or even that their primary methodology is anthropological. However, the basis of their narratives is an anthropologically grounded experience of being scholars who are active participants in some phenomenon related to the practice of religion, which they are attempting to learn about, understand, and eventually convey to others.

Studying religious practice can be a messy and challenging process. One does not always know what to expect, where to go to best observe it, where to situate oneself during a rite, the degree to which one should participate in the practice, the amount of primary preparation needed, or the amount of descriptive content to provide when sharing the experience with others. One does not always understand aspects of what one has observed, what certain actions and activities might mean, and how other participants, particularly insiders, are experiencing the processes. One does not always have the best attitude, the most open-mindedness, optimal physical health, and other such attributes when actually engaged in the process of research. It may take many hours, days, weeks, years, and even decades of experiential immersion in a culture, and painstaking study of texts and other material, for scholars to deepen their understanding sufficiently to report on it. And even that is always regarded as a work in progress, a contribution that may be refined by the subsequent work of the same or other scholars. The contributions in these anthologies are written from the disposition that the scholarly study of religion is an ongoing process. And it is a process in which we invite the reader to participate by revealing aspects of the research process often concealed from view in most scholarly literature. Moreover, these contributions are not exclusively written by outsiders for outsiders. They are written by scholars, who, whether or not they belong to the religious tradition under study, assume a scholarly stance of engaged objectivity and empathetic distance with that religion as they engage in their research. Through their descriptive narrative vignettes, they invite the reader to share in their experiences, however briefly and partially, while they were engaged in some features of their research.

Almost anyone who has some experience with teaching about religion and culture knows the efficacy of storytelling. Not only is it an ancient and well-tested technique through which religious beliefs are conveyed and culture transmitted, but also the narrative is equally effective in eliciting and maintaining the attention of a student audience. The first-person story is one of the most engaging forms of the narrative. Tell a person what you did, saw, thought, and felt, and you are much more likely to garner their interest. Within that encounter there is the possibility for learning to occur.

The objective in these chapters is primarily pedagogic. These are true stories of the experiences of real persons engaged in some of the activities of their discipline. It is hoped that they convey to the reader not only some details of what the study of religion entails but also, as significantly, the rich textures of humanity's religious life. One might find within these narratives revelations that the author did not always use good judgment in certain instances, that they initially misunderstood what was transpiring, and so on. The honesty within the narrative portion of each contribution would likely be suspect if these stories did not contain features of surprise, puzzlement, or missteps. However, these narratives are not relatively superficial journalistic or travelers' accounts of adventures written to satisfy the reader's need for entertainment or to satiate some passing curiosity. Embedded within the narrative descriptions and in the discussions that follow the reader will also find remarkable details and useful information that derives from corollary facets of solid and rigorous scholarly work. It is hoped that the reader comes away with an enhanced appreciation and understanding of the religious tradition they are studying, as well as of the disciplines and methodologies through which it is studied.

Acknowledgments

I wish to thank the authors of these essays for their willingness to participate in an atypical project, their openness to the challenge of revealing their processes and even missteps in service to mentoring and pedagogic purposes, and for their many contributions linked both to research and teaching about Buddhism. I would also like to express gratitude to several other key people, whose vision, work, and support made this collection possible. Hillary Rodrigues, the editor of the *Studying Religions in Practice* series and of the *Studying Hinduism in Practice* volume, deserves particular thanks for his vision for the larger project and expertise in guiding it to fruition. We have discussed the merits and potential pitfalls of this undertaking for the last six years, and this volume has been beneficially shaped by his influence. We co-wrote the introduction to this volume so that it closely mirrors the structure and intent of the series while responding to dynamics unique to Buddhism and specific to the contributions to this compilation. Lesley Riddle, the senior publisher in religion and anthropology at Routledge, warrants special mention as well for her patience and steadfast and enthusiastic support of this concept and series from the beginning.

I also appreciate the warm reception that other scholars have extended to the purpose and potential of this volume on Buddhism and the larger series to which it belongs. Some offered to contribute a chapter, but then had to withdraw from the project. Most regrettably, William LaFleur was writing a chapter for this volume when he unexpectedly died in late February 2010. In sadly parallel circumstances, Leslie Kawamura had agreed to write a chapter but then reconsidered for health reasons before passing away in early March 2011. Neither of these eminent scholars had retired; instead, both were very much engaged in their many projects and with the innumerable people to whom they meant so much. Both deaths were a great loss to Buddhist scholarship, but were felt more deeply within and beyond academic communities because each was also such a remarkable human being. A version of LaFleur's autobiographical essay included in this volume came to light courtesy of Richard A. Gardner during preparations for sessions in Bill's honor at the 2010 American Academy of Religion annual conference. Three panels commemorated his remarkably diverse, imaginative, and influential scholarship as well as his thoughtful mentorship, warmth, and good humor. I would like to thank Rich Gardner for providing that version of LaFleur's retrospective essay, which is included at the end of this volume. I also appreciate Mariko LaFleur's permission to use her husband's essay posthumously in this book.

Finally, I would like to express my gratitude to Lisa Kozleski. I owe her thanks for many reasons, ranging from her support and patience as a spouse when I have been too occupied by this project to her invaluable role as the editorial assistant first for *Studying Hinduism in Practice* and then for the current volume on Buddhism in this same series. She has improved both volumes with her expertise as a writer, an editor, and an instructor in academic writing. Moreover, she has helped our efforts to keep our targeted non-specialist audience in mind. As affirmed also in the introduction to *Studying Hinduism in Practice*, we collectively hope that instructors and students, through being entertained, informed, instructed, and inspired, find as much satisfaction in using *Studying Buddhism in Practice* as we did in constructing it.

On transliteration and pronunciation

Transliteration is the method by which words that are typically written in foreign scripts are depicted in the English or Latin-based alphabet. The scholarly convention is to use diacritical marks to represent sounds of characters from other languages that do not always correspond with the English alphabet. Buddhism spread across many Asian countries for more than two millennia. It proved adaptable, including prompting major translation projects and adopting local languages for daily practices, new texts, and new layers of commentary for older texts. As a result, a number of Asian languages are important for the study of Buddhism. For access to early texts during its development in India, Pāli and Sanskrit are useful. For later influential textual collections, Buddhologists often spend countless hours mastering Tibetan, Chinese, Korean, and Japanese. Of course, these languages from Central and East Asia are also important modern languages for understanding contemporary Buddhist practices and worldviews, as are Sinhala, Vietnamese, Thai, Burmese, Lao, Khmer, and additional languages of Buddhist communities. English and other "Western" languages are becoming increasingly important as a result of the spread of Buddhism beyond Asia, as well as for access to scholarship and popular writing about Buddhism in these languages.

For most foreign terms, it is preferable to employ diacritics – dots and dashes that are placed above or below a character giving it a sound variant. When you see a diacritical dot under a letter, place your tongue near the roof of your mouth, and then say it as you would in English. If you see a dash over a vowel, as in Mahāyāna, for instance, just extend the sound of that vowel, so it sounds like "Mahaayaana." There are some words that have become increasingly common to read in English without the precision of diacritics. For example, the word "mandala" (cosmic map or similar symbolic geometric figure used in Buddhist and Hindu ritual) has become common in English dictionaries and little is gained by using diacritics to keep closer to the Sanskrit *maṇḍala.* However, we do use diacritics for most relevant terms throughout the volume, because these marks indicate to the reader how to pronounce the foreign terms once the diacritics themselves become less foreign. They are also used in this volume (and the series as a whole), with its attention to the practice of the study of religion, because diacritics are widely used by most scholars and can signal a more exacting, academic approach.

The chapters in this volume address a number of different Buddhist traditions located in at least nine language contexts – Japanese, Chinese, Vietnamese, Tibetan, Sanskrit, Pāli, Thai, Sinhala, and English. The different countries and languages encountered in each scholar's study require some variation in terminology. Even within a Buddhist language, country, or tradition, there can be further variety because of multiple systems for transliteration, as well as regional conventions. So although the terms will be spelled consistently the same way in a particular essay, on occasion you might find variations in the spellings of the same term or name in different essays within this volume or in other sources. For instance, *nembutsu* and *nenbutsu* are both common transliterations for writing the name of the recitation practice central to Japanese Pure Land Buddhism; whereas "kamma" and "karma" are examples of variants of the same ethical doctrine concerning the consequences of intentional action from different but related languages (Pāli and Sanskrit respectively).

Introduction

Studying Buddhism in practice

John S. Harding and Hillary P. Rodrigues

This book, which is the second volume in the Studying Religions in Practice series, is a collection of contributions written by specialists expressly for readers relatively new to the academic study of Buddhist religious tradition(s). This introduction to *Studying Buddhism in Practice* mirrors that of *Studying Hinduism in Practice.* In accord with the intent of the series as a whole, the essays in this compilation are designed to serve two purposes. These are: (1) to highlight features of Buddhism as it is actually practiced, and (2) to illustrate some of the authentic experiences of researchers engaged in the study of those practices.

These contributions have other features that make this collection distinct. Although many of the authors may have strong affinities for the Buddhist tradition, and some may even be deeply immersed in aspects of its practices, these are not articles by Buddhists telling the reader how they practice and experience their faith, and then explaining how or why these practices might make sense to non-Buddhists. This book is grounded in the secular, scholarly study of Buddhism. It is also focused on the doings of Buddhists, that is, their practices. This is because even well-written comprehensive introductory textbooks cannot adequately convey the life of the Buddhist religious tradition as it is experienced by Buddhists. A textbook typically describes the life of the Buddha, foundational teachings, the development of Buddhist communities, and influential figures, texts, and schools formative to the development and spread of Buddhist tradition(s) for more than two millennia. Even where textbooks do address some Buddhist practices, these descriptions of what Buddhists do rarely transport the reader into the midst of practitioners' experiences. After all, textbooks are typically designed to convey information and serve as useful and relatively comprehensive references on Buddhism. They serve a necessary function in introducing Buddhist tradition(s). However, such books almost never reveal to the reader anything about the experiences of the researchers as they are making those discoveries. This volume, and the series to which it belongs, does try to introduce readers both to the practice of religions and to how the study of religion is practiced.

This collection is intended to serve as a complement to a good textbook about Buddhism and a knowledgeable instructor. It makes no pretensions to providing a comprehensive coverage of Buddhist practices. Frankly, one should be highly suspicious of any book that makes such a claim. Buddhism is a complex and rich tradition. Furthermore, Buddhism can be described as a family of related traditions with shared characteristics and traits that have been passed down through generations but also exhibit significant variety as Buddhism has spread across Asia and beyond for more than 2,000 years. Although its expressive forms vary considerably across various regions of Asia, there is greater overlap of shared features within certain regions. For example, the family resemblance is particularly notable within the Theravāda traditions of South and Southeast Asia, within the Mahāyāna traditions of East Asia, and within the Vajrayāna traditions of Central Asia. Naturally, the divisions are more complicated than this description suggests. For example, although both China and Japan are most characteristic of Mahāyāna, Shingon Buddhism in Japan remains a vibrant descendant of Vajrayāna from the time when that tradition was especially prominent in the capital of Tang China at the beginning of the ninth century C.E. Moreover, the global spread of Buddhism and surge in academic and popular engagement with the tradition in the last 150 years have produced a wealth of study topics that cannot be surveyed exhaustively in a lifetime, much less within a single compilation of essays. Any attempt at an all-encompassing treatment of Buddhist practices would require a small library of volumes. Nevertheless, this concise collection of articles is felicitously broad in its temporal and topical coverage as well as its distribution among Buddhist traditions and countries.

Consistent with the design of the Studying Religions in Practice series, the chapters in this volume on Buddhism are weighted toward contemporary practices from recent decades to the present day, as they were actually observed. The accounts of contemporary practices nevertheless refer to people and places from earlier periods of Buddhist history, including sites from the story of the historical Buddha's life approximately 2,400 years ago, customs that can be traced back to commentaries of Buddhaghosa 1,600 years ago, Kūkai's extensive influence in Japan 1,200 years ago, criticism and reform of Buddhism in Vietnam during French colonial rule 120 years ago, and funeral practices in Sri Lanka 12 years ago. Within its corpus the authors discuss various rituals and diverse topics such as ordination, oral traditions, sermons, ceremonies, performance, pilgrimage, food, funerals, modernization, merit making, gender roles, social changes, secret societies, esoteric initiations, village life, miracle working, women's practices, animal release, devotional worship, festival traditions, film-making, coping with crisis, competition among sacred sites, political appropriations of Buddhism, relations and responsibilities of lay and monastic Buddhists, and rites related to abortion, birth, aging, and death. This array encompasses multiple perspectives as well as the voices and practices of women and men, monastics and lay followers, old and young practitioners, villagers and city dwellers, initiated and non-initiated practitioners, and various levels of wealth, literacy, religious education, and interest in Buddhism. Theravāda, Mahāyāna, and Vajrayāna traditions are each represented by multiple essays. Moreover, the geographic range of the chapters includes Buddhist research, practice, and participants from Sri Lanka, India, Tibet, Thailand, Myanmar (Burma), Laos, Vietnam, China, Japan, and North America.

This anthology is an excellent source for the study of contemporary Buddhism. Unlike other collections in which Buddhist practice is represented by translation of how classical texts prescribe Buddhist practice, the authors' contributions to this volume focus on how select groups of Buddhists actually engage in their religion today. This compilation is also different from most scholarly works on Buddhism in terms of its aim and the audience for whom it has been written. Articles are not culled from larger works written by academics for the benefit of their scholarly peers. These are pieces written by highly trained, professional researchers and instructors specifically for readers who may have little or no background knowledge of the Buddhist tradition or the academic study of religion. The contributors span a range from relatively early stages of their professional careers to well-known and highly esteemed senior scholars, with the balance in established positions closer to mid-career. Some tell stories about their journey through academia. Others tell stories of times they faced a change in their professional lives. All tell stories about their discoveries and processes of learning about Buddhism. Moreover, research material not published elsewhere is contained within some of these essays. Apart from other volumes in this series, there is currently no other published collection of contributions of this sort.

Another distinctive feature of this collection is the form in which the articles are written. We encouraged authors to comply with an innovative, experimental, prescribed structure, allowing moderate flexibility for the subject matter and the dispositions of the contributors. Hillary Rodrigues, the Studying Religions in Practice series editor, and I have discussed this unique format from the time we were en route to meet Lesley Riddle, the senior publisher in religion and anthropology for Routledge, at the 2005 International Association for the History of Religions (IAHR) conference in Tokyo to the Spring of 2011, when this *Studying Buddhism in Practice* volume was sent off to the publisher. Dr. Rodrigues, who also edited the first volume in the series, *Studying Hinduism in Practice*, is an acclaimed and effective teacher who trained in both textual and anthropological methodologies. He has been the chair of both anthropology and religious studies departments. Additionally, he has received the highest teaching awards at the University of Lethbridge and has also developed pedagogic resources for the study of Hinduism and the academic study of religion. Moreover, we collaboratively produced a textbook and reader to introduce students to religious studies. I am reporting this information about anthropological and religious studies disciplinary orientations, teaching excellence, and the pedagogic purpose of this Studying Religions in Practice series to better familiarize readers with how and why essays are in this unique form.

Storytelling is not only important to religious traditions, but it is also an effective device for teaching. Stories engage students' interest and are more likely to be retained than non-narrative lectures, lists, terms, and facts from the classroom or textbook. When we offer personal vignettes about our fieldwork, travels, or the context in which an image was taken long before it was inserted into a PowerPoint presentation, students often respond more actively. Some are even inspired to travel the world or journey into an academic career. It is our hope that the unique format of this series can stimulate student engagement by beginning with first-person narrative accounts of studying some aspect of religious practice that can then be contextualized through discussion.

For this volume, the story of the scholar's raw experience while engaged in the study of Buddhist practice transitions into analysis of that experience and of certain aspects of Buddhism and its study selected by each scholar. Rich narrative can lead to many different discussions. Students and instructors are encouraged to address any themes that are facilitated by the narrative or suggested in the discussion. Each author, however, was asked to select just one aspect that emerges from the narrative – or a couple of related topics or themes – to discuss. In this way, the initial story is used to illustrate pertinent topics about Buddhism, Buddhist practice, the practice, nature, and development of religion more generally, or critical issues of theory and method in the practice of the academic study of religion.

Although this prescribed format may sound simple, it can be surprisingly difficult to break with convention and keep an undergraduate audience in mind rather than one's fellow academics. I appreciate the enthusiasm of the authors for the project and their willingness to modify their usual style for this experimental approach. We asked the authors to tell their narratives not in a form that is typical in scholarly papers, where narrative is often wholly absent. But even in such papers that include narratives, the story is kept brief, mostly stripped of its colorful descriptors and with little or nothing revealed of the researchers' personal responses to the experiences. Embedded within or immediately after the narrative, scholars typically provide extensive interpretations and explanations often derived from their years of subsequent painstaking analytic work. There are obvious merits in that design, one of which is its effectiveness in conveying information to academic peers. Among its demerits are the distance it constructs between the specialist and the novice, and the illusion it can perpetuate that the researcher possesses a mature understanding in the midst of raw experience. It is more akin to a polished performance. In contrast to that format, the intention in these essays is pedagogic. Here the authors tell about their experiences in as honest a manner as they remember, including indications of their thoughts, and their sensory and emotional states. What were they seeing and hearing, what did the experience cause them to feel, and what did it make them wonder about? In so doing, and by minimizing specialized terminology, the aim is to first draw the reader into the experience alongside the researcher. The narrative is intended to be more of a description of raw experience than a well-processed explanation of the observed practices. This is because experience, whether it is that of the researcher or the observed practitioners, has a potency that derives from its immediacy. It is compelling because it carries qualities of sensory, emotional, and intellectual stimulation. Explanation, by contrast, is secondhand, a reflection upon experience.

By being drawn into companionship with the author through the narrative, readers may be better able to share vicariously in the experience of observing and participating in the religious practices that are being described. They may find themselves having emotional responses, such as excitement and awe, or even fear and revulsion, which resonate or contrast with those experienced by the researcher. Readers may discover that they start to ask questions about features of the experiences described in the narrative that the researcher does not appear to ask. This openness to multiple questions and discussions is consistent with our pedagogic strategy. Moreover, the discussion that ensues in the article may not address the questions that most interest the reader. We asked the authors to use the narrative as a launching point for any of a number of related topics. They might contextualize some features of the narrative with additional information. Alternately, they may pursue a discussion about certain aspects of the experience, providing a much broader context and explanation about the phenomena described in the narrative. Some choose to touch on theoretical issues, while others offer advice to novice researchers – as well as to more established scholars who are newly incorporating ethnography into their repertoire of practices for the study of Buddhism.

Whichever features of the narrative the author selects for analysis, there are many more potential topics that are not addressed in the discussion section of each chapter. Each author does provide information about further readings and may even signal some of the potential topics that the narrative account illustrates but that were not pursued in the discussion section. Thus, readers are offered some guidance but are not presented with a neatly packaged story with its authoritative explanations and interpretations seemingly providing answers to all anticipated questions and an end to all further discussion. Instead, they are encouraged, if not induced, to turn to their instructors, read their textbooks more pointedly, and consult the suggested readings where many of their unanswered questions might be addressed in much greater detail. This process will have already transformed them into inquiring agents rather than passive recipients of knowledge. Readers may also find some answers to their inquiries, but certainly more questions, in other contributions in the anthology, because a discussion provided in one article may have instructional value and explanatory relevance for other narratives in the collection. Similarly, various narratives may touch upon overlapping subject matter, similar themes, and describe related forms of practice.

Let me now turn to a brief account of the contents of this collection. My brevity is deliberate, because I do not wish to preface the authors' stories with lengthy summaries and analyses, which can diffuse their impact. Our intent is to let the phenomena of religious practices and their study take the lead, and to let reflections by the reader follow in their wake.

Pamela Winfield describes her first participant-observation experience when she seizes the opportunity to take part in an elaborate ritual initiation on Kōyasan, the mountain headquarters of Shingon Buddhism in Japan. In the aftermath of her illuminating ritual empowerment, she discovers surprising revelations that link esoteric ritual and imperial symbolism to pre-modern government strategies employing Buddhism for the health and protection of Japan.

Lina Verchery reviews the processes of making her documentary film about Buddhism, *The Trap* (*La Trappe*), which focuses on the lobster-release ceremony at Gampo Abbey, the monastic headquarters of Shambhala Buddhism located on Canada's east coast. She discusses "truth through artifice" by connecting her experience to Buddhist philosophy and a growing awareness of the creativity, subjectivity, and conventions of crafting both films and scholarship.

Alexander Soucy recounts three days in particular from among his years of ethnographic fieldwork in northern Vietnam as illustrative of gender differences in Buddhist practice. He uses interviews and observations to analyze how men and women not only diverge in their practices but also in their views about Buddhism and the corresponding sense of their roles and goals in relation to the tradition.

Rita Langer relates her experiences and observations of Theravāda Buddhist funerals in Sri Lanka with occasional reference to funerals within this tradition that she has observed in Laos, Thailand, and Myanmar (Burma). In addition to providing insights into the roles of lay and monastic participants, her chapter draws attention to practices of providing and sharing food as part of these Buddhist funeral rites.

John Clifford Holt portrays the impact of social change on religious culture, such as transformations since his first visit in 1979 at the main ritual and pilgrimage site for Sinhala Buddhists: the Dalada Maligava ("Temple of the Tooth-Relic") in Kandy. He shares with the reader how it was only after arriving in Sri Lanka that he began to appreciate how the Buddha is understood culturally there. Moreover, his repeated visits over ensuing decades reinforced the notion that these cultural appropriations of the Buddha continue to change with social and political developments.

In my own chapter, I explore conflict and modifications in the route of Japan's 88-temple Shikoku pilgrimage to illustrate the theme of change within religious traditions. In this essay, I navigate the shifting religious landscape to show how this famously "traditional" Buddhist practice was disrupted by the persecution of Buddhism in the late nineteenth century and continues to be shaped by unintended responses to that inequity.

Mavis Fenn recounts her unexpected shift from the study of Buddhist texts to acquiring new scholarly skills better suited to interviewing Buddhist practitioners and engaging in participant observation. Through her new forays into ethnographic study of Buddhist women in Canada, she analyzes shortcomings and successes in order to offer advice for others taking up similar approaches for the study of contemporary Buddhism.

Monica Lindberg Falk describes the devastation of the 2004 Indian Ocean tsunami and how Thai survivors have used Buddhism in the recovery process. Her account of temporary ordination ceremonies as a source of merit that is transferred to the deceased transitions into a discussion of gender and merit. The ceremonies remain primarily the domain of school-age boys, but some instances of temporary ordination for women and girls speak both to mechanisms to cope with crisis and to the recent push for a return of female ordination in Theravāda Buddhism.

Jason A. Danely reveals the unexpected role of Jizō Bodhisattva as an informant to his anthropological study of an aging Japan. Better known as a protector and guide of travelers and children, including aborted fetuses who overlap both categories, Jizō is also invoked by the elderly. From this discovery about Buddhist practice, Danely draws insightful connections between generations and life-cycle rites while also indicating benefits of fieldwork methods in cultural anthropology, including remaining open to chance encounters.

Paul Crowe takes readers to Gold Buddha Monastery in Vancouver to illustrate how Buddhist practice is very much a communal activity in Chinese temples and monasteries – both daily practice and special occasions in the Buddhist festival calendar. He depicts festivities for Amitābha Buddha's birthday and a "Liberation of Life" animal-release ceremony and contextualizes both Buddhist practices.

Clark Chilson discloses conventions of a secretive Pure Land Buddhist group that scholars had mistakenly assumed died out long ago. Shin Buddhism is the largest Buddhist denomination in Japan and is often represented as the most resistant to hidden meanings. Thus, Chilson's discovery of the secretive Shin Buddhist tradition of Urahōmon is unique. However, his discussion of sermons as pedagogical performances with multiple meanings resonates with religious practice throughout, and beyond, Buddhism.

James B. Apple recalls his participation in a ritual in the year 2000 outside Sujātā village, a site in India associated with Siddhārtha Gautama embarking on a Middle Way between his princely and ascetic pursuits just before awakening and becoming Śākyamuni, the historical Buddha. Apple analyzes his role and position as a North American scholar chanting Tibetan in the middle of a Buddhist ritual conducted by Tibetan monks in India. He invokes the scholar J. Z. Smith in his thought-provoking discussion of the important, and problematic, insider/outsider relation in the study of Buddhism(s) and other religions.

And finally, the last essay, written by William R. LaFleur, differs in format from the other dozen chapters and offers reflections on his academic journey, including a discussion of the practice of the study of Japanese Buddhism as well as some of the Buddhist practices he researched. His insightful perspectives have produced groundbreaking studies of Buddhist dimensions of Japanese culture from medieval literature to contemporary bioethics. Although the benefits of reflections on such a renowned legacy are manifold, this was not the original plan. LaFleur was writing a chapter for this book on Buddhism, abortion, and related *mizuko-kuyō* ritual practices for aborted "water children" (*mizuko*) when he unexpectedly passed away in February 2010. He was a warm and inspiring friend, an insightful and selfless mentor, a philosopher and poet whose depth of thought and deftness with language elucidates his scholarship and illuminates whichever of the wide-ranging topics he fearlessly engaged. He had not yet retired or written any autobiographical reflections that we knew of at the time of his death. However, as noted in the acknowledgment to Richard Gardner and the preamble to LaFleur's essay in this compilation, he had worked on just such an autobiographical reflection and we appreciatively include it in this volume. Bill LaFleur's chapter concludes this book, which is dedicated to him.

The contributors did not read one another's works and did not deliberately craft their contributions to resonate with them. And yet, as was suspected, thematic relationships and connections are evident everywhere. Holt and Harding both discuss social changes that reshape major pilgrimage sites. The transformations described by Holt are located in late twentieth-century Sri Lanka in contrast with Harding's emphasis on late nineteenth-century changes to Shikoku pilgrimage in Japan. Both invoke the intersection between politics and Buddhism, as does Winfield in her analysis of imperial symbolism in Shingon ritual and the use of Buddhism for the protection of the nation.

Themes about gender and the practices, contributions, and roles of Buddhist women are especially prominent in the contributions by Soucy, Fenn, and Lindberg Falk. Additionally women are central to Buddhist practices described in many of the essays – including those by Verchery, Langer, Danely, Harding, and Crowe. Buddhist practices in response to death connect the essays by Langer, Danely, and Lindberg Falk. These three also all address making and sharing merit, as do the chapters by Soucy, Verchery, and Crowe, among others.

All the essays reveal assorted Buddhist practices. Rituals and ceremonies are central to the narratives in Winfield, Danely, Langer, Apple, Crowe, Verchery, and Lindberg Falk, for example. Also, all of the chapters address contemporary realities and provide valuable resources for the study of modern Buddhism. Instructors should find *Studying Buddhism in Practice* easily adaptable to organizational schemes of their Buddhism courses, including most introductory textbooks. For instance, courses organized by tradition might place Winfield, Verchery, and Apple with Vajrayāna (representing Shingon in Japan, Tibetan Buddhism, and Western Shambhala respectively); Soucy, Harding, Danely, Crowe, Chilson, and LaFleur with Mahāyāna (representing Vietnamese, Chinese, and Japanese forms); and Langer, Holt, and Lindberg Falk with Theravāda (representing Sri Lanka, Thailand, and other Theravāda countries of Southeast Asia). Fenn is harder to place, as the Buddhist women she interviewed belong to different traditions. She could even be placed in what is sometimes labeled as a fourth vehicle of Buddhism in the West, in which case Verchery, and to an extent Crowe, could be brought into that category as well.

As indicated by the countries placed in parentheses in the above categorization by vehicles of Buddhism, it would also be reasonably adaptable to fit this volume to a geographic arrangement, or the common hybrids that move with the spread of Buddhism arranged in variations that are partially attentive to historical timelines, partially mapped by geographical spread through Asia, and, in some cases, partially arranged by emphasizing one vehicle at a time. For example, Apple's essay would provide a good starting point both for its location in India and emphasis on a site linked to the story of the Buddha. The spread to Sri Lanka, Thailand, and other Theravāda countries in Southeast Asia, Vietnam, China,

Japan, and the West could then follow with Holt, Langer, Lindberg Falk, Soucy, Crowe, Winfield, Harding, Chilson, Danely, LaFleur, Fenn, and Verchery.

The essays in this volume are also synergistic for discussions of method and theory. Reflections on method arise in most of the essays, including advice about and modeling of ethnographic practices such as "participant observation" and the techniques, advantages, and ethical concerns most closely associated with anthropological research methods. These remarks range from those of scholars whose graduate training was in cultural anthropology and/or whose long-term research practices have relied on anthropological methods, such as Soucy, Danely, Langer, Chilson, and Lindberg Falk, to those of scholars like Winfield and Crowe reporting relatively early experiences of study in this mode, as well as Fenn reflecting on the transition from textual to ethnographic practices.

In addition to this unusually robust treatment of method in an introductory book, some issues of theory and the overlap of these categories arise as well. Verchery brings Buddhist philosophy and reflections on film-making and fiction to bear on how she addresses theoretical concerns about the constructed nature of scholarship. Apple dives more directly into related theoretical concerns central to current debates in religious studies about "insiders," "outsiders," and the role and position of the scholar. LaFleur's essay is compelling in this regard as he reminisces about what drew him into the field, including the influence of his key advisors, Joseph Kitagawa and Mircea Eliade, at the University of Chicago. The "Chicago School" has been, and remains, central to critical discussions about actual practices in the study of religion as well as disciplinary ideals. This is evident in Apple's essay, where the prominent role of J. Z. Smith in that chapter mirrors his standing in larger discussions about theory and method in religious studies for several decades. LaFleur's essay demonstrates his academic origins in the "History of Religions" tradition with broad comparative and humanistic interests, but also traces a unique, diverse, and influential career as a Japan specialist and scholar of Buddhism. His awareness of Buddhism's wide-ranging influence on culture, literature, various arts, and even bioethical decisions and medical practices informed his scholarship, which included, but also extended far beyond, innovative insights about religious practices.

As the topical overlaps, thematic links, and synergistic reflections on theory and method mentioned above indicate, there were many options for how to order the contents of this volume. However, no particular grouping seemed adequate. Ordering essays geographically or by tradition admittedly fits textbook organizational schemes; however, it would often conceal the thrust of the discussion. Moreover, each narrative is rich with examples of Buddhist practice and possible points of departure for further discussion. One could categorize Langer, Lindberg Falk, and Danely under ritual responses to death, but this would ignore Langer's focus on food, Lindberg Falk's discussion of ordination, and Danely's emphasis on the unexpected dimensions of Jizō practice beyond what was expected. It would also exclude synergistic essays such as Soucy's, which connects to Lindberg Falk's discussion of gender and attention to making and sharing merit in several chapters. In other words, just as with *Studying Hinduism in Practice* in the same series, any viable grouping seemed to diminish the richness of the constituent essays, undercutting potential benefits derived from such categorizations. Instead, the order is more arbitrary. With the exception of LaFleur's chapter, which is deliberately positioned at the end of this volume, the essays have been placed in reverse alphabetic order of authors' surname. This inverts the arrangement, but preserves the underlying logic, of *Studying Hinduism in Practice*.

Chapter 1

Coronation at Kōyasan

How one woman became king and learned about homeland security and national health care in ancient Japan

Pamela D. Winfield

Preamble

Technically, I was not trained as an anthropologist of religion. I was just in Kyoto conducting my dissertation research on esoteric Buddhist art and doctrine when I learned that the nearby mountain monastery of Kōyasan was offering lay initiations into the Diamond World mandala. This mandala is one of the two most important images in Shingon Buddhism, which is an early form of Vajrayāna or Tantric Buddhism that is characterized by elaborate rituals, secret initiations, symbolic hand gestures (*mudrās*), chanted mantras, and colorful mandalas. In Japan, this form of esoteric Buddhism is designed to connect the practitioner to Dainichi, the cosmic Buddha whose name means Great Light. It was October, and I learned that initiation into Shingon's other main mandala called the Womb World would not be offered until May. I therefore jumped at the chance to witness this unique biannual event, even though I had never done participant observation before.

The irony is that I did not witness or observe much of anything for a large portion of the ceremony. This is because for most of the time, I was actually walking blindfolded through the ritual hall. Despite my covered eyes, however, I did learn something – more than something, in fact. I walked away from that experience with a firsthand understanding of this famous Shingon initiation rite, a deeper awareness of the imperial imagery in the Two World mandalas, not to mention the symbolic role that these two paintings played in maintaining the health and safety of Japan throughout the pre-modern period. But let us begin at the beginning.

Narrative

I arrived in the mountain town of Kōyasan in the evening and stayed in one of the many temple-lodgings that serve the town's famous spongy kind of tofu – a key ingredient in local Buddhist (i.e. vegetarian) cuisine. The next day I walked to the main temple compound at the heart of Kōyasan, took my shoes off outside the Lecture Hall, climbed the wooden stairs rubbed smooth by centuries of stockinged

Figure 1.1
The author at Kōyasan's great pagoda

feet, and joined the line of complete strangers waiting outside along the hall's elevated portico. I was the only foreigner in a group of about 25 Japanese men and women of all ages. When the monks signaled that it was time for us to enter the Lecture Hall, I was temporarily disoriented as my eyes adjusted from the brilliant autumn sun outside to the dark, candle-lit interior. Like everyone else, I just followed the silhouettes in front of me and sat down. My reliance upon these fellow strangers before me would become even more pronounced as the ceremony progressed.

We sat in a formal seated position with our calves tucked directly under our thighs on the tatami mat floor. A priest in mustard-colored robes explained the ceremony to us and delivered a short dharma talk. He informed us that the *kechien kanjō* initiation rite is designed to tie a karmic bond between oneself and a Buddha or bodhisattva figure that is pictured in the mandala. *Kechi* means to tie and *en* means karma, he explained, so getting initiated (*kanjō*) into the Diamond World mandala meant karmically sealing our connection to one personified aspect of Dainichi's enlightened nature. We were to establish this bond by randomly tossing a sacred *shikimi* leaf onto a raised mandala altar with all of the Diamond World deities painted on top, but to do it blindfolded so that whichever figure it landed on was destined to be our special "patron saint" or Buddhist deity who helped advance our practice in exchange for our special veneration. The priest mentioned that in fact Kūkai (774–835), the founder of Shingon Buddhism in Japan, actually hit Dainichi Buddha at the lucky center of the mandala when he was initiated while studying abroad in China in 806, thereby indicating his predestination to greatness. The priest then taught us to chant the mantra "*Om samaya satoban*," which roughly translates as "Om hail to Buddha's symbolic form-being" (i.e. Dainichi's embodied aspects in the mandala). He also taught us how to clasp our hands in the special initiation mudrā, with both hands folded together and fingers interlaced as in prayer, with just the third (middle) fingers extended to hold the waxy evergreen leaf between them. He then expounded upon the Shingon doctrine that one can become a Buddha in this very body, in this very lifetime, by engaging in these kinds of Vajrayāna "quick-path" esoteric rituals. Then the ceremony commenced.

As we all stood up, assistant monks inserted a leaf between our pressed third fingers and told us to start chanting the mantra out loud and in unison. Then they blindfolded us and arranged us into a line so that the tips of our third fingers pressed up against the back of the person in front of us. I was completely blind in the dark hall, with absolutely no light even filtering in through the bottom of my blindfold. My sole navigational cue at this point was the person in front of me, and I knew I was the only guide for the person behind me. We were thus linked to one another physically, verbally, and by extension mentally in the pitch-black space of sightlessness. I assume that the blindfolded individual at the head of the conga line was led by a Shingon monk. I do not even know how long we snaked through the hall, but it seemed like an eternity. After the initial novelty of the situation wore off, I soon began to wonder when all this repetitive chanting and aimless, sightless walking would ever end.

Suddenly, someone broke my connection to the person in front of me and just held my hands, still clasped in the special initiation mudrā. After a few minutes this person then led me a few steps forward and told me to open my hands and let the leaf go. He removed my blindfold, and I was dazzled by the light and bright colors of the mandala altar before me. The altar was square, divided into a three-by-three grid of nine mini-mandalas with numerous little white moon disks – the symbol for enlightenment – painted within each tic-tac-toe square. There was my leaf, lying squarely in Dainichi's center circle. I am under no illusion; I am no Kūkai. I just assume it was the monk's job to brush each initiate's leaf into the center before lifting our blindfolds. He told me to look up. There before me was an enormous painted version of the Diamond World mandala hanging from the ceiling. Its dimensions were overwhelming. My eyes were still adjusting to the light, and my brain was still processing the rapid and vast influx of data after such a long period of sensory deprivation when the monk delivered the surprising news that I was the cosmic Buddha, Dainichi. I was nothing other than the personification of universal Buddha-nature. I had "become a Buddha in this very lifetime"

Figure 1.2 Dainichi Buddha of the Diamond World mandala

as the Shingon phrase goes. This was a lot to digest. Somewhat stunned, I think I returned his bow, a Japanese social cue that this portion of the ceremony was over.

Another monk then began to escort me away toward a side area of the sanctuary that served as a kind of empowerment station for all of us new lay initiates. This second part of the ceremony was totally unexpected – the mustard-robed priest had said nothing about this when he first explained the ritual to us.

Five or six priests sat on chairs facing a new initiate seated before them. I took a vacant seat, and the Shingon priest smiled and bowed forward in his seat, greeting me with a kind *konnichi wa.* Then he immediately changed his demeanor. He furrowed his brow in obvious concentration and seriousness, lowered the register of his deep voice and began intoning a series of mantras or longer protective blessings. I couldn't understand a word he was saying. Shingon Buddhism transliterates Sanskrit words with approximate Japanese pronunciations (the Sanskrit word for "master" or *acharya* becomes *ajari* in Japanese, for example), so unless you know the Sanskrit, you're lost. As this nice yet formidable priest was rapidly reciting this incomprehensible Japanized Sanskrit Buddhist jargon over me, he crowned me with a paper crown. He blessed a long piece of folded white paper with some rapid movements of his *vajra*, a double-ended, five-pronged, hand-held ritual implement that ostensibly empowers anything it touches with Dainichi's invisible cosmic force. In the center of the paper strip there was an orange ink-stamped block print of Dainichi Buddha with his hands formed in the distinctive Diamond World mudrā. He was pictured wearing royal garb, a crown, precious jewels, and other kingly regalia. While continuing to intone the incomprehensible mantras, the priest centered the Dainichi-emperor image on my brow and tied the two ends of the paper strip at the back of my head. With Dainichi strategically placed on my forehead, I immediately grasped the symbolism that we were literally of one mind. While still reciting the words of empowerment, he simultaneously indicated that I should put my hand on his as he pointed the *vajra* to the four directions. First we pointed to the left and right, and then we pointed it between him and me. The empowerment ended when he told me (in Japanese) that again, I was Dainichi Buddha, the ruler of the cosmos. This time, however, I had the paper crown to prove it.

As soon as he completed my ritual coronation, he urged me in polite Japanese to please look at the painted portraits of Shingon's first eight patriarchs before I exited from the back of the hall. He used the honorific form of the verb "to look at," indicating that these large painted images of the masters deserved the highest respect. Indeed small votive candles were placed at the foot of these floor-to-ceiling portraits, and some new initiates were kneeling before them in prayer. I followed them out to the back exit, where two young novices were tasked with stamping our paper crowns with the date and official temple seal. Those who had brought personal temple pilgrimage journals could also have the novices record their visit with calligraphic flourishes and the temple seal for a token donation. I squinted as I stepped out into the afternoon light.

Discussion

As a scholar, there are several different ways one might analyze the above ritual. A feminist analysis might question what it means for a twenty-first-century American non-practicing laywoman to be initiated into an esoteric, secret tradition historically reserved for males, while a scholar of ritual studies would probably use Victor Turner's concepts of liminality and communitas to analyze how the clergy and my fellow initiates facilitated ritualized communion with a cosmic deity and with Shingon's much more human patriarchs. A focus on material culture would look at the ritual paraphernalia, the "smells and bells" and the ritual structures of the sacred spaces I encountered that day, while a psychological investigation might examine the subjective experience of ritual time that seemed to either drag on or speed up at key points in the ceremony. A philosopher of religion would examine the phenomenological dialectic of perception that moved from everyday vision, to no-vision, to transformed vision before the mandala, and also might think about the overall symbolic trajectory of the ritual that progressed from blind ignorance to revealed truth to empowered rulership.

All of these topics are possible avenues to pursue. However, what I wish to focus on here is what I found to be the most surprising and intriguing aspect of the ritual. The overt imperial symbolism of being crowned at Kōyasan has led me to look more deeply into the imperial iconography of these Buddhist images and to investigate the broader interactions between religion and politics in Japan during the pre-modern period. Many, if not most North American readers presuppose that church and state do – or at least should – remain separate. These readers do not realize that this assumption is a relatively recent socially and politically constructed ideology born out of Western European Enlightenment ideals and a quite specific historical context of religious persecution in Western Europe. None of these considerations have any bearing on pre-modern Japan, or on the pre-industrial histories of most other world cultures for that matter. As a result, the remainder of this chapter will focus on the historical treatment of Buddhism in the service of the state in early Japan. Specifically, I would like to investigate the ways in which esoteric texts and images like the mandalas helped further Japan's perennial concern with homeland security and national health care throughout its history.

By necessity, both the tone and the approach of the remainder of this essay will significantly differ from those of the first half. I consider these two parts to be connected, however, as I believe any present-day experience can and should be understood within the contours of its history, ideology, and concrete visual and material expressions. It is in this spirit of contextualizing my observations that we begin de-coding the secret symbol system of Shingon Buddhism and unpacking its symbiotic power relations with the state.

Buddhism and the state in early Japan

Even before Kūkai introduced the Diamond and Womb World mandalas to Japan in 806, Buddhism had traditionally served the needs of the state. Beginning in 741, for example, Emperor Shōmu (r. 724–49) issued a series of imperial edicts to establish a provincial network of national Buddhist temples and nunneries called Kokubunji (*koku* means country, *bu* or *bun* means Buddha and *-ji* means temple). Emperor Shōmu established this network throughout the land to unify, pacify, and protect the entire country against a series of famines, the smallpox epidemic of 735–37 and a revolt against the central government in 740 by a disgruntled nephew of the Empress. Shōmu's imperially sponsored temples were headquartered in the capital of Nara at Tōdaiji temple, whose radiant gilt bronze Vairocana "Sun" Buddha would help to insure the health and safety of the body-politic. Emperor Shōmu commissioned this monumental 16-foot-tall statue in 743 and its eye-opening ceremony was held almost ten years later in 752. The symbolic power and ritual logic of this image invoked the Buddha's illuminating and purifying rays to discern, shed light on, and purge the dark, offending spirits that were believed to cause illness, epidemic, pestilence, and misfortune throughout the land. The apotropaic and healing properties of Vairocana's light were literally and metaphorically reinforced throughout the land on doctrinal, political, ritual, and iconographic levels.

Doctrinally speaking, Vairocana Buddha embodies the *dharmakāya* or the cosmic world-body of universal enlightenment. Politically speaking however, Shōmu's bronze Vairocana metaphorically cast the emperor as a universal world ruler or *cakravartin*, one who virtuously maintains the health and prosperity of his land. By identifying Vairocana's world-body with his own body-politic, Emperor Shōmu was able to unite the land under one symbolic figure and extend his imperial influence through the circulatory system of Kokubunji temples. Therefore, just as Vairocana extends his hands in fear-dispelling and boon-bestowing mudrās that interpenetrate all lands without obstruction, so too would Shōmu extend his hands to sponsor imperial rites for protection and health in every province without obstruction.

Ritually and textually speaking, moreover, these Buddhist rites for homeland security and national health care invariably involved the ritual chanting of the *Golden Light Sūtra of the Four Heavenly Kings*. This scripture was an appropriate choice, for it guarantees the peace and wellbeing of the people in all four directions, provided that a virtuous king promulgates it with pure intention. (This was the key caveat that insured the Buddhist establishment's continued imperial patronage. If their rites and rituals did not succeed, they could blame the failures on the Emperor's lack of sincerity, not their own shortcomings.) In this sūtra, which appears on page 98 in Theodore de Bary's *Sources of Japanese Tradition*, the Four Heavenly Kings vow:

> [If] this sūtra of the Golden Light is transmitted to every part of a kingdom … if the king of the land listens with his whole heart to these writings … and supplies this sūtra to … believers, protects and keeps all harm from them, we Deva Kings, in recognition of his deeds, will protect that king and his people, give them peace and freedom from suffering, prolong their lives and fill them with glory.

Later in the sūtra, on page 99, the Buddha himself rejoins:

> If any king upholds this sūtra and makes offerings in its behalf, I will purify him of suffering and illness, and bring him peace of mind. I will protect

his cities, towns and villages, and scatter his enemies. I will make all strife among the rulers of men to cease forever.

Thus Buddhism's role in homeland security, i.e. in protecting it from harm and promoting its health, is known as *chingo kokka bukkyō*, that is, "Buddhism for the pacification and protection of the family state."

Iconographically speaking, furthermore, these state-protecting and health-promoting rituals at imperially sponsored Buddhist temples were performed before sculpted images of militant and medical power. At temples such as Yakushiji (est. 718) and Shin-yakushiji temples (est. 747), the Four Heavenly Kings dressed in military armor are strategically placed at the four corners of the altar platform so as to symbolically keep watch over all four corners of the earth. In addition, the Twelve Heavenly Generals of the Chinese zodiac appear to regulate the smooth rotation of the seasons, which by extension ensures crop productivity and a reliable food source for the entire population. The protective and productive functions of the Four Kings and Twelve Generals extend throughout the land and throughout the 12 months of the year. They thus personify and indemnify the safe and proper functioning of the state throughout space and time, as they operate everywhere, always.

In addition to these ancillary figures, the main deity of these temples is the dazzling gold Yakushi "Medicine" Buddha, who heals patients and penitents alike of their physical and mental dis-ease. Moreover, Yakushi is almost invariably flanked by Nikkō and Gakkō, representing the purifying and healing light of the sun and moon, respectively. Since its very inception, Buddhism has linked illumination with the cessation of suffering, and enlightenment with the Great Medicine that heals us of all our afflictions. For this reason, many of the Kokubunji temples quite literally served as hospital-temples, free dispensaries or hospices of compassion for those about to die.

These well-established doctrinal, political, ritual, textual, and visual formulae for light-filled state-protection would not be lost, but would soon be supplemented and further empowered when Japan's first Shingon patriarch Kūkai introduced his esoteric teachings to Japan in 806. As a powerful insider in the state's main religious institution (he became the main administrative head of the old guard at Tōdaiji in 810 and built a Shingon chapel there in 822), he was able to insert his new esoteric forms into the old familiar ones with ease.

Kūkai and the shift to esoteric state-protection

When the capital moved from Nara to Heian (present-day Kyoto) in 794, the court wished to distance itself from the growing influence of the Nara clergy. The emperor still needed to sponsor Buddhist rituals to protect and promote the wellbeing of the land, but he sought a new religio-political method of statecraft that was no longer beholden to the Buddhist establishment in Nara. In a fortunate confluence of mutual needs and good timing, Emperor Saga (r. 809–23) read Kūkai's appeal for government support and recognized the potential for constructing a new form of political Buddhism that could serve the needs of his newly established regime. Kūkai's compelling appeal, called the *Catalogue of Imported Items*, reads almost like a patent disclosure. It details all the new Buddhist texts, relics, images, and implements that he had acquired in China from 804 to 806, and explains many of their real-world applications (e.g. rain-making, state-protection, calamity-aversion, etc.). His writing effectively markets his new brand of Buddhism as being the latest, greatest, new and improved scriptural, ritual, visual, and religio-political technology from the continent to date. Kūkai casts himself as its key ritual technician and monopolistic holder of Japan's latest R&D efforts in China, since he alone was initiated into both the Diamond and Womb World mandalas by China's then-eminent "national teacher," Hui-guo. With an impeccable pedigree, a treasure trove of esoteric texts, images, and accoutrements in his possession, and Saga's imperial patronage behind him, Kūkai was instrumental in the shift from exoteric to esoteric discourse regarding *chingo kokka bukkyō*.

How did Kūkai's new esoteric imagery and ritual initiations help to enhance the old exoteric means for healing and protecting the national body? In terms of public health improvements, the old exoteric forms healed well, but these new esoteric images, Kūkai claimed, could help cure the state's perennial ills better and faster than before. Yakushi Nyorai could still fulfill his familiar function as the healing Buddha of Medicine, but now Dainichi was seen as the ultimate source of Yakushi's derivative power to cure. Kūkai rhetorically asks in his *Secret Key to the Heart Sūtra*, "If they do not go seeking for the remedies of the King of Medicine, when will they ever be able to see the Light of the Great Sun?" (p. 263 of Hakeda's 1972 translation 2:350 in *Kōbō Daishi Kūkai zenshū*, hereafter KDZ). Stated in more affirmative terms, Kūkai subtly proposes that seeking remedies through Yakushi Medicine Buddha would eventually lead one to the great light of Dainichi Buddha. This is not just Emperor Shōmu's familiar solar deity of Vairocana, but rather it is *Dai*-nichi or *Mahā*-vairocana in Sanskrit, the *Great* Sun whose universal power and illumination is as infinite as the cosmos itself.

In addition, Yakushi's subordinate figures of Nikkō and Gakkō used their solar and lunar light to exorcise harmful spirits before, but now the solar and lunar imagery of the two mandalas could help to do it better. In the Womb World, Dainichi is pictured at the center of a sunlit lotus blossom, and in the Diamond World he is pictured fully enlightened in the middle of full-moon disks. The mandalas therefore show Dainichi's powerful light as both the enlightening cause as well as the enlightened effect of awakening. (The sun can make lotus flowers blossom, and, conversely, a fully illuminated moon, it should be remembered, is but a reflected result of the sun's rays). Dainichi thus becomes the a priori source for both Nikkō's and Gakkō's purifying and curative powers, just as in Yakushi's case. Finally, the color coding of the Womb World's red lotus blossom and the Diamond World's white moon disks resonates with and further enhances the already well-established color associations of Nikkō's and Gakkō's hand-held attributes of a red sun disk and a white moon disk, respectively.

In this same vein, exoteric scriptures such as the Golden Light sūtra had been recited for apotropaic purposes before, but with the advent of Shingon Buddhism in Japan, esoteric mantras and *kaji* hands-on healing techniques could now better purge the body-politic of harmful elements. Kūkai versifies in "The Precious Key to the Secret Treasury" (*Hizō hōyaku*) as found on page 34 in Anesaki's 1931 translation of KDZ 2:16.

> The healing power of exoteric doctrine has wiped away all dust.
> Now opens the store of the True Word (*Shingon*)
> In which all hidden treasures are brought to light
> And there embodied are all virtues and power.

Thus in Kūkai's view, the "healing power" of Nara's old exoteric Buddhist methods cures well, but the "virtues and power" of Shingon's new esoteric methods can cure even better. By claiming to open Shingon's heretofore hidden treasure house of healing mantras, Kūkai thus successfully was able to market his new brand of Buddhism to the newly established Heian court without simultaneously alienating the Buddhist establishment in the old capital of Nara.

In terms of state-protection, moreover, how did Kūkai's esoteric doctrines, rituals, or texts supplement and improve the pre-existing Nara methods for averting harm to the nation? In this regard, it is important to note that Kūkai continues to acknowledge the potency of the Golden Light sūtra, but also elevates the status of an esoteric sūtra called the *Sūtra of the Virtuous Kings Who Protect the Country*. As noted on pages 175–6 in M. W. deVisser's 1935 work, *Ancient Buddhism in Japan*, Kumarajiva first translated this sūtra into Chinese between 402 and 412 and the esoteric master Amoghavajra used his own translation of it in 765 to suppress barbarians and successfully produce rain upon the request of China's Emperor Tai-tsung. This scripture specifically claims that it can avert the seven calamities of the sun, moon, and stars (i.e. eclipses, comets, and other inauspicious disruptions of the heavenly order), water (floods), fire, storms, drought, war, and robbery (p. 182). In addition, this sūtra's prayers are specifically designed to remove such calamities, increase wealth, foster reverence and love and/or subjugate demons (p. 166). The text had been known and used in Japan since 660 for state-protecting ritual assemblies called Ninnō-e, but Kūkai was the first in Japan to write commentaries on it. Although he never stopped chanting and expounding upon the Golden Light sūtra, he supplemented his exegesis with material culled from this esoteric scriptural source.

In terms of exoteric–esoteric material culture, furthermore, the official title of Kūkai's own renowned Tōji temple (est. 823) is Kyō-ō gokokuji, meaning "the State-Protecting Temple (*gokokuji*) of the Sūtra's Kings (*kyō-ō*)." This generic namesake simultaneously invokes the protection of both sūtras' kings (i.e. the exoteric four heavenly kings of the Golden Light sūtra as well as the newer esoteric powers of the Virtuous Kings sūtra). This double combinatory strategy translates directly into the iconographic program of Tōji temple as a whole.

In Tōji's Golden Hall, an altogether conventional configuration of exoteric deities fills the ritual space. The healing Yakushi Buddha is flanked by the solar Nikkō and lunar Gakkō figures, with 12 diminutive generals supporting Yakushi's circular lotus throne. This supporting circle of generals (symbolizing the rotating zodiac) constitutes the one creative iconographic variation on the standard Nara-period configuration of deities. Directly behind the Golden Hall, however, lies Tōji's Lecture Hall with its altogether new mandalic arrangement of deities that was in part inspired by the esoteric Virtuous Kings sūtra. At the four corners of the altar platform appear the standard Four Heavenly Kings (and Indra and Brahma), but within their purview appear three main "pentads" of deities: Dainichi and four wisdom buddhas in the center, five wrathful wisdom kings to the viewer's left, and five great bodhisattvas from the Diamond World to the spectator's right. Cynthia Bogel, in her 2009 book, *With a Single Glance: Buddhist Icon and Early Buddhist Vision*, demonstrates on page 322 that at least from the early tenth century onwards, this arrangement was explicitly associated with the Virtuous Kings sūtra, as an altar diagram dated 922 specifically labels this configuration of deities a "Benevolent Kings sūtra mandala."

Finally, Kūkai also "esotericized" the annual Golden Light state-protecting rituals. In 835 Kūkai inaugurated a week-long series of elaborate rituals to complement other ceremonies taking place during the first week of the New Year. This Latter Seven-Day Rite pacified, protected, and promoted the well-being of the state by the power of the Golden Light sūtra. This ritual used the Two World mandala paintings and altars (as well as relics, five other paintings of the wrathful wisdom kings, and other altars for purification and fertility) to empower the sacred space. Most central to this ritual of national importance is the explicit imperial imagery in the Diamond and Womb World mandalas. Both mandalas are two-dimensional floor plans for three-dimensional palaces and/or imperial cities. These architectural constructs provide visual metaphors for the majesty of the macrocosmic universe, the country, the capital, the imperial palace, and the sovereign himself. The colorful Buddhas and bodhisattvas who reside within these mandala-palaces are accordingly dressed in imperial or princely garb and wear crowns and jewels as befitting any *cakravartin* or virtuous world-ruler. In short, they represent sacred geography and enlightenment by sampling visual cues for secular power, control, authority, and ideal space. As a result, to pump up the power of Nara's old state-protecting rituals, Kūkai insisted that *kanjō* initiations involving the Two World mandalas like the one I experienced at Kōyasan were essential to ensuring their efficacy. As translated by Yoshito Hakeda on page 41 in his 1972 volume, *Kūkai: Major Works*, Kūkai writes the following memorial to Emperor Saga dated 810:

> These sūtras are the essentials of the teachings of the Buddha and are sacred treasures of the nation. Therefore, since the K'ai-yuan era (713–41) in China, each emperor and his three highest ministers have received *abhiṣeka* and have recited and meditated on the mantras. ... Within and without the

> capital they built monasteries where mantras are recited in order to pacify the nation. There are such examples in the Buddha's own country as well ... The Buddha preached these sūtras (regarding mantra recitation) especially for the benefit of kings. They enable a king to vanquish the seven calamities, to maintain the four seasons in harmony, to protect the nation and family, and to give comfort to himself and others. For these matters these texts are sacred and excellent. ... For the good of the state I sincerely desire to initiate my disciples.

The rest, as they say, is history. Kūkai continued to initiate disciples into the esoteric path, and the Shingon school grew to exert major influence on Japanese politics and culture throughout history. Naturally the full scope of this religious, political, and cultural development is far too substantial to address here, or even within a single tome. However, this brief look into Shingon's early religious and political developments – and how these were accomplished through both textual and visual means – has helped us to better understand not only my own surprising coronation experience at Kōyasan, but also the imperial imagery and political functions of the Two World mandalas and other important esoteric Buddhist imagery in Japan.

Conclusion

The shift from exoteric to esoteric Buddhist methods for protecting the health and safety of the nation was accomplished not only through textual discourse, as Abe Ryūichi has shown, but also through material objects, iconographic symbolism, and ritual initiations like the one I experienced at Kōyasan that brisk October day. In particular, the addition of the Two World mandalas to pre-existing Yakushi sculptural groups pumped up the power of the old Nara-period deities' ability to heal and protect. In a kind of medical technology upgrade, these Vajrayāna microchips helped Yakushi, Nikkō, and Gakkō heal faster and better than before. As a kind of new powerful security surveillance system, Dainichi provided the light with which four divine sentinels would patrol the national borders and 12 heavenly generals would maintain the proper rotation of the seasons, thereby insuring agricultural prosperity and by extension, peace and tranquility throughout the land. Thus this public health and welfare committee was enhanced by the latest, greatest apotropaic measures *du jour*, since again homeland security and national health care were inextricably linked at the time.

My ritual coronation and our pointing of the *vajra* to the four directions at Kōyasan is overtly imperial in its symbolism, and was probably intended as the first step in a neophyte's future career dedicated to the protection of the state. I had no idea that becoming king of the cosmos at a religious rite in modern Japan would ultimately lead to a greater appreciation for the major objectives and historical developments of Japan's pre-modern religio-political governance methods. You never know what a blindfold can reveal.

Readings

Several notable publications have made Kūkai's doctrinal writings and Shingon's elaborate rituals and symbols accessible to English-language readers. All of Kūkai's pre-modern writings were fully compiled and translated into modern Japanese in the eight-volume *Kōbō Daishi Kūkai zenshū* (KDZ) published by Chikuma Shobō, 1983–85, but to date, Yoshito Hakeda's *Kūkai: Major Works* (New York: Columbia University Press, 1972) remains the standard primary source in translation for Kūkai's most famous writings (this essay, however, also used one translation from M. Anesaki's *History of Japanese Religion* [Tuttle Publishing, 1931]). M. W. de Visser's historical treatment of the Ninnō-e and the *Sūtra of the Virtuous Kings* appear in his *Ancient Buddhism in Japan* (Leiden: E. J. Brill, 1935) and Theodore de Bary's *Sources of Japanese Tradition*, vol. I (New York: Columbia University Press, 1958) also translates the *Golden Light Sūtra* and other Japanese primary sources related to Kūkai and his times.

In terms of secondary sources, Ryūichi Abe's *The Weaving of Mantra: Kūkai and the Construction of Esoteric Buddhist Discourse* (New York: Columbia University Press, 1999) is by far the most comprehensive analysis of Kūkai's major contributions to Japanese Buddhism and society. His approach is textual-philological, but other scholars have approached Shingon differently. Taikō Yamasaki's *Shingon: Japanese Esoteric Buddhism* (Boston: Shambala, 1988) is a general introduction aimed at the average reader, Minoru Kiyota's "Shingon Mikkyo's Twofold Mandala: Paradoxes and Integration," *Journal of the International Association of Buddhist Studies* 10(1) (1987), pp. 91–116, analyzes the mandalas' iconography in terms of Buddhist philosophy and phenomenology, and Robert Sharf's final chapter in *Living Images: Japanese Buddhist Icons in Context* (Stanford, CA: Stanford University Press, 2001) deconstructs some of the assumed ritual uses of the Two World mandalas. Art historians have also done much to elucidate Shingon's visual culture, e.g. Ryuken Sawa, *Art in Esoteric Buddhism* (Tokyo: Heibonsha; New York: Weatherhill, 1971), Elizabeth ten Grotenhuis' *Japanese Mandalas: Representations of Sacred Geography* (Honolulu: University of Hawai'i Press, 1999), and most recently Cynthia Bogel's *With a Single Glance: Buddhist Icon and Early Buddhist Vision* (Seattle: University of Washington Press, 2009). My own publications mentioned below also attempt to combine religious studies with art history and introduce Shingon's elaborate symbol systems to the average reader.

Author

Pamela Winfield is Assistant Professor of Religious Studies and Coordinator of the Asian Studies Program at Elon University in North Carolina. Her research focuses on the study of Japanese Buddhist art and doctrine, especially in the Shingon and Zen traditions. Other related publications include "Mandala as Metropolis," in Charles D. Orzech, Henrik H. Sørensen, and Richard K. Payne (eds.), *Esoteric Buddhism and the Tantras in East Asia* (Leiden: Brill Publishers, 2010), "Philosophy of the Mandala," in Gereon Kopf (ed.), *Dao: Companion to Japanese Buddhist Philosophy* (Dordrecht: Springer Publishers, forthcoming). and *Icons and Iconoclasm in Japanese Buddhism: Kūkai and Dōgen on the Art of Enlightenment* (NY: Oxford University Press, forthcoming). She is grateful to the Cross Cultural Institute of Kobe College Corporation (KCC), whose Margaret S. Foley Graduate Fellowship supported her dissertation research in Japan from 2001 to 2002 and provided much of the material for this essay.

Chapter 2

Buddhism through the lens

A study of the study of Buddhism through film

Lina Verchery

> The question of fiction's referentiality – does fiction make true statements about the world? – is the wrong one, because fiction does not ask us to *believe* (in a philosophical sense) but to *imagine* (in an artistic sense).
>
> James Wood, *How Fiction Works*

Preamble

When I began making my first professional documentary film, *The Trap*, I held the naïve idea that to make a documentary, all I needed to do was go out and "document" real life. The camera would act like a transparent window through which viewers could gain direct access to reality the way I saw it, the way it *really* was. I quickly realized, however, that the semblance of realism achieved in documentaries is often artificially constructed; what the audience sees on the screen is generally very different from what was actually filmed. But this made me wonder: if documentary films do not represents real facts about the world, then what makes them different from fiction? And, even more problematically, how can documentaries teach us anything true about the world? What follows is an account of my gradual realization that truth is different from fact. Indeed, I hold that it is *because* film can dispense with mere factuality that it can reveal different and deeper levels of subjective truth, which are just as true and empirical, if not more so, than so-called empirical factuality.

Narrative

Seeing the artifice in reality

> SHOT 4: UNDERWATER
> Traveling shot through murky waters at the bottom of the sea. The camera follows a thick white rope that emerges from beneath green algae and rocks leading to a lobster trap. A muffled gong is heard as a monk, off camera, describes the Buddhist view of life, suffering, and death. We circle the lobster

> trap, lingering on the decomposing body of the fish used as bait. Buddhist chanting fades in and intensifies as we reach the lobster in the trap. Chanting crescendos and the lobster turns directly to the camera just before the trap is hauled out of the sea.

This is a script excerpt from a documentary film I wrote and directed entitled *The Trap* (*La Trappe*) about the annual lobster-release ceremony at Gampo Abbey, the monastic headquarters of Shambhala Buddhism located in the backwoods of Pleasant Bay, a small fishing community on the coast of Cape Breton Island, Nova Scotia, Canada. Since 2000, on the last day of the lobster-fishing season, the monks and nuns of Gampo Abbey buy the final catch of a local fisherman who then takes the lobsters, monastics, and – as was the case on June 31, 2007 – my film crew and me out to sea to release the lobsters back into the ocean. At the time I wrote this film script, I couldn't help feeling ill-prepared. Although I had read about the ceremony online, I had never actually been to Gampo Abbey; I had never witnessed a Buddhist animal-release ceremony; I had never directed a professional film crew, and, most unsettling of all, I had never "scripted" a documentary film. This was my first job as a writer/director and, despite the producers' insistence that I script every last detail, I couldn't shake the feeling that a *scripted documentary* was an oxymoron. After all, I thought, don't documentary films just *document* real life? Life is spontaneous and unforeseeable. Wouldn't scripting a documentary ruin its authenticity and make it artificial? Little did I know that my angst about planning out "reality" would only intensify as I moved from writing and research into shooting and post-production.

It took several months of correspondence and phone calls to gain permission to shoot at Gampo Abbey. Understandably, the monastics were apprehensive about allowing a camera crew to intrude on the rhythms of their daily practice, especially since the abbey is deliberately located in the remote countryside, far from the distractions of secular life and society. I had proposed to arrive alone, a week before the rest of the crew, to familiarize myself with monastic etiquette and reassure the abbey residents that I would respect the boundaries of their sacred space. My proposition was also in part self-serving: the time spent getting to know the monastics and gaining their trust would also give me a chance to scope out who and what at the abbey would look good in the film. Upon my arrival at the abbey, I was given a sleeping mat to set up in the "guest cubby" located in the attic beside the curtained cubbies of the junior nuns. My cubby was about four by seven feet – just big enough to lie down in – and was fitted with an alarm clock and a small lamp. Wakeup was around 5.30 a.m., which allowed just enough time to get dressed, line up for use of the shared bathroom, and make it in time for 6 a.m. meditation and chanting. The abbey has a daily period of ritual silence, beginning at 6 p.m. and lasting until noon the following day. Since I could not rely on speech to help me navigate the many rules of monastic etiquette, I had to simply observe and imitate those around me. I watched how the group lined up for breakfast and then fell into line myself. I saw that after removing their shoes, the monastics bowed to the Buddha on the altar before entering and exiting the shrine room, so I did the same. I noticed that the seating for chanting and meditation was arranged by seniority, with the eldest monastics nearest to the shrine, so I set up my cushion at the back of the room.

As I became accustomed to the patterns of abbey life, I also got to know the monastics. Many of the conversations that spontaneously arose while I was helping with chores like cooking, gardening, and washing dishes were exactly the kinds of testimony I wanted to capture in the film. I began to see everything around me as though I was already looking through the camera lens. Though half of me was in the present, the other half was in the future, already shooting the film in my mind. When the crew arrived, however, the relaxed atmosphere that had been so conducive to spontaneous conversation quickly changed in response to the pressures of filming. In addition to the constant artistic decisions I had to make as a director – which alone felt overwhelming – I had to resolve a myriad practical problems, like convincing the monastics to allow us to film inside the shrine room while they were meditating, developing a method of clandestine communication with my crew (a combination of charades and muffled whispering) so as not to conspicuously break ritual silence, and ensuring that all crew members took off their shoes and bowed (even while carrying armfuls of sound and video equipment!) whenever entering or exiting the shrine room. I also began to notice that the presence of the crew was affecting the behavior of the monastics. They became self-conscious, acting either more reserved or more boisterous than before. I gradually realized that it would be impossible for me to simply *document* real life at the abbey because "real life" had changed in response to my documentation of it.

The day of the lobster release began in the usual fashion: wakeup shortly after dawn, the ceremonial raising of the flags, morning chanting and meditation, and the observance of ritual silence until noon. Although afternoons were usually dedicated to individual study or communal chores until dinner, when ritual silence begins again, on this particular afternoon we all piled into the monastery's minivan and headed down the unpaved forest road to Pleasant Bay, about 20 minutes away. Sporting maroon "Gampo Abbey" baseball caps to protect their shaved heads from the bright June sun, the monastics gathered on the dock, where the captain escorted them aboard his boat. We quickly packed the 42-foot double-decker cabin cruiser and, as the motor revved up, a celebratory atmosphere swept over the group. Although the director of photography had secured the camera to a specially crafted harness around his torso, he still struggled to get a steady shot on the rocking boat. As some monastics crawled up perilous ladders to perch atop the boat's 20-foot-high lookout, others stealthily scaled the front railing to sit on the bow, bare feet splashed by the chilly waves below. Despite the excitement, however, the group never lost sight of the trip's soteriological purpose and, once we reached the right spot to drop the anchor, the ritual began. The abbey's administrative director, its ritual director, and a senior monk opened the ceremony by chanting Sanskrit mantras and an English translation of a Tibetan blessing. As they chanted, an ornately decorated ritual wand was used to drip special blessing

Figure 2.1 Monastics participating in the annual Gampo Abbey lobster release

ambrosia, called *amrita*, over the lobsters. After the chant, the monastics each took one of the lobsters and, carefully removing the rubber bands from around the claws, gently deposited the crustaceans back into the sea. Some did this solemnly, while others were more playful, sometimes whispering a few fond words of farewell to the animals. Even the fisherman released a lobster and, after planting a couple of kisses on its back, jokingly exclaimed, "See you next year!" After the last lobster was set free, the monastics closed the ceremony by singing a musical arrangement of a poem by the eleventh-century Tibetan monk Milarepa. They then set off for home while I set off for the editing studio.

When I first watched the rough footage for *The Trap*, I thought every shot was visually interesting; the editor, however, quickly set me straight. There is a maxim in film-making that an editor should never be present at a shoot. That is, the editor must be free of all preconceived ideas about the footage – how it was gathered, who is depicted, what the shoot was like – and simply let the material speak for itself. In this sense, the editor is the film's first audience. While I thought the footage was fascinating because I was intimately involved in the process of its creation, editors – like audiences – do not benefit from that personal backstory; they see only what is on the screen. But this raised a problem. If the reason I loved the footage was that I had a personal connection with its characters, how could I make audience members who had never met the characters in person feel the same kind of emotional connection? This is where the editor comes in. It is the editor's job to *create* moments of emotional connection for an audience through the skillful manipulation of cinematic language – that is, by strategically constructing, cutting, recombining, and enhancing the film's content, color, composition, and sound to deliberately evoke a certain affective response.

For example, one of the major challenges we faced while editing *The Trap* was to make the audience feel sympathy for the lobsters despite the fact that, with their beady eyes, wiry antennae, and sharp claws, lobsters are certainly not the most affable of creatures. Yet the success of the film depended in large part on the audience's reaction to the first shots of the lobster trapped in its cage; it was imperative that these first few seconds stir the audience's sympathy such that they remain emotionally involved for the rest of the film. To achieve this, the editor deployed specific cinematic techniques. In the film sequence quoted above, for example, our addition of off-screen narration about topics like suffering and death immediately establishes a serious and somber tone. As the narration plays, the camera slowly approaches the lobster trap, lingering on the morbid detail of a small crab eating away at the corpse of a dead fish. Having already introduced the themes of suffering and death, we arrive at a close-up shot of a lobster trapped in the cage. The use of close-ups suggests feelings of claustrophobia, subtly making viewers themselves feel trapped, thereby inciting their sympathy for the lobster.

Editing also works on an audience by manipulating the pace of the story, in particular by omitting all but the most interesting and essential of information. These omissions do not only serve to speed up the story, such that we can recount the events of a whole day in less than 20 minutes, but are also a salient narrative

Figure 2.2 A novice nun releases a lobster during Gampo Abbey's annual lobster release

tool in their own right. That is, they draw viewers into the narrative by forcing them to imaginatively "fill in the blanks" when certain information is deliberately omitted from the story. For example, although I explain above that we took a minivan from the abbey to the dock and that a fisherman brought us out to sea, the film omits all these details and replaces them with four carefully chosen shots. First, we see a young nun sitting before a window in the abbey's shrine room. As she strikes the prayer bowl to end the chanting, we see a flag flapping in the wind behind her. We then cut to a wide exterior shot of the flagpoles, then to an extreme wide shot of the flagpoles, the abbey, and the sea on the horizon. The final shot in the transition shows the abbey from even further away, but this time the camera zooms out to reveal that we are actually looking at the monastery from aboard the boat where the lobster release is about to begin. In merely nine seconds, we jumped ahead in space and time: we omitted all uninteresting transitional facts – driving to the dock, getting on the boat, sailing out to sea – and instead moved the story immediately into the lobster-release ritual. Strictly speaking, this confounds our ordinary sense of sequential logic – after all, did we not see the same monastics now on the boat in the shrine room only moments before? – but most viewers do not consciously notice the omission because they automatically "fill in the blanks" as the action unfolds. That is, just as the ear automatically generates missing overtones in a musical harmony, we instinctively generate explanations for these kinds of narrative jumps in a story: moment by moment, we must be actively engaged in the creative exercise of interpretation to understand what is happening on-screen, and this keeps us interested. By deliberately omitting just enough information to keep an audience imaginatively engaged, an editor can change an audience of passive viewers into active interpreters who then become, in a sense, co-creators of the story.

In addition to manipulating the content and pace of the film to evoke certain emotions in the viewer, the editor and I also worked to create specific aesthetic effects. Part of this had already been accomplished during filming: all the scenes inside Gampo Abbey, for instance, were shot with a warming filter over the camera lens. This highlighted subtle tones of red and orange, giving the image a feeling of warmth and enclosure. Conversely, the digital editing systems we used in post-production enabled us to cool down the colors in the fishermen's scenes to emphasize drab grays, browns, and earthy greens. This color palette is designed to evoke the harsh elements that the fishermen face every day: the salty winds, the sharp rain, the perpetual dampness, the dirt, and the mud. Adjusting color temperature in this way subtly enhances the dramatic intensity of each shot. Whether it actually *was* warm in the monastery or cold on the dock on the day of filming does not matter; what matters is that viewers watching the edited footage have the *feeling* of warmth or coolness. In this sense, the reality created by the film was becoming as important as – or perhaps more important than – the real events the film was supposedly depicting. I was now far from my initial belief that documentary film is simply about *documenting* real life. In fact, as the editors and I began to piece together the final cut, I realized that virtually everything that looked like "real life" was artificially constructed. The film was not, as I had previously imagined, a transparent window onto factual reality. Rather, it was depicting reality – both literally and metaphorically – though the mediation of a lens. I began to realize that documentary film is often indistinguishable from fiction, and thus had to ask myself: if the "reality" in a documentary film is artificial and constructed, how can documentaries teach us anything *true* about the world?

Discussion

Seeing the truth in artifice

In a work called *The Dioptrics*, René Descartes compares what he calls the "very perfect image" – the image supposedly perceived inside the eye – and the real outside objects being perceived. He states, "Very often the perfection of an image depends on its *not* resembling the object as much as it might." He gives the example of etchings which, following the laws of perspective, depict circular or square objects not with circles or squares, but with oval and diamond shapes. In other words, the "very perfect image" is not an exact mimetic reproduction of objects in the world; rather, its perfection depends on depicting a certain *perspective* of the outside world that, in some cases, may not factually resemble the outside world at all.

Descartes' analysis gives us a fruitful way to think about different ways one might understand the notion of "truth" in documentary film. If, on the one hand, we espouse a positivist definition of truth – that is, one that takes empirical factuality as the sole criterion by which something can be deemed "true" – then documentary films have very little to offer. As I have argued, so much material in a documentary film is artificially constructed that it would be naïve to assume it reflects how the world *really is* in an empirical sense. If, on the other hand, we understand "truth" in a way akin to Descartes' "very perfect image" – that is, if we allow the possibility that a representation best reproduces its object when it does not resemble the object at all – then documentary films can teach us a great deal. A question, however, remains: if what documentary films show us are not the empirical facts of reality mimetically reproduced, then what "reality" do they show us? I contend that what they show us is not a reproduction but a *perspective*. It is the world through a lens. This subjective perspective is neither less true nor less real than so-called factual representations of the world. Even if an etching depicts a circular object as an oval, it does not follow that the circle is real while the oval is not. Rather, the etching accurately represents the human experience of perceiving circular things; after all, as is true of the rules of perspective, in everyday life we *do* perceive circular objects as ovals. We must, in other words, adjust the criterion by which we evaluate reality. The goal is not to represent objects as they empirically exist in the outside world, but to represent our subjective perception of them. Similarly, I suggest that a "very perfect film" is not – as I had initially imaged when working on *The Trap* – a transparent window through which to see the outside world; it is, rather, a lens through which we see *ourselves* seeing the world. Film is a means to see subjective, rather than objectivist or empirical, truth; film does not present truth *about* the outside world, but about our place *in* it.

As I thought about these issues, I found they had several parallels in Buddhist understandings of truth and reality. A foundational tenet of Buddhism is that all things are impermanent. By extension, ordinary perceptions of reality as static and enduring – the idea, for instance, of a unified and enduring self – are illusory and the cause of human suffering. Strictly speaking, there is no permanent objective reality behind our subjective perceptions. However, even though Buddhism asserts the illusory nature of so-called objective reality, it does not follow that our subjective perceptions of reality *per se* are untrue; rather, the error lies in the assumption that these subjective perceptions have objective external referents. In other words, taking subjective perceptions to be empirical fact is erroneous; seeing subjective perceptions as subjective perceptions, however, is to see reality as it really is. The Buddhist philosopher Nishitani Keiji explained the relationship between perception and "factual" reality through a salient metaphor. He said our perceptions of the world are like a mask, only the mask has no face underneath it; they are like an "appearance with nothing at all behind it". Put another way, the goal in Buddhism is not to reject perception – after all, Nishitani exalts the notion of the mask as a supreme virtue – but instead, the goal is to stop the mind from assuming that subjective perceptions must correspond to an independent, objective referent. In sum, one must see the mask simply as a mask, not as something that conceals an underlying reality that is "more true" than the mask itself.

Documentary films present us with a similar challenge: namely, to stop taking as one's criterion for truth the degree to which a film mimetically resembles some independent, objective reality. Instead, we must see films for what they are: truthful representations of subjective perceptions of the world that, by virtue of the subjective points of view they depict, help teach us about our own subjectivity. This idea plays into the Buddhist notion of the bodhisattva. A bodhisattva is an enlightened being who postpones his or her entry into *nirvāṇa* to usher other beings to *nirvāṇa* first. To do this, the bodhisattva takes on whatever mundane forms are most expedient for leading others to liberation. The character of the bodhisattva Vimalakīrti is a quintessential example. Although Vimalakīrti was an enlightened being, he took the form of a sick layperson to lead those around him to the teachings of the Dharma. His illness attracted the attention of his neighbors, who, concerned for his health, visited him. Once he had lured them to his home, Vimalakīrti was able to teach them the Dharma and lead them to liberation. A central question this story raises is, first, whether Vimalakīrti's illness was real. From the positivist perspective that takes empirical factuality as the sole criterion for truth, it was not. We know that Vimalakīrti's illness was simply a temporary appearance he took on for salvific purposes, like a mask donned by an actor. Yet, insofar as it helped lead others toward enlightenment, it was an illusion that produced *real* results. This is like Nishitani's idea of the mask with no face behind it; even if there is no ontologically "real" illness underlying the appearance of Vimalakīrti's illness, it does not follow that the appearance itself is untrue. As Nishitani writes, Vimalakīrti's

> illness is indeed a real illness, albeit an occasion for showing Great Compassion for all living things. There is not the slightest hint here of a feigned illness. ... So long as the illness that all living things suffer is real, the suffering that Vimalakīrti undergoes ... is no less real.

In other words, Vimalakīrti's illness is both artificial *and* true. Because it is primarily a tool for saving beings, the illness is merely the appearance of an illness, a kind of temporary mask that serves a specific purpose. Despite this artificiality, however, the mask produces *real* results: it saves sentient beings and, in this respect, its soteriological effects are absolutely real. A bodhisattva, thus, might be defined as one who uses the *illusory* world of appearances to produce *real* experiences of enlightenment. The skill of the bodhisattva is to produce real results with illusory means. It is, in other words, to make truth out of fiction.

Truth, artifice and the "magic" of cinema

The film-maker Werner Herzog makes what might be conventionally described as documentaries, as well as fictive narrative films. However, he describes his work – and cinema in general – as striving to achieve a level of truth that does not resemble conventional reality, that is deeper than the mundane reality of everyday experience. "Cinema," he writes, "is inherently able to present a number of dimensions much deeper than the level of truth that we find in reality itself, and it is these dimensions that are the most fertile areas for film-makers". This is what Herzog calls "ecstatic truth": a truth that, like Descartes' "very perfect image", can perfectly represent reality without *resembling* reality. In other words, ecstatic truth is a deeper truth that is achieved through artifice. It is, he describes, "mysterious and elusive, and can be reached only through fabrication and imagination and stylization."

Herzog's notion of ecstatic truth has at least two important consequences for how we evaluate the pedagogical value of documentary film. First, it means that what may look like reality in a documentary film is not a direct and unmediated representation of reality. What appears to be real, in other words, is often artificial. Learning to see the artifice in what looks "real" is important for developing critical discernment – a skill that is as imperative for scholars as it is for amateurs of film. It is like looking at an Impressionist painting: we must not content ourselves by standing at a distance and admiring only the "big picture." We must also step closer to see the coarse brushstrokes that make the picture possible. We must learn to see not only what the film wants us to see but also how the film's deployment of cinematic techniques *makes* us see what we see. This is also true when reading a scholarly essay. We must train ourselves to recognize the rhetorical tools used by the author to convince us of his or her point. In this sense, a well-argued thesis is much like a well-made film. Like film, scholarship uses its own techniques and conventions to demonstrate the truth of its claims, including styles of argumentation, citation of supporting evidence, and methods of gathering data. And, like film, the more skillfully a piece of scholarship uses these techniques of argumentation, the more invisible they become. In fact, we might say that an argument is truly *persuasive* when its argumentative techniques are so masterfully constructed that we stop seeing them altogether and the argument simply seems true of itself.

To be discerning scholars, however, we must step back and not only consider *what* the argument is but *how* the argument is made, and not only ask ourselves whether we are persuaded but *why* we are persuaded. The more scholarly works we read, the more attuned we become to the conventions of scholarly style. With practice, we learn to recognize a thesis, analyze supporting evidence, and adjudicate whether data is being used responsibly. We must, in other words, learn the "tricks" of the trade; we must recognize that, like film or painting, scholarship, too, employs its own techniques to make its audience believe in the veracity of its claims. In addition to being pedagogically important, practicing this kind of critical discernment is also of personal value: by recognizing and deconstructing the techniques we find rhetorically persuasive – whether in writing or in film – we come to better understand ourselves. Our deeply held views of "truth" and "falsity," or "right" and "wrong" are often the product of persuasion. Thus, reflecting on why we find certain views more persuasive than others is an invaluable step in better understanding ourselves, our cultures, and the world around us. In addition to teaching us to see the artifice in what looks like reality, documentaries can make a second – and, I think, even more valuable – contribution to the pedagogical process: they teach us to recognize the truth in artifice.

This means redefining the notion of artificiality – not as the opposite of sincerity or truth, but as a means through which truth, or what Herzog might call "ecstatic truth," can be approached. This is akin to the Buddhist notion that illusory means can produce real results. As Herzog puts it, good film-making does not simply present life as it is, but "intensifies truth by invention." Learning to see this invention – that is, the constructed cinematic techniques that generate certain feelings in the viewer – does not ruin the so-called "magic" of cinema. It does not ruin the temporary suspension of disbelief that enables us to be swept away by a story. Rather, in my view, the real magic of cinema is not the experience of being swept away at all. We can illustrate this by again referring to the metaphor of Impressionist painting. When we study an Impressionist canvas from up-close, all we see is a mass of brushstrokes, abstract shapes, and colors; the likeness of the picture is not apparent at this proximity. Once we step back, however, and look at the whole canvas at once, a recognizable picture – a bridge, a forest, a cluster of lily pads – emerges. Having seen the brushstrokes, one is aware of the techniques that generate the image, but this does not diminish the beauty of the image itself. Instead, it increases it. Thus, the magic of Impressionism is not merely the beauty of its images but, rather, it is seeing how deliberate and calculated technique – often rough and abstract blotches of paint that do not mimetically resemble the objects they depict – can generate a recognizable image. Similarly, the magic of cinema is not dependent upon ignoring the "brushstrokes" – that is, the use of artificial techniques and cinematic conventions – but on appreciating the many ways in which truth and artifice work together. Although the events in a film might be staged, the emotional response of a viewer is nonetheless real; like the illness of Vimalakīrti, cinema uses artificial means to generate real results. The "magic" of the craft lies in this interplay of artifice and reality.

An important consequence of this is that we must reconceptualize the notion of subjectivity and, by extension, expand the definition of empiricism. Subjective reality – that is, the *perspectives* that are presented in films, novels, works of scholarship, and even scientific theories – are not the opposite of or less valuable than so-called empirical or factual reality. In fact, as Herzog reminds us, subjective reality can point to a deeper truth than mundane, factual reality itself. Van Gogh once reflected that Impressionism attains a deeper life-resemblance than photography because it captures the truth of how we *experience* reality more accurately than can verisimilitude; that is, it is by virtue of its subjectivity that it is more truthful. It is what James Wood calls *lifeness*, not mere mimesis, "lifelikeness or lifesameness but … life brought to different life by the highest artistry." This redefinition of subjectivity also calls for a redefinition of empiricism. That is, if we recognize that the subjective is not the opposite of the empirical but is, rather, a valuable avenue to truth in its own right, then empiricism can no longer exclude subjectivity but must encompass it. If we hold to the formal definition of empiricism as knowledge that derives from experience, then a view of reality that takes subjective experience into account is not *less* but *more* empirical than one that excludes subjectivity. Documentary film allows us to engage this subjective reality.

Concluding remarks

While asking the local lobster fishermen who live near Gampo Abbey about their impressions of the lobster release, I collected a host of responses – many of which never made it into the film. One of these was a vexing question: what is the point of releasing lobsters if they will probably just get caught again the following year? This question revealed the potential futility of the lobster release, so I asked the monastics at Gampo Abbey about it.

One of the most salient responses I received was that the lobster release reflects Buddhism's position as a middle way between two philosophical extremes: eternalism, the view that action is absolutely meaningful and enduring, and nihilism, the view that action is fleeting and therefore meaningless. On one hand, the monastics of Gampo Abbey understood that their act of releasing lobsters, albeit a meritorious act, held no guarantee of eternal salvation. Practically speaking, everyone knew that the ritual really only ensured one extra year of life for each lobster, even less if other threats arose before the next fishing season. On the other hand, even though the lobster release was of only short-term practical benefit for the lobsters, none of the monastics therefore concluded that the act was meaningless. They knew that the lobster-release ritual was – like all things and all actions – impermanent. But this impermanence was not grounds for a nihilistic view of the world; as embodied by the bodhisattva ideal, our task is to work with illusory and impermanent forms to produce real benefit for others.

As I wrestled with the tension between truth and artifice during the making of *The Trap*, I, too, confronted a kind of nihilism. The realization of how much artifice is involved in creating the appearance of reality in film made me question the value of documentary film. It also affected my view of academic scholarship, for if, like film, scholarship employs its own rhetorical conventions and techniques to construct a persuasive argument, then how can we ever know if something is really true? In the end, however, I concluded that we can never know if something is *really* true because – as Buddhism teaches – absolutely objective truth cannot be attained; every argument inevitably presents the truth through a certain lens. But this does not mean there is no such thing as truth. Rather, it means that factual objectivity is not a precondition for truth and that subjectivity holds its own kind of reality.

In a sense, documentary films tread the same thin line between eternalism and nihilism as did the lobster release itself. Films are never unmediated depictions of reality and, thus, are never absolutely true in the objective or positivist sense. Yet this does not mean that there is nothing true we can learn from them. Even though films represent subjective perspectives, they still have the capacity to convey truth – not about some objectively existing external reality but about the many subjective ways in which humans experience the world. In the words of Wood, film captures life's *lifeness* itself. Documentary film is neither absolutely true nor absolutely artificial but, rather, reflects the fundamental fact that truth and artifice are inextricably linked in our experience of the world.

Readings

The Trap/La Trappe is available through the National Film Board of Canada's website and can be viewed online (French version only) at www.onf.ca/film/la_trappe as part of the NFB's extensive online library of documentary films. Those wishing to learn more about the tradition of animal release in Buddhism might begin with Duncan Williams' "Animal Liberation, Death, and the State: Rites to Release Animals in Medieval Japan," in Evelyn Tucker and Duncan Ryūken Williams (eds.), *Buddhism and Ecology: The Interconnection of Dharma and Deeds* (Cambridge, MA: Harvard University Press, 1997) and Henry Shiu and Leah Stokes' "Buddhist Animal Release Practices: Historic, Environmental, Public Health and Economic Concerns," *Contemporary Buddhism* 9(2) (November 2008), pp. 181–96. Further readings on the topic of fiction and documentary film include James Wood's *How Fiction Works* (New York: Farrar, Straus, and Giroux, 2008) and the writings and interviews of Werner Herzog, including his infamous "Minnesota Declaration," his interview with Paul Cronin, "The Ecstatic Truth of

Werner Herzog," in *Films in Focus* (www.filmsinfocus.com, accessed January 23, 2009), and the latter chapters of Paul Cronin (ed.), *Herzog on Herzog* (New York: Faber and Faber Inc., 2002).

Author

Lina Verchery is a doctoral student in Buddhist studies at Harvard University, where she is also a Frank Knox Fellow and a Fellow at the Harvard Film Study Center. Before writing and directing *The Trap* (*La Trappe*) for the National Film Board of Canada, which won the prize for Best French-Canadian Short Film at the 2008 Festival International du Cinéma Francophone en Acadie (FICFA), Lina co-wrote and co-directed *De Midi à Minuit*, a documentary short about cab drivers in Montréal which won first prize in the Alliance Française's Concours Senghor. Lina has over ten years of professional performance experience in film, television, theatre, and dance, working both in North America and Asia. In addition to assistant-teaching film studies and visual rhetoric at the Harvard Extension School, she is currently working on several films, including a documentary on the intersection of fiction and non-fiction.

Chapter 3

Voice and gender in Vietnamese Buddhist practice

Alexander Soucy

Preamble

Being a Buddhist in Vietnam means very different things to different people. There is no firm consensus on the kinds of rituals or practices that must be carried out to follow Buddhism. Nor is there much consensus on the kinds of goals people try to achieve through their practices. Contrary to the portrait that many Buddhist textbooks paint of practitioners searching for self-perfection with an eye to enlightenment, or being reborn in the Pure Land by the grace of the Buddha Amitābha (called A Di Đà Phật in Vietnam), the aim of devoted followers of the Buddha in Vietnam more often centers on mundane concerns of improving one's life here and now. Sometimes practitioners allude to a more vaguely stated idea of trying to improve their chances for a good rebirth in the future, or averting an extended stay in hell before rebirth occurs, but for most these goals remain secondary to more immediate concerns.

Vietnamese Buddhism, like many religious traditions in Asia, focuses more on correct practice (orthopraxy) and much less on the correct meaning or ideas of the religion (orthodoxy). There is very little structured attempt to teach people Buddhist doctrine. Instead, some people read about it in books, while many others are not concerned with meaning at all. This chapter will look at the highly individualistic way that Buddhism is practiced and interpreted on the ground in northern Vietnam. Particular attention will be given to how these variations are played out differently by men and women in ways that make their religious practice tightly connected with the overall construction of gender identities in the Vietnamese context.

I spent 18 months doing fieldwork in Vietnam in 1997–98, and returned after completing my PhD for an additional two years. My description comes from my memory, photographs, interview material, as well as field notes and journal entries. The ethnographic methodology is a slow process that gives the researcher the opportunity to get to know people very well. The process is intended to gain the trust of informants and to learn how different aspects of their lives relate to each other in a holistic manner. In my research, it was often a laborious process that required repeated, often unproductive, visits to various pagodas and time spent chatting and observing, rather than only interviewing. Sometimes I witnessed periods of excitement and effervescence when much was happening, as during festivals, special rituals, or pilgrimages, but a lot of the most fruitful work and best information was harder earned. In this chapter I will focus not on one event, but on three separate and unrelated days in a period of four months in the spring of 1997 when I visited Quán Sứ Pagoda almost daily.

Narrative

Most pagodas in Hanoi are quiet sanctuaries where one or two monks or nuns live and perform the daily rituals in relative seclusion. Devotee traffic is limited on most days, and if you go into one of them you will likely find only an older woman doing some cleaning. The lights to the main sanctuary will be turned off and a deep quiet will pervade the whole area. However, on the first and fifteenth of every lunar month there is an eruption of religious activity that erases all notions of the Vietnamese being irreligious.

The lack of activity on most days, and at most pagodas, was a source of frustration for me. I had gone to Hanoi to research Buddhist practice and found that, for the most part, nothing happened except on these two days of every month, when offerings were understood as being particularly efficacious, and the supernatural beings – whether buddhas, gods, or other spirits – were thought to respond to the entreaties of the devotees. At the beginning of my research I took to stopping at Quán Sứ Pagoda almost every day because, as the largest and politically central pagoda in northern Vietnam, it was exceptional for its activity. Every day there I saw vendors of religious articles, with their wares laid out on the sidewalk, hawking flowers, fruit, incense, and spirit money to offer to the buddhas; beggars hung around the courtyard hoping for donations from devotees who trickled in by ones and twos; various offices in the temple complex bustled with monastic and lay workers taking care of the official functions of this central pagoda; people wandered up to the bookstore counter from the street to buy Buddhist books, magazines, or ritual paraphernalia; young monks came and went to their classes that were held in the lecture hall towards the back of the complex; and others did various jobs like taking care of the library, guarding the motorcycles and bicycles parked on the side, or taking care of the maintenance. All of these people came to the pagoda for the same reason I did: Quán Sứ Pagoda was a hub of activity, and therefore had a steady stream of traffic all the time, and this activity signified its importance, which in turn drew others.

Here I will describe three separate days when I went to Quán Sứ Pagoda. The first day was on the first of the lunar month in the spring, and I went to participate in the sūtra-chanting ritual that is the mainstay of Buddhist practice for older women, who become more devout in their retirement. The next two days were not special in any way, but days when most pagodas would be inactive. So, I went to meet with men who presented themselves as knowledgeable "experts."

Figure 3.1 Woman praying in front of Quán Sứ Pagoda

Day one

The day was a relatively cool one, as the summer heat and humidity had not yet arrived, so it would be a comfortable day to attend the sūtra recital ritual that takes place on these special days. This is no small consideration, for when the warmer weather started the pagoda sanctuary would become nearly unbearable, with incense smoke hanging in the still, humid and hot air of the crowded hall. The long brown robes that Buddhist devotees wear in northern Vietnam over the top of long pants and a shirt made the setting even more difficult to bear; wearing shorts in public was considered rude, and especially so at religious sites, and so all of those at the temple arrived well covered.

I put on my brown robe, took out my prayer beads and sūtra book, and sat near the back of the room, where I could watch the ritual. The old women around me urged me to sit up front with the men. While not required, there was an expectation that men sit at the front and women sit behind them. I explained that I preferred to sit near the back, where there was more air from outside to make it easier for me. They eventually agreed, which was not always the case; several times my protests were overruled by the women who sat around me.

The woman on my left told her prayer beads, quietly saying the name of Amitābha Buddha – the Buddha who had vowed to have the faithful reborn in his Pure Land. With the sound of "Nam mo A Di Đà Phat" (pronounced Namo A Zee Da Fut), the woman on my right leaned over and started to ask questions of me in Vietnamese. The women on all sides leaned in to hear what I had to say. She asked me my name, how old I was, what I was doing, and whether I was Buddhist. I told her all, saying that I was doing research on Vietnamese Buddhism and culture and that I was sympathetic to Buddhism. I asked her in return why she came to the pagoda, and she replied that it was to give her a peaceful heart and that it would bring good luck to her family. This was a response that I had frequently heard from women to explain their Buddhist participation.

As usual, the service involved reciting sections from a few sūtras, culminating with the recitation of a list of buddhas and bodhisattvas, and finally in the recital of the name of Amitābha Buddha 100 times. The sūtras were collected in a cheaply bound red book called *The Sūtra for Daily Use* (*Chư Kinh Nhật Tụng*), which was used in pagodas throughout Hanoi, and could be bought at the bookstore. The sūtras themselves, though written only in the modern Vietnamese script based on the Latin alphabet, were still largely unintelligible to the people who chanted them, as they merely provided the Vietnamese pronunciation for Chinese characters. Thus the activity of chanting sūtras in no way imparted Buddhist teachings to the vast majority of chanters, and was therefore not a learning opportunity.

During the entire time we were reciting the sūtras, younger women (who did not wear brown robes) would approach the main altar from the side, place some flowers in the vases, light an incense stick, and place a tray on the altar, piled with fruit and spirit money. After five minutes or so they would reclaim their trays, burn the spirit money in a furnace in the courtyard, put the fruit in a bag, and pay the motorcycle watchmen before riding out into the bustling streets of Hanoi. As with the woman who sat next to me, their main purpose revolved around getting favors from the buddhas; young women would pray to pass exams, to meet a nice young man and get married, to have a baby boy, or to bring health and luck to their families.

At the end of the service I took off my brown robe and spoke with some of the women around me. They asked me the standard questions – where I was from, how old I was, and whether I was married. They were pleased to see that a young man (and a Westerner no less) was chanting sūtras. While I knew some women who came to Quán Sứ Pagoda, I did not know these women. There were 18 different groups that took turns chanting sūtras at this central pagoda, so the chances of forming relationships were not great. There were no places to sit and socialize over tea, so the crowd of devotees removed their robes and disappeared quickly on bicycles and motorcycles. I climbed onto my motorcycle, paid the watchman, and joined the traffic leaving the pagoda precinct.

Day two

A week later I pulled up to the front gates on my blue Russian Minsk motorcycle that looked like a Cold War relic and dripped oil wherever I parked. Arriving a few minutes before ten on a drizzly, cool morning, I shut off the engine and pushed it into the courtyard to park. There to greet me, as always, was the old man who watched visitors' bikes and motorcycles for a small fee. We had spoken often in the past. He was 68 years old and employed by the pagoda to do this job. It afforded a lot of time to sit and chat, and he could often be seen drinking tea with the caretaker, who was paid by the government rather than the pagoda. I had spoken to him in the past about his beliefs and he was peculiarly emphatic that he was not a Buddhist devotee (called a *phật tử*, a child of the Buddha). However, he did say that he believed in the teachings of the Buddha. He even participated in his own way, by going to listen to the Buddhist sermons that were delivered every Sunday at the pagoda and by reading about Buddhism. When he first insisted that he was not Buddhist I could see that for him it was an important distinction, though at the time I was not clear what it signified.

The purpose of my visit to the pagoda on this day was to meet a man who could often be found in the office of the Vietnamese Buddhist Research Institute (Phân viện Nghiên cứu Phật học thuộc Giáo hội), located on the second floor of the building to the right of the main shrine. It was in this office that one of the two Vietnamese Buddhist magazines is published, the *Journal of Buddhist Studies* (*Tạp chí Nghiên cứu Phật học*). It was a stodgy publication that reported on the activities of the government-run Buddhist association, as well as publishing articles on Buddhist history and philosophy. The room was dominated by a long, heavy, wooden table, which took up the center of the long room. Not having a firm appointment, I was happy to see that the man I had been hoping to meet was indeed there, sitting at the far end of the table with a copy of the latest edition of the magazine opened to his newly published article. I had met Colonel Tịch (pronounced "tick") briefly on a previous occasion, and he had given me a short, impromptu lecture on the importance of Buddhism to Vietnamese culture. He had presented me on the first occasion with a business card – a practice that is very common in Vietnam – that was intended to establish him as an expert on Vietnamese Buddhism. The card, in Vietnamese on one side and English on the other, read:

Tam – Tich
COLONEL (RETIRED)
– Senior Editor Editorial Board of
VN ENCYCLOPEDIA
– Journalist (since 1945)
– Researcher on Buddhism

He was well educated and proud of the fact that he could speak some English, French, and Chinese. As his card indicated, he wrote about Buddhism for several publications, including the *Journal of Buddhist Studies*.

The reason that I wanted to meet Colonel Tịch this day was to ask him more questions about his own religious practices and beliefs. I had learned that it was more productive in the Vietnamese context to get information from informal discussions than formal interviews, because the formal interview made many people (especially men) feel as though they should behave formally. They acted stiffly and were therefore less inclined to give their personal opinions, instead repeating official views taken from books they had read. I had previously informed Colonel Tịch that I was doing research on how people practice Buddhism in Vietnam, so this time I simply slipped into a discussion with him about how different people practice Buddhism.

We spoke for around 15 minutes, though the conversation was very one-sided, with the Colonel replying at length each time I was able to get in a question. He told me that he never went into the main sūtra hall of the pagoda; nor did he spend any time reciting sūtras. Instead, he felt that these practices were superstitious, and that they achieved nothing. The women who were primarily engaged in this activity, in his opinion, were wasting their time if they thought that there were any supernatural powers – like buddhas and bodhisattvas – who could help anyone with their problems on earth or with salvation. He instead felt it more important to try to understand the teachings of the Buddha. To that end, he spent a great deal of time reading about Buddhism and writing about Buddhism in Vietnam for the magazine.

Day three

When there were no rituals taking place at Quán Sứ Pagoda, I would often go to the library – the only Buddhist library in Hanoi – to look for information about Buddhism in Vietnam and to talk with the librarian there. The library is located on the ground floor of the building that surrounds the main temple, close to the road. It is not large, consisting of one room with some shelves and cabinets placed against the walls, and with a large table in the center of the room. On this day I arrived mid-morning to meet the librarian and to go through back issues of the *Journal of Buddhist Studies*. The main librarian in this small, one-room library was a gentle and intelligent man named Mr. Đức (pronounced to rhyme with "nook").

On this day I arrived wanting to learn something from Mr. Đức about his view of hell. The commonly held belief was that when you die most people have to atone for their sins by going to hell for a stint before being reborn in a new life. The souls of dead relatives can be helped to some extent by burning spirit money, which they can use to bribe the officials in hell so that they receive a lesser sentence. His response to my questions, however, followed reasoning that conformed to elite skepticism regarding the supernatural. Mr. Đức insisted that hell was merely symbolic, meant to teach people to behave morally (or perhaps frighten them into doing so). When I asked about people burning spirit money he told me that it did not help in any way: "The truth is that you only have yourself. So you need to have a good heart and behave correctly. That is the only thing that helps." This response followed a pattern of his that tended to follow a rationalist view that stressed self-cultivation while diminishing the role of faith and devotion. Thus, like Colonel Tich, Mr. Đức felt that the people who recited sūtras misapprehended the purpose of their activity:

MR. ĐỨC: After you recite sūtras you will feel joyful, you will promise to follow the Buddha forever. But there are some people who do it wrong. They hope that when they recite sūtras they can wish for things like health, wealth, or success in business from the Buddha. This way of thinking is wrong.

ME: Do you think that most people do it correctly or not?

MR. ĐỨC: That depends on the level of enlightenment of each person. If their level of instruction is enough … then they are "cultured" (*có văn hóa*) and will be able to understand that you have to rely on yourself to gain enlightenment (*tự mình tu lấy mình*) ... and those who have only studied a little in the village think that reciting the sūtras alone is enough to bring happiness.

Also like Colonel Tịch, Mr. Đức did not chant sūtras, feeling that moral behavior and study were the essential practices for a Buddhist.

Discussion

Quán Sứ Pagoda is the most important Buddhist center in Hanoi. It is a large and untraditional structure in the heart of the city. Whereas most pagodas in Hanoi are one-story and have curved tile roofs, Quán Sứ Pagoda is two stories and has unique architectural features that distinguish it from all of the others. The main sanctuary is surrounded by offices that house the various committees and functions that are needed as the headquarters of the Vietnamese Buddhist Association – the only legal Buddhist organization in Vietnam. It was rebuilt in 1941 during a period when there was a movement on the part of some elite monks to reform Buddhism. The movement was a response to the position in which the Vietnamese found themselves during the late nineteenth century, when they were subjugated and colonized by the French. As a result there was a broad re-examination and self-criticism by the Vietnamese elite that extended to their society and culture. One object of this self-criticism was religion. Many renounced religion altogether in favor of Western secular rationalism. The Buddhist reformers' response viewed Buddhism in Vietnam as having been corrupted over time by false cultural accretions and superstitions. The main thrust of the reform movement was to, ostensibly, purify Buddhism of these aspects and bring it back to the original teachings of the historical Buddha. At the same time, this movement was international – Vietnamese Buddhist monks and scholars were participating in conversations with Japanese and Chinese reformers as well. Nonetheless, the reform movement did not trickle down to most Vietnamese Buddhists, and instead remained mostly at the elite level.

Quán Sứ Pagoda was the center of this reform movement and of attempts to bring unity to the independent Buddhist pagodas in the north. After the Communist government took over in 1954, Quán Sứ Pagoda became the headquarters of the new Buddhist organization founded and controlled by the state, and it remains in this position to this day. This organization reflects the state's desire to conform to religion (as defined in Western terms) as opposed to superstition, and is therefore (in an odd way) heir to the form of Buddhism proposed by the reform movement of the 1930s. This is especially seen in the opinions of Mr. Đức the librarian and Colonel Tich, who felt that reciting sūtras was at best misunderstood by most practitioners, and at worst a complete waste of time. It also underlies a more widespread masculine view of Buddhism that associates the practice of reciting sūtras with devotional practices and understandings of women.

Nonetheless, and despite the centralizing attempts by the state to organize and control Buddhism in Vietnam, Buddhists continue to practice of their own accord and in their own way. The lack of authoritative direction and dogma means that there is a great deal of individuality in the way that people practice Buddhism and conceive of their practice. Despite the heavy stress on orthodoxy at Quán Sứ Pagoda, the more mainstream forms of devotional activities are also practiced here, as they are practiced throughout Vietnam and by overseas Vietnamese around the world. Groups of devout Buddhists – mostly women – show up twice a month to recite sūtras and chant the name of Amitābha Buddha. Others, frequently younger women, do not have the time or the devotion to take part in this core activity, and instead simply make offerings at the altar to the buddhas.

The most prominent distinction in practices is, thus, between the way that men and women engage in Buddhist activity and think of themselves in relation to their Buddhist practices. The men at Quán Sứ Pagoda respond in a typically masculine way to Buddhism. For example, the elderly gentleman who watched the bikes and motorcycles at the pagoda was clearly interested in Buddhism, demonstrated by the fact that he read books about Buddhism and listened to Buddhist dharma talks. However, he resolutely refused to declare himself a Buddhist. This reflects the overall view in Vietnamese society that Buddhism is for women because it shows weakness – a characteristic that was desirable in women but was a serious character flaw in men. Others, like Colonel Tịch and Mr. Đức in the library, were more forthright in declaring themselves Buddhist, but they did it in a way that drew a clear distinction between their Buddhism and the Buddhism that was practiced by the women in the sūtra hall.

The women who made offerings and the women who recited sūtras had similar explanations for why they engaged in these activities. I was most often told that the motivation for their Buddhist practice was to bring good luck to their families. This intention for practice on the part of women was recognized by both men and women, who used it as the foundation for their explanations for why it was overwhelmingly women who could be seen at pagodas. There were some men who took part in the sūtra chanting, but they generally represented only 10 percent of participants. They also differentiated themselves from the women by usually sitting in the front and taking a more active part in leading the ritualistic elements, such as reading the petition to the buddhas and playing the percussion instruments that accompanied some of the chanting.

The reason that women gave as the motivation for practicing Buddhism stems from an understanding of women's roles in the family and in society. Women usually construct their identities around their perceived role as caregivers for the family, in fulfillment of behavioral prescriptions placed on them by Vietnamese society. Women who are seen to be neglecting this role are frequently disparaged, along with women who are seen to be overly assertive. Vietnamese culture has inherited much from China, including Confucian dictates regarding women. Traditionally, women were expected to follow the Confucian rules for proper behavior, which dictated that women acted gently and maintained a subservient demeanor to men. Modernity has somewhat eroded the forcefulness of these dictates, and certainly influences some people to view the actual formulation as a backward aspect of their feudal past. Nonetheless, societal expectations still require that women act quietly while men can be loud, that women serve instead of receive service, and that women follow the decisions of others rather than be forceful about their own views.

There are, however, subversive ways that play on this overall structure and allow for women to gain substantial power, especially within the family. The success of particular strategies to gain authority within the overall system can be seen through casual observation of circumstances in which women often wield considerable power. This is reflected in the popular aphorism of wives being "generals of the interior."

The way that this is principally carried out is through cultivation of a sense of obligation, termed *ơn*, which is a pervasive aspect of all relationships in Vietnamese culture. There is an overt understanding that gifts and favors need to be repaid, and that the balance of power tips towards the one who is owed. Thus, people carefully calculate these debts to prevent being overly obliged, for too much debt will create resentment, but the right amount can warm relationships and draw people together. The extent to which people track these debts is amply demonstrated at weddings, where guests usually give money in an envelope as a gift, and the size of the gifts is carefully recorded so that they can be exactly repaid on a later occasion.

Within the family the rules of obligation are somewhat different. Notions of filial piety obligate children to respect parents unconditionally and permanently. However, it is the father, as part of the patrilineage, who demands greater respect in terms of the hard power structures of family in Vietnam. Mothers, in a way that resembles the situation found by anthropologists in China and Taiwan, hold a marginal position relative to the patrilineage, and therefore are psychologically prone to creating their own families based on the children that come from them rather than the ancestors of the family which they have joined through marriage. The effect of this is that mothers tend to make greater efforts to engender affection in their children and to create more overt ties of reciprocal obligation. These ties of obligation are also useful for balancing male authority within the family; by being good mothers/wives, they rightfully oblige husbands to reciprocate. One way that this is often done by wives/mothers is by performances of caring and sacrifice, which serve to stress obligation owed for their role as caretakers of the family. One can frequently hear mothers attempt to instill guilt in children, by making statements about the efforts and suffering that they have undergone on behalf of their children and their husbands. At the same time, women are seen to be fulfilling their role as good mothers and wives by putting their family above all else.

In this light, it makes perfect sense that women accentuate the benefits that religious practice has, not for their own salvation, but for the good of the entire family. Thus, most women I spoke with, whether they principally practiced by making offerings a couple of times a month or became more involved by reciting sūtras at the pagoda, claimed that their efforts would bring good luck to their families, and especially their children. Being Buddhist, in essence, was an extension of their roles as primary caregivers in the family.

The concerns of men were quite different, and this was also reflected in their Buddhist practice. It is not a coincidence, therefore, that it was men at Quán Sứ Pagoda who showed a tendency towards scholarship rather than the devotional practices of reciting sūtras and making offerings. Most men who would describe themselves as Buddhist would not participate in the signature practice of Buddhism in Vietnam – chanting sūtras. They would describe this practice as often misinterpreted by women, saying that it has no effect whatsoever on a person's luck (never mind a whole family's) other than giving the opportunity to learn the teachings of Buddhism. (Of course, this view is compromised by the fact that the sūtras are largely unintelligible to most practitioners.)

In fact, there is a concern that Buddhist practice as constructed by women (the primary practitioners) is too devotional and has a sense of reliance on an exterior force, which goes against masculine ideas of strength and self-sufficiency. For example, the caretaker at Quán Sứ Pagoda once explained to me the reason for the heavy presence of women at pagodas by saying that women go to pagodas more than men because they are weaker, and so need to ask for external help to solve their problems. On this basis, most men avoid Buddhism altogether. Those who do identify themselves as Buddhist take pains to distinguish themselves from women and their practices. Rather than engaging in Buddhist practice as a way to display concern for the family, men tend to stress aims that are more fitting in the construction of masculine identity. While the level to which Confucianism has infused the Vietnamese way of being is debated, masculinity and power tend to reflect a Confucian view, which stresses personal cultivation. Thus, men I spoke with tended to say that the aim of their Buddhist practice was to cultivate themselves intellectually and morally, and perhaps eventually to be in a situation where they could gain enlightenment.

Not only were their views different, but the forms of practice that they undertook were also distinguished from those of women. Colonel Tịch and Mr. Đức were both examples of this. While both claim to be fervent Buddhists, neither one ventured near sūtra-chanting rituals. Instead, they both preferred to read, write, and talk about Buddhism as their principal practices. They maintained that it was absolutely essential to understand the Buddhist sūtras, and that, in the opinion of Mr. Đức, chanting without understanding was of no benefit. It would have no effect whatsoever upon a person's luck, or even their karma, if they did not also try to understand what they were reading and to live a moral life. The men who actually engaged in chanting sūtras distinguished themselves from women in other ways, but that is a discussion for another time.

Readings

Writings on Vietnamese Buddhism are few and far between. Most have tended to treat Buddhism in Vietnam as an ideology that has been transmitted from China, and very few of these descriptions are based on original research. The result is that there has been an idea that has been perpetuated that Vietnamese Buddhism is best represented as Zen. The first study to challenge this idea is Cuong Tu Nguyen's important textual analysis, *Zen in Medieval Vietnam: A Study and Translation of the Thiền Uyển Tập Anh* (Honolulu: University of Hawai'i Press, 1997). The same thesis is presented more concisely in his "Rethinking Vietnamese Buddhist

History: Is the *Thiền Uyển Tập Anh* a 'Transmission of the Lamp Text'?" in K. W. Taylor and John K. Whitmore (eds.), *Essays into Vietnamese Pasts* (Ithaca, NY: Southeast Asia Program, Cornell University, 1995), pp. 81–115. Shaun Kingsley Malarney has contributed an essay that describes Buddhism as it is practiced on the ground in a northern Vietnamese village: "Buddhist Practices in Rural Northern Viêt Nam," in Philippe Papin and John Kleinen (eds.), *Liber amicorum: mélanges offerts au Professeur Phan Huy Lê* (Hanoi: Nhà xuất bản Thanh niên, 1999), pp. 183–200. Alexander Soucy has contributed several essays that deal with gender and Buddhist practice in northern Vietnam, including "Masculinities and Buddhist Symbolism in Vietnam," in Katherine Biber, Tom Sear, and Dave Trudinger (eds.), *Playing the Man: New Approaches to Masculinity* (Sydney: Pluto Press, 1999), pp. 123–34; "The Problem with Key Informants," *Anthropological Forum* 10(2) (2000), pp. 179–99; "Consuming *Lộc* – Creating *On*: Women, Offerings and Symbolic Capital in Vietnam," *Studies in Religion / Sciences Religieuses* 35(1) (2006), pp. 107–31; "Language, Orthodoxy and Performances of Authority in Vietnamese Buddhism," *Journal of the American Academy of Religion* 77(2) (2009), pp. 348–71. On Vietnamese Buddhism as it is practiced in North America, see Cuong Tu Nguyen and A. W. Barber, "Vietnamese Buddhism in North America: Tradition and Acculturation," in Charles S. Prebish and Kenneth K. Tanaka (eds.), *The Faces of Buddhism in America* (Berkeley: University of California Press, 1998), pp. 129–46; and Alexander Soucy, "The Dynamics of Change in an Exiled Pagoda: Vietnamese Buddhism in Montreal," *Canberra Anthropology* 19(2) (1996), pp. 29–45. For the role that Buddhism has played in helping Vietnamese refugees settle in the United States, see Paul Rutledge, *The Role of Religion in Ethnic Self-Identity: A Vietnamese Community* (Lanham: University Press of America, 1985), though this is somewhat outdated.

Author

Alexander Soucy received his PhD from the Australian National University in 2001 and is currently Associate Professor of Religious Studies at Saint Mary's University, Halifax (Canada). He has conducted research on Buddhism in Vietnam, where he lived for four years, as well as on Vietnamese Buddhism in Canada. He is the author of *The Buddha Side: Gender, Power, and Buddhist Practice in Vietnam*, forthcoming in early 2012 from the University of Hawai'i Press, and has recently co-edited, with John S. Harding and Victor Sogen Hori, a book called *Wild Geese: Buddhism in Canada*, published by McGill-Queen's University Press in 2010. His current research focuses on global Vietnamese Buddhist connections and the changes that are occurring in practice as a result of the meeting of Vietnamese traditional Buddhism with Westernized forms in the Vietnamese diaspora.

Chapter 4

Feasting for the dead

Theravāda Buddhist funerals

Rita Langer

Preamble

The countries of South and Southeast Asia that belong to the Theravāda school of Buddhism (Sri Lanka, Burma, Thailand, Cambodia, and Laos) share the reliance on the version of the Buddhist canon and its commentaries that is composed in Pāli, the sacred and ritual language of the Theravādins. Despite the fact that not all monks and indeed very few laypeople know Pāli, these texts have shaped the religious outlook of that region. They also play an important part in the liturgy of Theravāda Buddhist funerals, when monks chant canonical verses (e.g. for protection or blessing), retell Pāli stories (such as the Vessantarajātaka) in the local vernacular, and draw on topical verses to provide a theme for their sermons (e.g. on suffering or impermanence).

Most people would regard the participation of monks as essential at key moments of Buddhist funerals, and considering that traditionally death rituals are the only life-cycle ritual in which Theravāda Buddhist monks are actively involved, funerals are a great opportunity to observe the monk–laity relationship. There are, however, still other, complex layers to the funeral rites, which do not require the participation or presence of monks at all. The Theravāda Buddhist funeral consists of practices as diverse as confusing the spirit of the dead, feeding crows and ancestors, protective chanting, feeding Buddhas, gambling and dancing, feeding monks, giving of merit, feeding hungry ghosts, etc.

I will describe in some detail the burial of a laywoman and the two follow-up rituals (the sermon on the sixth day after the death and the alms-giving on the seventh day), which I observed in 1998 and 1999 in Sri Lanka. This will be supplemented by occasional glimpses into other Theravāda funerals, which I observed in Luang Prabang (Laos) in 2007, in Chiang Mai (Thailand) in 2008, and in Sagaing (Myanmar) in 2009. For my description of events in Sri Lanka I rely on my field notes, audio recordings, and photographs. On my more recent trips to Laos, Thailand, and Myanmar, I started filming as well as taking photographs.

Figure 4.1 Laypeople and monks work together ladling food onto the plates of the invited monks. The monks indicate "enough" by covering their plate with one hand

Narrative

In 1998, I spent six months with my husband and our two-and-a-half-year-old son in a small village in Sri Lanka (Gampaha district) researching Buddhist funeral rites. I had friends there who generously let us occupy a small house next to their home. The two houses were surrounded by a beautiful garden with old trees including coconut palm, banana, jackfruit, and even a roseapple tree. After setting up house I tactfully spread the news that I was interested in Buddhist rituals in general and funeral rites in particular. Even though most people found my interest somewhat peculiar, to say the least, they were nevertheless very supportive and patiently answered all my questions on funerals while I was waiting for an opportunity to observe these rituals at first hand. Finally one Saturday morning, about a month after our arrival, our friend's uncle very excitedly popped his head through our kitchen door and announced that an old lady, one of his relatives, had died in a village not too far away. As she was originally from our village there would be a little group of people going to the funeral. He was obviously very pleased to be the bearer of such "good news."

On Monday morning our small party of eight made its way to the train station, stopping at the local shop on the way to buy some milk powder and sugar. It is customary to bring something for the bereaved family, and I was told packets of milk powder and sugar are always appreciated. (In Laos and Thailand, incidentally, people bring envelopes with money, and the donor and amount donated are announced to the deceased and recorded in a book.) At the last minute a retired English teacher from our village (another relation of our friend's) was summoned to join our party to assist me in case my Sinhala was not up to the job. During the next few months he became a good friend and helped me transcribe and translate some of the sermons that I had recorded. After a short train journey, a longer bus ride, and another short three-wheeler ride we spotted the tell-tale signs of a funeral: white flags along the roadside, white banners with messages of sympathy, and metal chairs arranged in front of the house.

Funerals in Asia are very public affairs, but, of course, it is still essential to ask permission to observe and document the proceedings. Ideally someone known to the family should make the introduction, but that is not always possible. In Myanmar I went with the volunteers of the local funeral society – many towns, not only in Myanmar, have these societies to help with the organizational and financial side of funerals – which is the next-best thing. In Laos and Thailand my colleague and I visited temples with cremation facilities, and when there was a funeral in preparation we approached the families and explained that we were researching Buddhist funerals. So far my request to observe has never been refused; on the contrary, more often than not I have been invited back for some follow-up ceremony, such as a special alms-giving on behalf of the deceased. However, as this was the first funeral that I documented, I was very glad to be part of a group.

We arrived at about 11.00 a.m. and were formally greeted by the family in front of their house. The daughter and son-in-law, both in their seventies, told us that the mother had died very peacefully at the age of 94. The body was lying in a fold-out coffin in the front room, all dressed in white, with folded hands and a calm look. Two enormous artificial elephant tusks flanked the coffin, and an oil lamp was burning at the head end. We paid our respects and I was encouraged (urged, actually) to take a picture. My worries were unfounded and everyone was very friendly and helpful. The front room was bare of furniture and most pictures had been removed. From the moment someone dies his or her home becomes a "home of the deceased" (*malagedera*) and certain rules apply: there is a wake as the body must not be left alone, mirrors and shiny surfaces are covered, doors and windows are kept open at all times, and no cooking takes place inside the house. Most of these customs are easy to miss and the details might vary slightly, but the underlying concerns are not to frighten the spirit of the deceased or hinder its movements and separation from his or her home.

As the next guests arrived, dressed in formal white, we were moved along through the house into the garden. The setting was rather beautiful: a small, simple house (no show of wealth) at the end of a village surrounded by a garden. It looked as if major cooking activity was about to happen: several fireplaces were set up, huge clay pots were brought out, and pumpkins and mountains of beans and dried fish were piled up. Still, for a long time nothing seemed to happen and we chatted and drank orangeade while the hottest time of the day approached. I took the opportunity to walk around the house and garden to see what, if any, other activities or preparations were going on. Then somewhat abruptly at about 2.00 p.m. the daughter and son-in-law of the deceased urged everyone to go to the neighbors' house, where a buffet lunch had been prepared for the 20–30 people (family, friends, and neighbors) who had been at the *malagedera*. After a delicious lunch we returned and serious cooking began in the garden: vegetables were washed and chopped for the traditional funeral meal (*malabata*) of rice, pumpkin, cooking bananas (or green beans), and dried fish. Fires were lit and children were sent off on errands, and everyone who offered to help was given some task or other by the daughter of the deceased. Steadily the number of people increased until well over 100 mourners of all ages were present. The granddaughters were busy walking around with trays, offering fizzy drinks to the guests.

Funeral ceremonies in this region do not have to be held at home, but can be conducted in various locations. In Myanmar I observed funerals in a pavilion at the burial ground, and, in one case, in a temporary shelter set up at the roadside (when someone dies away from home the body can only be taken as far as his neighborhood boundary). The funerals I observed in Laos and Thailand were held at the temple and at the crematorium in a purpose-built hall or a pavilion. However, in this case the ceremony was taking place at home, and while the cooking went on in the garden, the front of the house was prepared for the arrival of the monks. The funeral society, which is run by volunteers, had provided chairs and a corrugated iron roof as shelter from the sun. Four chairs were lined up facing the house, and a piece of white cloth was tied underneath the roof to create an awning for the monks. A small table was arranged with four bottles of orangeade for the monks and a tray with betel leaves and areca nuts. Chewing betel, or paan as it is often referred to, is very popular in South and Southeast Asia, particularly with monks.

At 3.45 p.m., four monks (the minimum number required) arrived in a van and were formally greeted by the family. People stopped their activities and gathered at the front of the house. The president of the funeral society welcomed the monks and people sat down on the floor. The mood changed from relaxed banter to respectful silence. Six men took the coffin outside and placed it on a stand in front of the monks. There was some hesitation because the body had to be taken over the threshold at a precise moment, which had been established by an astrologer. This is meant to ensure that the spirit of the dead will not return to the house. The family sat down on the floor between the monks and the coffin. The monks and laypeople began the ceremony with the salutation to the Buddha, Dhamma, and Sangha and by reciting the Five Precepts. This was followed by a brief sermon and the offering of the "cloth of the dead" (*matakavastra*), a piece of white cloth in a brown paper bag, to the chief monk. The monks chanted in a very sorrowful voice a canonical Pāli verse about impermanence: this is chanted at nearly every Theravāda Buddhist funeral. It is always a very poignant moment and has a certain finality.

After a brief sermon the family gathered around a bowl and took hold of a jug of water, which they poured very slowly into the bowl until it overflowed. This signified the giving of merit to the deceased and was accompanied by the monks chanting. The three bases of merit in Buddhism are: generosity (*dāna*), morality (*sīla*), and contemplation (*bhāvanā*); by donating the cloth, taking the precepts, and listening to the sermon great merit had been accumulated for the deceased by her family and friends. The chief monk then chanted Pāli verses of blessing for everyone and continued his good wishes and aspirations in Sinhala. The president of the funeral society thanked the monks, who rather abruptly got up and left, taking the parcel of cloth with them. The whole ceremony from arrival of the monks to their leaving lasted only about 30 minutes. Funerals in Thailand and Laos often have additional chanting and, if organized by a well-to-do family, there might be more than one group of monks and the ritual sequence of chanting (by the monks) and offering the cloth (by the laypeople) is repeated.

Now the president of the funeral society introduced a number of people, one after the other, who gave speeches. People relaxed and started milling about again. Time passed slowly and the shadows grew longer. Finally the president of the funeral society announced the dates of the follow-up ceremonies and with that a sudden hub of activity started. The coffin was briefly opened one more time and women cried as it was swiftly taken away, a white umbrella held over it. Only men accompanied the coffin to the cemetery, but as a foreigner I was in the fortunate position that I could choose my side. On another occasion I stayed back to watch milk being boiled in the front room to cleanse the space where the coffin had been, but in this case I opted to join the funeral procession. By the time we arrived at the cemetery the shadows were very long. The men carried the coffin clockwise around the open grave three times before opening it one last time. With its long white tassels it looked beautiful in the late sunlight. After a few moments of silent respect the coffin was closed again and quickly lowered into the grave, which was then closed and decorated with a green coconut.

In Sri Lanka and Myanmar burials are more common than cremations; the latter are reserved for monks and the well-to-do. A few weeks later I observed a cremation in our village. The preceding funeral ceremony conducted by the monks was largely the same, but the prospect of a cremation attracted more people to the cemetery (including women and children, but not monks). The pyre is traditionally lit by two nephews of the deceased, facing away from it, by throwing torches over their shoulders. In Thailand and Laos cremations are the norm and these can take place either at the temple, with a cremation platform, or, in big cities, at the crematorium. If the cremation takes place outside, the pyre is sometimes lit by a rocket shooting across the cremation place on a wire with great noise. These indirect ways of lighting the pyre seem meant to put a distance between the living and the departed.

On the way back we collected the poles with white flags that had marked the way to the cemetery. Back at the house the grave-diggers (neighbors who had volunteered for this honorary job) were "paid" with local liquor and cakes. The cooking in the garden complete, everyone was invited to the simple but delicious funeral meal, served in the traditional way on banana leaves. Everyone was in a rush now to get going before the last of the sunlight had gone. Tropical twilight is brief and power cuts are frequent. We were offered a lift, but before we left we had to promise to be back for the next event, the sermon on the evening of the sixth day after the death has occurred.

On Thursday I had to bribe my friend's aunt to go with me. She had not actually intended to go, but there was no way I would have found the house by myself and besides I was still somewhat unsure of the dos and don'ts of such an event. After I had promised that we could take a three-wheeler all the way there and back, Auntie finally agreed to come with me. Again a big crowd of 70 to 80 people had gathered, and this time most people greeted me like an old acquaintance. We arrived a bit early, so I had a chance to look around. In the garden behind the house the cooking was in full swing, but here a bewildering array of dishes was prepared: fish and chicken curries, soup, various vegetable dishes, cashew curry, papadams, sweets, and cakes. Today our contribution was a bunch of bananas. We found the daughter and son-in-law in the kitchen, busy filling a big cone made from a banana leaf with their dead mother's favorite dishes. In the garden at the side of the house a little square, about 1 meter by 1.5 meters, was fenced off with young coconut leaves. Someone had lovingly arranged the sleeping mat and pillow of the deceased as well as a glass of water. I was intrigued to find out what was going on as no one had ever mentioned this to me before. When I later asked people about it, it turned out they just thought it unimportant, as the offering for the spirit of the deceased did not involve monks.

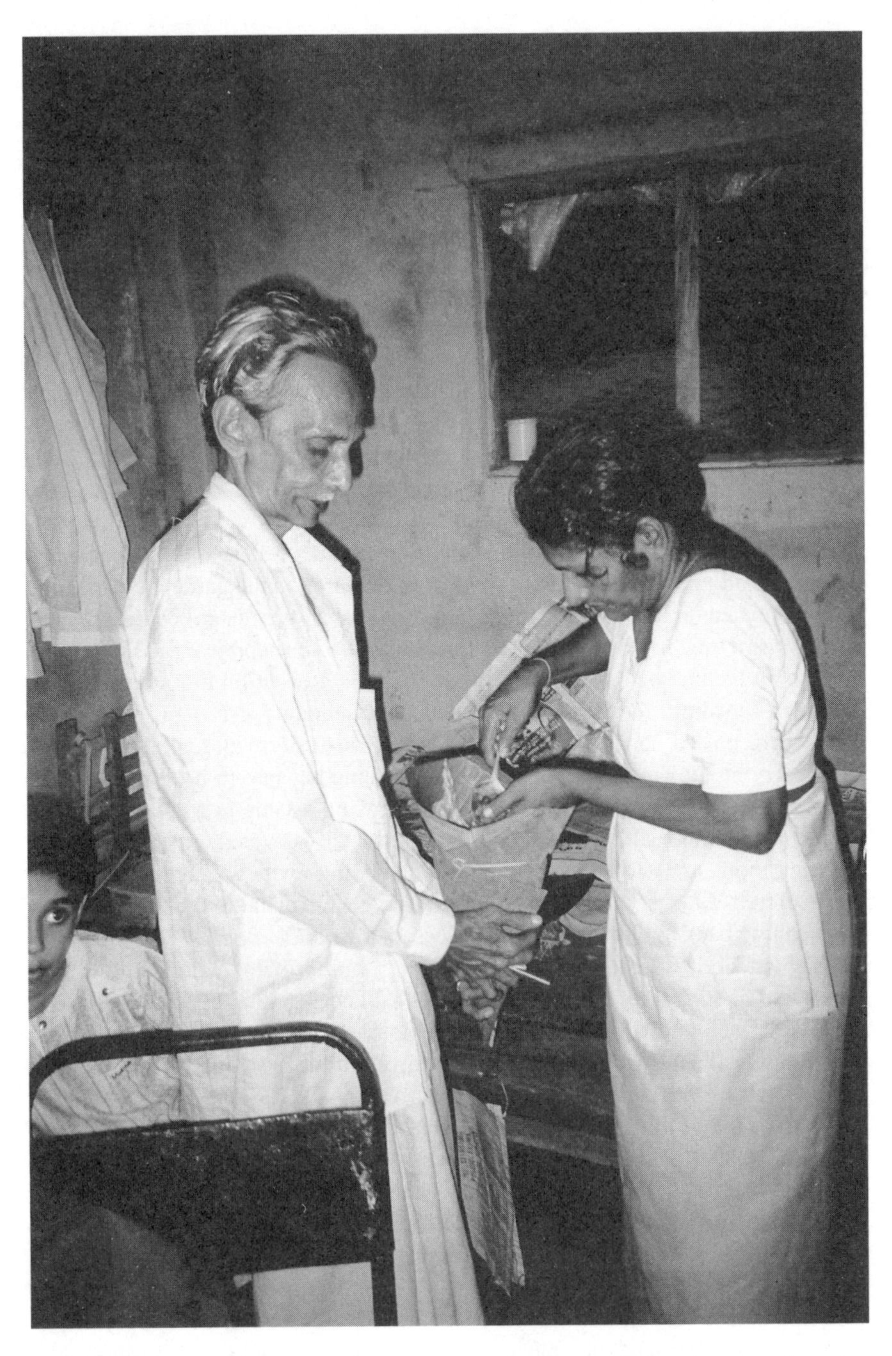

Figure 4.2 A cone made of banana leaves sewn together is filled with rice and curries, salads and papadam for the spirit of the deceased

At about 7.45 p.m. a single monk arrived in a three-wheeler. While he was being shown to his seat in the front room the son-in-law took the banana leaf cone with food into the garden. He stepped into the little square, placed the cone on a bamboo stand, lit an oil lamp, and called the spirit of the dead mother. He invited her in very affectionate terms to come and listen to the sermon, which was about to begin. He also told her about the alms-giving the next day and that all the merit accruing from this would be given to her. Then he went to the front room, where the monk now began to preach with more sympathy than regard for doctrinal issues. His sermon lasted exactly one hour; a big alarm clock on the table in front of him made sure of that. After the monk left (monks are not supposed to eat after midday), everyone was treated to the most delicious meal. Before we left I had to promise to bring my family along when I came back the next day for the traditional alms-giving.

On Friday morning again a small party from our village headed for the *malagedera*, buying vanilla ice cream (our contribution to the alms-giving) on the way. This time my husband and son joined us, which proved to be a real success (doing fieldwork with a small child is highly recommended, as it does open many doors). Again great clay pots with food were prepared in the garden. For the first time it dawned on me just how important food was in the funeral context, as this was the third time in seven days that a great feast had been prepared. This was not only about feeding people, though. In the morning a beautiful brass bowl, which had been sent from the temple, was filled with delicious dishes and sweets and cakes were placed on top. We piled into a three-wheeler with one of the grandsons, carrying the brass bowl, a coconut, and some bananas to head for the local temple. There we placed the various food items on a table in front of the main statue in the shrine hall, a recumbent Buddha partially covered with a net curtain. A young monk assisted us by chanting the Pāli verses with which the food items were offered. After no more than 10 minutes we were again in the three-wheeler and heading back to the home of the deceased, the *malagedera*.

At about 11.30 a.m. nine monks arrived in a van, bringing with them the relic receptacle. Every temple in Sri Lanka has what is believed to be a bodily relic of the Buddha, the most famous being the temple of the tooth-relic in Kandy. The son-in-law walked over to the van with a towel on his head and carried the relic on his head to a makeshift "altar" in the front room. This "altar" occupied the position of the most senior monk, and the other monks were seated in order of seniority next to it. Again food items were offered with the same Pāli verses that were chanted before at the Buddhapūjā. This was followed with a brief sermon, religious wishes, and blessings. Family and friends then lined up to serve the great variety of dishes. As the monks started eating one of the sons went around with a banana-leaf plate to collect little handfuls of food from every monk. He then took the plate outside and carefully placed it at the foot of a tree for the hungry ghosts or crows (both explanations are common). After the monks had finished their meal the son offered to the most senior monk a dome-shaped parcel containing the eight requisites for monks (three robes, an alms bowl, a waistband, a razor, a

Figure 4.3 The brass bowl filled with food is taken to the local temple for the Buddhapūjā

sewing kit and a water strainer) before placing it on the "altar." The family then joined in the distribution of parcels containing useful household items such as umbrellas, buckets, and washing powder. The chief monk next preached a brief sermon of "appreciation after the meal." Again relatives assembled to pour water and give merit to the dead mother. The monks chanted the accompanying verses, followed by more blessings for the family and everyone present. When they left they took the relic and parcels with them.

Now everyone relaxed and the children were the first to start eating. The mood was quite different from the two previous events and rather more celebratory. For the past seven days the house had been a *malagedera* and a hub of activity. Three major events (funeral, sermon on the sixth day, and alms-giving on the seventh day) with feasts for great crowds had had to be organized; every night the men of the family and male friends had held a wake and needed to be catered for; relatives from afar had had to be put up, and a constant stream of visitors who came to pay their respects had been treated at least to a cup of tea. Everyone had pulled together to help with the enormous tasks and expenses of those seven days; neighbors had catered for the bereaved family as no cooking is done in the *malagedera*. Friends had come to lend a hand or keep the family company day and night, and the funeral society had provided the chairs, the awning for shade, and the speaker. Now with the monks gone and the seven-day period of mourning over, the household could finally get back to normal. The relief of the family and something akin to a sense of achievement were tangible. I have observed a good number of funerals in Sri Lanka as well as Thailand and Laos, but somehow this would turn out to be my "favorite" one, my benchmark for an ideal funeral. The village setting was beautiful and there was something rather old-fashioned in how the neighbors and friends stepped in to help with cooking and other tasks. It was almost like going back in time and getting a glimpse of a world that is fast vanishing. Nowadays, particularly in big cities like Colombo or Chiang Mai, the old social networks are disappearing and caterers, instead of neighbors, are called in to do the cooking. Funerals have, of course, always been occasions to assert the family's social status within the community, but there seems to have been very little of that on this occasion (just the minimum number of local monks were invited, no famous monks from afar, and there were no lavish gifts). Besides, the deceased was in her nineties and had died peacefully at home, which made the funeral sad, but not as raw and traumatic as another funeral I observed in Laos, which was for a young person who had died in a traffic accident. And I cannot even begin to imagine what a funeral for a small child or a young mother would be like; luckily I have never found myself having to observe one. But maybe this funeral was also special to me because it was the first I followed over seven days. I had a chance to get to know the chief monk and the family and even visited them again later when I brought them some photos. They seemed very affectionate and even joked that they had to let the son-in-law do all those tasks that are normally done by the eldest son because he was closest to their mother. But I think what set this funeral apart more than anything else was the fact that the

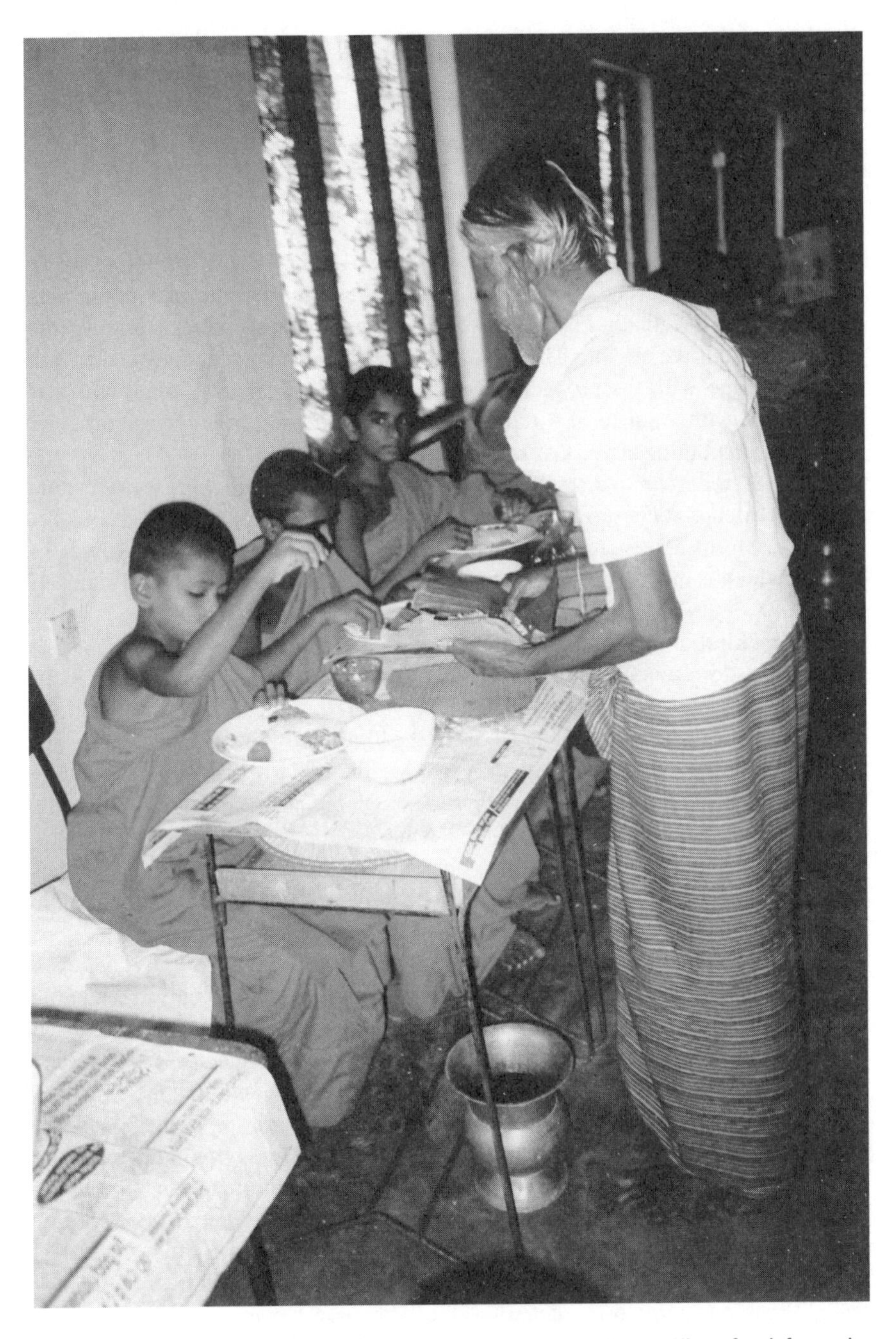

Figure 4.4 Two laymen go around with a "banana-leaf plate" to collect food from the monks for the hungry ghosts.

daughter and son-in-law were elderly themselves, which gave the proceedings a sense of poignancy. There was something rather beautiful and intimate in the way they had arranged everything for their mother, thought about her favorite dishes, and invited her spirit with kind words.

Discussion

The fact that the Buddhist funeral rites are so complex and comprise many different activities spread over several days makes it difficult to pick one aspect for discussion. Originally I had planned to concentrate on the Pāli chanting of the monks, as that is the obvious Theravāda part of the funeral proceedings. I decided, however, to go with the broader topic of providing and sharing food, which is of such great importance in a religious context generally (see for example the Eucharist, combining aspects of sacrifice and feast).

First, it is important to distinguish different types of feeding: there is (a) feeding the dead which is about providing for the afterlife; there is (b) feeding the Buddha, which is a form of veneration; and finally there is (c) feeding great crowds of people, which is mostly but not exclusively aimed at asserting the social status of the family.

The first kind of feeding – providing food and clothing for the dead – is a pre-Buddhist custom, which has been given a Buddhist twist in the shape of merit (see Holt's article "Assisting the Living by Venerating the Dead," for instance). The brahmanical rituals for the dead detail the kind of offerings needed at various stages: the first 11 days (a symbolic year) are particularly crucial as the newly dead (*preta*) is not only hungry, thirsty, and naked, but also in need of a new body. By way of a special ceremony on the eleventh day, he is turned into an ancestor, which is the climax and in a way the objective of the brahmanical funeral rites. Faint remnants of this shift from preliminary to permanent stage are still tangible in the Sri Lankan ritual, even though this is not made explicit and in fact goes against the Theravāda doctrine of instant rebirth. However, popularly it is believed that for at least seven days the spirit of the deceased is still around, so when the special offering of food and drink is made in the garden for the newly deceased on the sixth day it is a very personal offering and tailored to the deceased's tastes. When the monks are invited for an alms-giving on the seventh day the emphasis shifts quite clearly from personalized food offering to merit for the deceased and a token food offering for the hungry ghosts. The monks are invited for a meal and accept donations of useful items, thereby acting as mediators between the living and the dead, who benefit indirectly from this meritorious deed. Interestingly, even though canonical texts such as the Petavatthu (a collection of ghost stories) largely deny the efficacy of direct food offering to the dead and stress the importance of giving merit to the departed, the latter never completely replaced the former, but rather complemented it in that the food became the "carrier of merit."

The second kind of feeding – providing the Buddha statue or a relic receptacle with regular meals – is not only done in the funeral context but is part of the daily worship at the temple. Whenever laypeople send food for the monks to the temple or invite monks for a meal to their homes food is also provided for the main image in the temple or the portable relic shrine. This custom of providing the Buddha with food is not only very common, but also seems to have a long history, as it is already mentioned in a fifth-century commentary by Buddhaghosa. Both the statue and the relic are treated like a living presence, a very honored guest, the most senior member of the Sangha. Even though some contemporary Theravāda Buddhists will insist that the Buddha is never regarded as anything other than a very special man it has also been argued that this form of *pūjā* (worship) is akin to *deva* worship. To illustrate this point I will draw on another example: on certain occasions in Sri Lanka a family, or a group of people, decide to organize a worship (*pūjāva*) of the 28 Buddhas. I have taken part in one such event, which is a rather elaborate affair involving 28 identical, beautifully decorated trays of food. This *pūjāva* is usually done either in fulfillment of a vow, or with an agenda, e.g. the donors wish for something, and is not dissimilar to a *pūjā* at a Hindu temple. The difference, though, is that food offered to a Buddha statue or relic cannot be taken back, whereas part of the food given at a Hindu temple is regarded as auspicious when it is returned and consumed by the donor.

And the final kind of feeding involves the various other beings or groups that are fed. After the initial seven-day period is over, there is usually another almsgiving for the monks three months later, which is in some places even bigger and more elaborate than the one on the seventh day. It has already been mentioned that holding big funeral feasts goes some way to asserting the social status of the family, but this is not the only rationale here. One characteristic of these feasts is that no expense is spared and families do get into debt over these feasts. The general rule seems to be the more money spent and the more people fed, the greater the benefit for the deceased. But these feasts are not only for people. Hungry ghosts (or crows) are fed as well with little food scraps from the plates of the monks, as it would be inauspicious on such an occasion to feast while others go hungry. The Buddha functions as the head of a hierarchical, food-sharing "commensal community" (see Strong, *The Legend and Cult of Upagupta*, p. 51) which encompasses monks, laypeople, beggars, animals, spirits of the dead, and hungry ghosts. Funeral feasts are widely discussed in anthropology, where they are seen as part of a wider food exchange, but rarely get the attention they deserve in the field of religious – or more specifically Buddhist – studies.

Readings

While death has always been a popular topic in Buddhist studies, its practical side, the death rituals and the disposal of the dead, have only recently begun to attract scholarly attention. A very important volume edited by B. J. Cuevas and J. I. Stone, *The Buddhist Dead: Practices, Discourses, Representations* (Honolulu: University of Hawai'i Press, 2007), brings together a collection of articles from various Buddhist traditions. However, there are no books yet which are specifically devoted to Theravāda death rituals, a topic so far dealt with only in passing (usually under the heading of life-cycle rituals). A good example for this marginal treatment of death rituals is R. Gombrich, *Buddhist Precept and Practice: Traditional Buddhism in the Rural Highlands of Ceylon* (Oxford: Clarendon Press, 1971). The book combines historical and anthropological approaches and gives a good insight into the religious practices in Sri Lanka in the 1960s, but devotes only one chapter (chapter 5) to the issue of death rituals. Again, journal articles dealing with the topic are rare and tend to concentrate on doctrinal and historical, rather than contemporary issues (see the excellent articles by J. C. Holt, "Assisting the Dead by Venerating the Living: Merit Transfer in the Early Buddhist Tradition," *Numen* 28 [1981], pp. 1–28; and P. D. Premasiri, "Significance of the Ritual Concerning Offerings to Ancestors in Theravāda Buddhism," in D. J. Kalupahana (ed.), *Buddhist Thought and Ritual* [New York: Paragon House 1991], pp. 151–58). It is hoped that the situation is slowly changing and that the volume edited by Paul Williams and Patrice Ladwig, *Buddhist Funeral Cultures of Southeast Asia and China* (Cambridge: Cambridge University Press, 2011), will go some way towards closing this gap. John Strong's excellent study, *The Legend and Cult of Upagupta: Sanskrit Buddhism in North India and Southeast Asia* (Princeton: Princeton University Press, 1992), looks at a wide range of Buddhist rituals in South and Southeast Asia associated with the legendary monk Upagupta. It contains interesting observations on the Buddhist monastery as center and focal point of a commensal community which could serve as a starting point for more in-depth research into feeding and feasting in Buddhist practice (another area which has not yet received the scholarly attention it deserves).

Author

Rita Langer is Lecturer in Buddhist Studies at the University of Bristol (UK). Her publications include *Buddhist Rituals of Death and Rebirth: A Study of Contemporary Sri Lankan Practice and Its Origins* (Abingdon: RoutledgeCurzon, 2007). Her most recent research includes a comparative study of the funeral chants in Sri Lanka, Thailand, Laos, and Burma.

Chapter 5

Buddha for our time

Images of a Sri Lankan culture hero

John Clifford Holt

Preamble

In 1977, after years of failed socialism and the nationalization of the economy, a newly elected government of Sri Lanka with a pro-Western diplomatic tilt jump-started what was avowedly championed as a capitalistic "open economy." The new government initiated large-scale development schemes, including the construction of several reservoirs and irrigation projects by Britain, Sweden, Germany, and Canada. Other plans included establishing free-trade zones and nurturing what would become the spectacular growth of the nation's tourist industry. The consequence of the "open economy" was rapid social change, particularly in the Sinhala regions of the country. Westerners seemed to swarm over the island. In the following essay, I reflect on how social change impacts religious culture, specifically focusing on how this change registered at the most important ritual and pilgrimage site for Sinhala Buddhists: the Dalada Maligava ("Temple of the Tooth-Relic") in Kandy, the last of the traditional royal capitals. I also observe how social change in Sri Lanka is sanctioned by its rationalized associations with the Buddha.

Narrative

> Perception is the fore-runner of all mental formations.
>
> *Dhammapada* 1: 1

I first came to Sri Lanka some 30 years ago, a day after the Vesak celebrations of 1979. At the time, in spite of years of studying Buddhism in texts, I was almost completely ignorant of the manner in which the Buddha is understood culturally by various types of Buddhists in Sri Lanka. As ridiculous as it seems to me now, I don't think I was even very aware that Vesak was one of the most important holidays celebrated in Sri Lanka every year. Thirty years back, my knowledge of the Buddha was decidedly more philosophical in character, almost exclusively derived from scholarly books about religious ideas. The Buddha, in my own mind, was one of the great religious teachers of humankind, who had tried to show a way out of the unsatisfactory nature and calamities of the human condition. But religious festivities like Vesak and other important modes of popular ritual expression were not what I had studied before I first came to Sri Lanka. Had I known about the importance of Vesak back then, I certainly would have made an effort to get there in time to see the colorful panoply of lanterns, pandals (popular poster art depicting various *jataka* stories), and "electric Buddhas" and to listen to the sonorous melodies of young, white-clad women singing Buddhist devotional songs called *bhakti gee*. Experiencing Vesak close-up on my first visit to the island would have made for a fantastic introduction to the Buddhist people of this country and would have accelerated my understanding of how the Buddha has been understood within the Sinhala Buddhist culture of Sri Lanka. But I was late for Vesak, and so my learning curve with regard to the social and cultural significance of the Buddha was probably a little bit steeper than it might have been as a result.

Because of my "late" arrival, my initial impressions of Sri Lanka were based on my first visual encounters with the lifeless, vacant streets I saw in the Colombo Fort that day after Vesak: a few casual workers were taking apart the structure of a pandal which had been so brilliantly illuminated only the day before, and small clusters of people were peering through the windows of department stores, catching glimpses of the newest import from the West: television. I remember thinking that Colombo was really a very drab city, the Fort, the old administrative center of the county, being a former and thoroughly colonial place whose best times had probably passed by many decades before. In retrospect, my initial impression couldn't have been more erroneous. The following day, when the holiday hangover was gone and people had returned to work, Colombo turned out to be a thriving and teeming bustle of activity. I was overwhelmed by the beehive of work going on in the neighborhood of the Pettah and by the intensive varieties of business being transacted in the Fort. I made a quick deduction based upon my first observations from the day before: the taking apart of the pandal and the fascination with television were somewhat paradigmatic of a pattern I suspected was then afoot – tradition (pandal) was waning and change (TV) was arising in modern Sri Lanka.

Recently, some Sri Lankan government officials introduced a movement to have Vesak recognized globally as an international holiday – a very interesting idea that would lend greater visibility to the profound impact that the Buddha has made not only upon the Buddhistic cultures of Asia, but on world history in general. I can only wish now that Vesak and its significance had caught my attention earlier. What I didn't really understand when I made my first deduction about tradition and change in Sri Lanka was that although change may seem ubiquitous and inevitable, there is a staying power in traditional ways of apprehending life in general, and that this staying power is represented by the Buddha. That is, change and tradition stand in a reflexive relationship to one another.

From my formal studies in religion as an undergraduate and then as a graduate student, my perception of the Buddha had been conditioned first by my encounter with him in the relatively sanitized textbooks on "world religions" that I had read while attending college in Minnesota. These books reduced the distinctive philosophical orientations and rich varieties of religious cultures of Asia to an abstract and almost faceless common denominator. Later in my studies, I had been further influenced by impressions that had been formed as the result of studying Pāli Text Society translations, especially the Buddhist monastic code of regulations, the *Vinayapitaka* (Book of Discipline), and the principal *nikaya*s (didactic portions of the *Suttapitaka*) some years later while studying at the University of Chicago. For me, as I read and reflected on these texts, first in English and later in Pāli, the Buddha seemed to cut the figure of a strict (and sometimes, in the case of articulating monastic disciplinary rules in the *Vinaya*, a rather downright intolerant) pragmatic disciplinarian of monks on the one hand and also that of a profound philosopher/teacher dispensing the advice of prosaic wisdom to would-be converts on the other. I wouldn't go so far as to say that my image of the Buddha was that of a "Victorian gentleman," to borrow a phrase from an American colleague who I think has aptly commented on how some nineteenth- and twentieth-century British scholars, like T. W. Rhys Davids and I. B. Horner, had portrayed the Buddha. But I would say that I probably had been carrying around an image in my head that was something of a cross between Plato, Solomon, and Confucius. At the time I was blissfully unaware that my view of the Buddha, whatever it was exactly, was nothing more than a narrow scholarly rendering.

When I recall my culturally and historically rather innocent understanding of the Buddha at that time, I think it was also concomitantly the result of my own lack of awareness regarding the manner in which my Protestant Christian (Lutheran to be precise) upbringing had affected my general understanding of religion, as well as my rather uncritical imbibing of the manner in which other earlier American and European scholars of a Protestant inclination had bequeathed a legacy of understanding the Buddha in the West. So, my perception of the Buddha was not only that of stern and wise Confucian Plato speaking the truth about human suffering and its transcendence (through the vernacular of the late nineteenth-century "Queen's English" of the Pāli Text Society translations), but also a perception of a religious genius (yet in Protestant or Germanic/Puritan style) who had eschewed all mediated forms of religious pursuit (thought, rituals, symbols, myths, as well as other types of cultural media which combine to create the rich tapestries of social and historical religious expression). In my perception, the Buddha was among the greatest of human teachers, but surely not a god. I thought the Buddha had been above or beyond all of the usual religious paraphernalia, a rather otherworldly figure enunciating lofty philosophical maxims, whose sole purpose in life had been to point out an arduous spiritual path to the ineffable experience of *nibbāna* (Pāli for Sanskrit *nirvāṇa*). While I remain convinced, some 30 years later, that the ultimate significance of the teachings of the Buddha has to do with ending suffering, my perception of the Buddha is no longer that of a Confucian Plato, although I do continue to see some affinities with many of Confucius' moral maxims. My education leading to a transformed understanding of the Buddha

Figure 5.1 The Avukana Buddha statue

continues today, but it really began in earnest two days after my 1979 arrival in Colombo, when I first entered the Dalada Maligava in Kandy.

In 1979, the Dalada Maligava remained a genuine place of pilgrimage. During the four days I spent at the temple photographing rituals, recording their sounds, and doing my best to see how the formal orchestration of ritual activities in the temple facilitated different types of religious experiences, I met very few Western tourists and I, myself, remained relatively undisturbed by tourist hawkers. I absorbed as much as I could, from the early 4.30 a.m. *pūjās* or worship services to the last ritual at night. I recorded the various drumming cadences, tagged along with various types of worshippers, watching their every move, and pestered temple officials about what was done when and why. I came away from that initial visit with an understanding of how Buddhism, especially with regard to the rituals, symbols, and myths associated with the Dalada Maligava, formed a type of civil religion among the Sinhalese. The Buddha was not only a great religious teacher of the past, and a "thus-gone one" (*tathāgata*) but somehow, in this temple, there was still something of his presence to be felt. Here was a temple complex blended into a royal palace and a relic that was undisputedly regarded as the palladium of the Sinhalese people. If the Buddha was not actually present, then his legacy certainly was.

I studied the spatial symbolism of the city of Kandy and found that it reinforced hierarchical conceptions of power within the Sinhala Buddhist traditional socio-cosmic worldview. The Buddha and the king, in parallel fashion, had been placed at the apex of this hierarchy. I came to know clearly, and could see this with my own eyes, that Buddhism was a religion intimately bound up with the political history of the island and had made its pact consistently with the country's Sinhala kings, who had become the religion's chief patrons of support over many centuries.

I was also impressed with the devotional expressions of religious piety I observed at the Maligava, especially among villagers who had come to pay their homage in the company of friends and family. I attributed to these people the social virtue of "communitas," a term coined by anthropologist Victor Turner to describe a type of spiritual camaraderie that can be generated among collegial pilgrims, an egalitarian social mysticism of sorts.

Thus, my image of the Buddha began to change. I began to see him not only in relation to lofty philosophical ideals articulated in venerable religious treatises, but also in relation to the socio-political history of the island on the one hand, and as an object of personal veneration among the village laity on the other. I began to suspect that, regardless of class, background, or station in life, the Buddha represented a valorization of the sacred for people of all walks of life in Sri Lanka. He was a bona fide "culture hero" in this country.

When I returned to Kandy three years later in 1982, however, I witnessed an explosion of the tourist industry, not only in Kandy but throughout Sri Lanka. Almost at every *handiya* (intersection), a plethora of colorful homemade signs advertising the comforts of new guest houses with names like

"Paradise Garden," "Shanti Rest," "Golden Horizon," etc., filled the streets. Hawkers were in overabundant supply on the streets of Kandy. I felt as if I was consistently among the most hunted. The government's "Cultural Triangle" officials, with some loose affiliation to UNESCO, had secured control of some of the premises of the Kandy sacred area (I was unhappy that I had to pay to gain access to sacred shrines), and the ambience of Senkadagala (the central core of old Kandy town) had shifted inexorably, I thought, from the sacred to the profane. Though I realized that there is always an interesting connection between pilgrimage and tourism at most sacred places throughout the world, and that sometimes the lines between these two forms of social behavior are easily blurred, I was disappointed with what had happened in Kandy, and even more so in Anuradhapura and Polonnaruva, where exorbitant entrance fees had been introduced for foreigners. I am not arguing here that Kandy had lost its sanctity for the village pilgrims who continued to visit, nor that the Diyawadana Nilame (lay custodian) should have been faulted for permitting the Maligava to become such a tourist attraction, but now religious culture had to share the place with another sub-culture, one with an entirely different clientele whose presence suggested leering voyeurs rather than devout worshippers. At the evening *pūjās*, there were likely to be almost as many tourists in attendance as Sri Lankans. It began to dawn on me that to a certain extent, the marketing of Sri Lanka's new open economy included the marketing of the Buddha, and that this marketing was but part of the image of the "exotic East" sold through the media of the European tourist industry, an industry that some Sri Lankan government ministries and businessmen had so obviously and so eagerly begun to encourage. I recognized that the development of tourism was a useful strategy to help boost the fledgling Sri Lankan economy, to provide more jobs, and to raise the general standard of living. But I also lamented the cultural costs. Unlike my experience in 1979, I also became much more aware of myself as a foreigner within the context of my visits to the Maligava. I was assumed by both temple officials and tourist hawkers to be a mark, a potential cash cow. Scholars and students loathe being regarded as tourists. I felt insulted. But being scholars and students doesn't make non-tourist Westerners any less foreign, in spite of a desire to understand culture empathetically.

In 1979, because there were so few Europeans visiting the temple, think I must have forgotten what I, myself, had looked like on those occasions, or how I probably stood out in the temple crowd without even being aware of it. Then, I had had the sense that I was just blending in and that my presence was unobtrusive, precisely because there were no other foreigners around to remind me of my own "otherness." But at the Maligava in 1982, I could not help feeling that the place had changed. Certainly the social experience had changed and not only for me, but surely for Sri Lankans as well. Sri Lankans now had to share the presence of the Buddha with others, visitors for whom the presence of the Buddha was but one more stop on a fun-filled holiday. I somehow found this incongruous and lamented the passing of an era. I was pretty naïve in this regard, too.

Figure 5.2 The Temple of the Sacred Tooth-Relic (Dalada Maligava) in Kandy

A few years later, a Sinhalese friend of mine took a photo of me and my son standing in a queue waiting, along with a small crowd of Sri Lankans, for the Katugastota bus in downtown Kandy. In the photo, our dress and facial expressions correspond exactly to those of the Sri Lankans. At that moment, we (the Sri Lankans, my son, and I) were gawking in semi-amazement at two female German tourists dressed in very short shorts with skimpy tank-tops. As they sauntered down the street we stared, and our friend's camera caught us all in an attitude reflecting how profoundly amazed we were at these tourists' "otherness." Yet at the same time, we were also oblivious to what we looked like, too. We had become "indigenized" to some extent, wearing the same type of dress and sharing the same facial expressions indicating our similar reaction to that of the Kandyans; but for all of our acculturation, we also remained unmistakably different, despite our own desire to be differentiated not so much from the Kandyan Sinhalese as from the German tourists.

I can only guess what goes on in the minds of Sinhalese villagers on pilgrimage to the Dalada Maligava when they encounter tourists with foreign tongues, foreign skins, foreign dress, foreign body postures, etc. In a place that to them is a central symbol of their traditional culture and social identity, what they may encounter and what may be most memorable to them is their encounter with what is so distinctively foreign! While there is much irony here, it is also the case that the encounter with such foreign "otherness" only furthers, by contrast, the sense of one's own identity. That is, identity with the Dalada (Tooth-Relic) and simultaneously juxtaposition to the strange presence of foreigners at the Maligava both function in ways to sharpen an awareness of one's own distinctive identity.

In any case, my initial 1979 visit to Kandy, in contrast to my stay in 1982, had a far more profound impact on my understanding of the Buddha for Buddhists in Sri Lanka. It was then that I first began to come to terms with the complexity of ways in which the Buddha was understood in Sri Lanka. The Buddha was not just a profound teacher, but an object of veneration, and his symbolic remains were an emblem of religio-ethnic, or even, as I was about to see, of socio-political identity. I began to understand just how complex a role the Buddha had played in the unfolding of civilization on this island.

I would call the Buddha I met at the Dalada Maligava in 1979 a "royal Buddha." His presence, or more precisely his legacy, lived on in that hill-country palace, was feasted every day, enjoyed musical performances, and gave audiences to his reverent devotees, some of whom had come from quite far away. Once a year, during the July/August Esala *perahara*, his relic was mounted on the royal animal par excellence, the elephant, and paraded around his city attended by a vast retinue of officials and an array of entertainers, including enthusiastic Kandyan dancers, in the process symbolizing his spiritual and temporal lordship over the kingdom. I later learned from reading ethnographies that the relic was thought to have the power to bring rain and, in the process, to safeguard the material wellbeing of this predominantly agricultural society. I also learned that the *perahara* was a ritual about ordering society, an annual collective statement of the community's identity, the parts of it in relation to the whole.

Indeed, from this first royal impression, I later came to a more thorough awareness of the conflation of royal imagery with the figure of the Buddha, a conflation that probably goes back to the very beginnings of the Buddhist tradition in India some two and a half millennia ago. After all, the Buddha had been born as Siddhārtha, prince of the Śākyan clan, and at his birth it had been prophesied that he would become either a buddha or a *cakravartin* (a dharma-minded universal conqueror). That mythic association doesn't mean that the Buddha was inherently political. Indeed, he is thought to have rejected the kingship that was his rightful dharmic inheritance. But it does mean that the association was present from the beginning, if we take his mythic biography seriously. Or, if we keep in mind other indigenous frames of reference, the royal conflation actually antedates the beginnings of Buddhist tradition in the *jataka* stories (about the Buddha's previous incarnations). By this, I refer to the best-known of all these 547 tales of the Buddha's previous rebirths, the *Vessantara Jataka*. Here the Buddha, in his last rebirth, a royal one, before being reborn royally again as Siddhārtha, gives away everything in his princely kingdom, including his wealth, wife, and children, to epitomize the radical extreme to which he quested: the realization of selflessness and detachment. The story of Vessantara remains extremely popular and well known even today. It has also been adapted for the stage by the renowned playwright Saratchandra. Again, it can be pointed out that Vessantara was giving away his princely domain and royal prerogatives. But he was a prince, nonetheless. I also became aware, in my further studies of Sri Lankan cultural history, of how many Sinhala Buddhist kings had aspired to become buddhas themselves, often stylizing their methods of rule in conformity to the selfless and compassionate bodhisattva. These more traditional associations of the Buddha with royalty, along with royal aspirations to become buddhas, were but preliminary insights into a growing awareness about the centrality of the Buddha figure for Sinhala culture in general.

One night in Tangalle, a day after *Poson poya* (full-moon day in June) in 1982 when I had spent the day among religious *sil*-takers (keeping the five basic moral precepts and three other special rules of conduct) in a local *pansala* (temple), I spent the greater part of an evening on the green adjacent to the major *handiya* in town amidst a partisan political crowd of Sri Lankan Freedom Party (SLFP) supporters listening to anti-government speeches delivered from a blue-and-white-draped platform. At the time, my Sinhala was not good enough to follow the substance of these speeches in any great detail. But by the angry, denunciatory tone of the speeches, sprinkled with "UNP," "J. R. Jayewardene," "Premadasa," "Bandaranaike," etc., I understood the drift of what was going on, especially since I had been reading about Sri Lankan politics fairly regularly since my original 1979 visit. What struck me, however, was not the style and tone of these ferocious oratories, but the unforgettable image of many monks seated on both sides of the platform facing the gathered crowd of supporters, a brilliant saffron line embroidering the presence of important lay politicos. Herein I realized that the legacy of the "royal Buddha" in a more traditional context was the realization of a "political Buddha" in the contemporary context.

It seemed to me, as I pondered what to me was such an extraordinary sight – those monks, or "sons of the Buddha," sitting on the platform for the political rally as if they constituted a chapter of militant cadres – that politics amongst the Sinhalese, perhaps since the successful 1956 election campaign of S. W. R. D. Bandaranaike, had become a matter of who could represent themselves as being the most Buddhist. That is, political discourse, either explicitly articulated or implicitly symbolized by the ritualistic actions of politicians or leaders in government, was thoroughly entwined with socio-religious discourses of a particular type and a public contest or vying of sorts was continuously being played out through the media. I shouldn't have been so surprised. By this time, I knew that Buddhism wasn't just a religion of elite, select religious virtuosos who had renounced the world and lived in relative solitude in their concerted quests for a spiritually other-worldly realization of *nibbāna*. In retrospect, I shouldn't have been so nonplussed at what I was witnessing at the time. I had previously studied Gandhi's religio-political worldview while pursuing a master's degree and I had been a sympathetic supporter of the Rev. Martin Luther King, Jr., during my college days in the 1960s. Moreover, I had participated in a number of marches protesting American involvement in Vietnam and had marched side by side with many clergy of a variety of Christian persuasions. So I knew that religion and politics could be thoroughly related. In fact, I had thought that they should be. In writing my master's thesis, I had noted that Gandhi had said explicitly that the person who did not recognize that religion and politics were indelibly linked really didn't understand the meaning of religion. Still, I can remember how stunned I was to see all those monks up there on the political stage sanctifying the presence of those SLFP officials. This was the legacy of the royal Buddha I had not known before I came to Sri Lanka.

Discussion

Perhaps seeing contemporary politically active SLFP monks as a legacy of the royal Buddha is somewhat overly simplistic. Since those early days in Sri Lanka, I have read a number of Buddhistic political tracts. In addition to works on Buddhist socialism formulated in Burma by enthusiastic Buddhist Marxists in the 1930s, works that stressed affinities between Marxist positions on the individual, community, state, and private property and Buddhist positions staked out in the Pāli *nikayas*, a number of writers, the Indian scholar Gokaldas De among them, have tried to show how democracy has been part and parcel of the proceedings of the early Buddhist monastic *sangha* since almost its very inception. Variants on the theme of the royal Buddha could be the "Marxist Buddha" and the "Democratic Buddha" respectively. My point here is that being Buddhist does not really imply any particular political mindset. The Buddha's legacy could be appropriated by people of any given political persuasion. The same is quite obvious in America, where the recent spectrum of political persuasions of Christians runs the gamut from the evangelical Jerry Falwell's "Moral Majority" on the right to leftist Roman Catholic priests Daniel and Philip Berrigan. What is interesting to me, however, is that any politician or political ideology in need of legitimacy in Sri Lanka must somehow come to terms with the Buddha or Buddhist thought, which function as a kind of polestar, a fundamental directional force, for Sinhala culture as a whole. That is, whatever the ideology being proselytized or contested among the Sinhalese, it needs to become congruent with a vision, image, or understanding of the Buddha or what he taught. I would argue that in post-colonial Ceylon/Sri Lanka, this situation is perhaps even more compelling than before.

What I have observed about politics in Sri Lanka is not exclusive to that domain of human endeavor. I think that the same might be said about many other arenas of human life and discourse in Sri Lanka. I have come to learn, for instance, that there are particularly Buddhistic ways of understanding health or medicine (ancient or modern), that there are Buddhistic approaches to science, to economic activity, to the environment, to social roles among family members, to education, to art and music, and Buddhist dispositions towards war and peace. In saying this, I want to underscore that these approaches are neither monolithic in nature, nor are they always consistent with one another. There is not just one Buddhistic approach to war or peace, for example, but a plethora of positions that in one way or another, however, make an appeal to the example of the Buddha, to the Buddha's "canonical" teachings, or to various Buddhist cultural traditions that have been in place for centuries.

Here, I do not aim to make the case that Sri Lanka has always been and will continue to be only a Buddhist society and culture. History and demography are too variegated to make that naïve claim. Moreover, Sri Lanka has been the venue of a fantastic degree of cross-fertilization among the various religious and ethnic communities who have found its shores congenial. Its Sinhala inhabitants have absorbed much from Tamils, Muslims, Portuguese, Dutch, British, Americans, and Japanese. The current pace of modernization in general is also quite furious. What I have observed, however, is a historical pattern of inclusivity among the Sinhalese in which the Buddha or Buddhism functions as an elastic legitimating or rationalizing factor in determining what makes for inclusion. The converse of this may be true also; that which is excluded or rejected is often done so on Buddhistic grounds.

Since the 1950s, copious quantities of articles in scholarly journals and numerous books have been published in social science academic circles about the twin processes of modernization and secularization in South Asia. Nehru's post-Gandhian vision of a secular independent India, together with various plans for economic transformations in South Asian countries, seemed to be proclamations of a fundamental transition that many assumed would alter the ethos of South Asian societies. There is no doubt that economic development under the stewardship of both the United National Party and the various alliances with the

Sri Lanka Freedom Party at their core have contributed to sea changes in the basic social experiences of Sri Lankans over the past 40 years. Ultimately, these changes may be judged, in time, to be just as significant as those wrought by the British colonial experience. My reference above to what had happened in Kandy at the Dalada Maligava between 1979 and 1982 is but an anecdotal confirmation of just one sort of change that has occurred. But what is even more interesting to me is that economic development has not been necessarily the bedfellow of secularization in Sri Lankan society on the whole. While this may seem to be the case among certain sections of the urban Colombo populace, the diffused presence of a Buddhistic ethos remains throughout most sectors of Sri Lankan Sinhala society. My comments about a royal and "political Buddha," as well as about identity and secularization, represent my attempt to make this clear.

Too often, when social change is measured by Euro-American social scientists, it is with the assumption that types of changes that have already occurred in European and American contexts represent a kind of inevitable future for Asian societies to negotiate. The anthropologist Clifford Geertz once labeled this tendency critically as the "world acculturative approach," an approach that assumes that the standards and goals of Western societies comprise a type of norm to be emulated by the non-Western. Insofar as Europe and America have become increasingly secularized societies in which the sacred has been increasingly relegated (and with diminishing intensity) to specified and limited time frames (Sunday mornings and Friday evenings) and to specific places (churches and synagogues) among decreasing numbers of *religieux*, it is assumed that capitalistic economic and democratic social transformations afoot in non-Western societies will lead to a similarly enervated condition of religion in Asia.

Perhaps it is simply a by-product of my own humanistic inclinations and an unwarranted projection of my personal experiences and observations on to the general trajectories of social experience in Sri Lanka as a whole, but I suspect that these assumptions, especially the tendency to think that Sinhala Buddhist culture is headed in the uniform direction of secularization, may prove to be overly problematic. Yes, the experience of visiting the Dalada Maligava between 1979 and 1982 changed dramatically with the infusion of tourism into the local economy. But the same rites continued to be observed at the temple, and there remains no question that they will continue to be observed far into any foreseeable future. There is not only an overt and explicitly Buddhist cultic community of religious practice thriving in Sri Lanka, but there also remains the function of the Buddha and his teachings as a kind of polestar. This, I think, is the nature of the implicit presence of the Buddha in Sri Lanka, and this presence, I would argue, may actually be far more profound than the explicit one.

This presence is a kind of diffused ethos that has been woven into the cadences of growing rice, getting healed, attending to the dying or dead, etc., on one level, and deciding, for instance, on what moral bases the government needs to predicate its various initiatives on behalf of the people, on another. "Ethos" is a difficult word to define, and its presence even more difficult to locate or reify specifically. I hesitate to use it here because I cannot think of an exactly precise equivalent term in Sinhala, but I know there are terms that come very close to its meaning. I would attempt to describe it as the character of a people that is sown by the manner in which various ideals have been suffused into social and cultural constructs. In Buddhist Sri Lanka, that ethos has been conditioned by the countless ways in which the Buddha has been appropriated.

Images of the Buddha in Sinhala culture are not fixed and assured, but rather shifting and transforming, continuously refracted anew in relation to the changing contours of the historical dynamic. My observation is congruent with what the Buddha taught about human experience in general: "Whatever is subject to uprising is also subject to cessation." Even images of the Buddha are not exceptions to the verity of this observation. Yet, having assented to that truest of maxims, polestars exist over vast spans of time, and I have a feeling that the Buddha's star will not set on the Sri Lankan horizon for many eons yet. That is, I expect to see pandals being erected and lanterns lit for many Vesak celebrations still to come. And I expect the Buddha to figure prominently in defining the nature, inclusion, or exclusion of any social and cultural transformations in the making.

Readings

Most studies of Buddhism in Sri Lanka have not been written by "Buddhologists," but by historians, historians of religions, and anthropologists. Still, one of the best introductions to Buddhism in Sri Lanka remains Richard Gombrich's *Precept and Practice* (Oxford: Clarendon Press, 1971), which attempts to see how the doctrinal teachings of the Buddha are refracted in the popular religious culture of upcountry Sri Lanka. Gombrich's approach can be effectively contrasted to Martin Southwold's *Buddhism in Life: The Anthropological Study of Religion and the Practice of Sinhalese Buddhism* (Manchester: University of Manchester Press, 1983), a provocative study that remains a theoretically significant critique of and an alternative interpretation to Gombrich's approach insofar as Southwold stresses the morally inherent practice of "village Buddhism," which is not driven by doctrinal emphases or the practice of meditation. For an outstanding study of meditative traditions, see Michael Carrithers, *The Forest Monks of Sri Lanka* (Delhi: Oxford University Press, 1983). Cogent studies of contemporary forms of Buddhist practice have been provided by George Bond, *The Buddhist Revival in Sri Lanka* (Columbia: University of South Carolina Press, 1988), and Richard Gombrich and Gananath Obeyesekere, *Buddhism Transformed* (Princeton: Princeton University Press, 1989). Excellent studies of the political significance of Buddhism historically and in the modern period include Gananath Obeyesekere, "Religious Symbolism and Political Change in Ceylon," in Bardwell Smith (ed.), *The Two Wheels of Dhamma*, AAR Studies in Religion 3 (Chambersburg, PA: American Academy of Religion Studies, 1972); Michael Roberts, *Sinhala Consciousness in the Kandyan Period* (Colombo: Vijitha Yapa, 2004); H. L. Seneviratne, *Rituals of the Kandyan State* (Cambridge: Cambridge University

Press, 1978) and his *The Work of Kings* (Chicago: University of Chicago Press, 1999); S. J. Tambiah, *Buddhism Betrayed* (Chicago: University of Chicago Press, 1992); John Clifford Holt, *The Religious World of Kirti Sri: Buddhism, Art and Politics in Late Medieval Sri Lanka* (New York: Oxford University Press, 1996); and K. N. O. Dharmadasa, *Language, Religion, and Ethnic Assertiveness* (Ann Arbor: University of Michigan Press, 1992). Studies that are more focused on Buddhism, culture, and forms of Buddhist religious experience include James Duncan, *The City as Text* (Cambridge: Cambridge University Press, 1990); John Clifford Holt, "Pilgrimage and the Structure of Sinhalese Buddhism," *Journal of the International Association of Buddhist Studies* 5 (1982), pp. 23–40, and *The Buddhist Visnu: Religious Transformation, Politics and Culture* (New York: Columbia University Press, 2004); Anne Blackburn, *Locations of Buddhism* (Chicago: University of Chicago Press, 2010); and Kevin Trainor, *Relics, Ritual and Representation in Buddhism* (Cambridge: Cambridge University Press, 2007). Excellent doctrinal studies of Theravāda Buddhist articulated in Pāli literature are found in two books by Steven Collins. The first is *Selfless Persons* (Cambridge: Cambridge University Press, 1982) and the second, published by the same press in 1999, is Collins' *Nibbana and Other Buddhist Felicities*. The continuous historical significance of Buddhism in Sri Lankan history can be seen in Kingsley de Silva, *A History of Sri Lanka* (Delhi: Penguin, revised edition, 2005). An effective overview of religion, culture, and politics in Sri Lanka can be gleaned from John Clifford Holt, *The Sri Lanka Reader: History, Culture, Politics* (Durham, NC: Duke University Press, 2011).

Author

John Clifford Holt is William R. Kenan, Jr., Professor of Humanities in Religion and Asian Studies at Bowdoin College in Brunswick, Maine (USA). He has authored numerous books about Buddhism and religious culture including *Spirits of the Place: Buddhism and Lao Religious Culture* (Honolulu: University of Hawai'i Press, 2009), *The Buddhist Visnu: Religious Transformation, Politics and Culture*, *The Religious World of Kirti Sri: Buddhism, Art and Politics in Late Medieval Sri Lanka*, *Buddha in the Crown: Avalokitesvara in the Buddhist Traditions of Sri Lanka* (New York: Oxford University Press, 1991), for which he won an American Academy of Religion Book Award for Excellence, and *Discipline: The Canonical Buddhism of the Vinayapitaka* (Delhi: Motilal Banarsidass, 1981). He established the Inter-Collegiate Sri Lanka Education (ISLE) Program in 1982, has received an honorary doctorate from the University of Peradeniya in Sri Lanka, and, in addition to many research awards and fellowships from the National Endowment for the Humanities and the Fulbright Program, was the Alumnus of the Year at the University of Chicago Divinity School in 2007. His most recent book is *The Sri Lanka Reader: History, Culture, Politics* (Durham, NC: Duke University Press, 2011). He is currently writing a book entitled *Theravāda Traditions: Ritual and Power in the Religious Cultures of Sri Lanka and Southeast Asia*.

Chapter 6

Shifting signposts in Shikoku pilgrimage

John S. Harding

Preamble

Signposts can be quite useful to a traveler, pilgrim, or scholar. Both the literal and figurative meanings of this term can offer guidance. Physical signposts strategically placed where paths diverge can indicate direction and distance to one's destination. In a more figurative sense, signposts can signal that one is entering a complicated situation and may also help one navigate unfamiliar terrain. In this chapter, I will discuss observations about tradition and change in Japan's famous multi-site Shikoku pilgrimage. I will emphasize how practitioners respond to modifications in the route and how scholars perceive these transformations as signs of complex historical interactions that continuously reshape religious traditions.

The observations in this essay arose from my collaborative research with Dr. Hiroshi Shimazaki in Shikoku, Japan, in the spring of 2005. I used field notes, photos, video, surveys, and audio recordings for this exploration of change in the 88-site Shikoku pilgrimage. In particular, the following narrative and discussion sections of this chapter explore the relocation of Buddhist structures at Temple #27 (Kōnomineji) as well as competing claims by Zenrakuji and Anrakuji to hold the official designation as Temple #30. The collaborative nature of the project was central to its origins and potential.

Narrative

Although my research often focuses on modern Japanese Buddhism, I am also fascinated by seminal figures from earlier periods in Japan's history as well as by traditional practices such as pilgrimage and ascetic journeys in remote mountains. I felt drawn to the study of Shikoku pilgrimage, in part because of its connection to an especially remarkable foundational figure, Kūkai. Posthumously named Kōbō Daishi, the great teacher who spread the Buddhist law, Kūkai is Japan's most famous Buddhist virtuoso. Before my 2005 research trip, I had traveled to Mount Kōya, Kūkai's monastic headquarters from the ninth century C.E., where legend maintains that he remains in extraordinarily deep meditation. However, I had not been to Shikoku, where he is thought to have been born in 774 C.E. I was eager to see sites linked to this multi-talented genius and master of esoteric Buddhism, whose appeal includes cultural and religious contributions that extend far beyond his school of Shingon Buddhism. Shikoku pilgrimage has attracted a wide spectrum of pilgrims from varied Buddhist backgrounds. I was curious about the contemporary pilgrims, too. What motivates them? How do they differ from tourists visiting famous temples? What is their understanding of Kūkai, of pilgrimage, or of the claims that most temples on the pilgrimage route make about their direct connection to Kūkai's practice in Shikoku 1,200 years ago? As I began to explore the topic more fully, I noticed unlikely assertions about the past are joined by testimonials to Kūkai's continued activity in relation to the pilgrimage. The perceived ongoing role of Kōbō Daishi as a miracle-working saint remains an enduring focus and motivation for the pilgrimage around this mountainous island southwest of Osaka.

Further stimuli from sources ranging from academic articles to feature programs on Japanese television about Shikoku pilgrimage continued to stoke my curiosity. Moreover, I began to encounter signs of modern modifications closer to my more typical areas of research. My earlier assumptions about this multi-site pilgrimage trek proved to be somewhat off-track.

I assumed that for most Japanese pilgrims to claim they had "really" done the approximately 1,400-kilometer Shikoku pilgrimage (*henro*), they would deem it necessary to have walked – rather than driven – the route and to complete the entire sacred journey in one campaign. It seems I was wrong on both counts, though admiration remains strongest for the walking pilgrims. Shikoku pilgrims (*Ohenro-san*) can enter the pilgrimage at any of the official 88 temples and are welcome to return repeatedly to do different sections en route to completion of the entire *henro*. Although reports suggest that the path was at times hard to find or follow, now signs lead the *Ohenro-san* along the sacred circuit that circumambulates Shikoku – the smallest and least populated of Japan's four main islands. The signs reassure pilgrims that they are on-track and help them find the "right" temples, often in order, that constitute the official 88. This apparent certainty emphasizes continuity over the centuries for this well-known religious practice. Although intrigued by this Buddhist practice, I was also quite skeptical about claims of uninterrupted tradition. As a result, I felt that any potential Shikoku research would likely remain at the margins of my plans along with many other potentially fascinating projects that would have to wait for the right alignment of time and funding as well as fit with other scholarly pursuits.

The fortuitous discovery that a colleague in the School of Management at my university, Hiroshi Shimazaki, had researched this pilgrimage for his PhD in geography, had sketched the locations of key cultural markers, such as temples and statues, and had compared them with related sketches centuries earlier reignited my interest. He had walked the route several times and noticed changes to the location and status of some sites. Subsequent conversations and research suggested that the changes were most likely related to the turbulent period of Japan's rapid modernization that is a special interest and research pursuit of mine.

Now conducting Shikoku research was not only possible but also felt exciting and connected to my ongoing projects. Serendipity and the benefit of multiple perspectives can – and did – serve important roles in research. In this case, my interest related to Buddhist adaptation to persecution 140 years ago in the early years of the Meiji era (1868–1912). Hiroshi and I set off for Japan together in spring 2005 to combine different approaches and areas of expertise in an exploration of one of the most famous – and "traditional" – pilgrimage practices in Japan, including striking changes from the late 1860s to the present day.

Hiroshi and I pulled the rental car over by the beach before hiking up to the temple. It was starting to rain, but I wanted to be right at sea level to make sure the altimeter on my portable global positioning system (GPS) was correctly reading the altitude as zero. A GPS unit is not typically needed for studying Buddhism, but we were interested in mapping the shifts of position of pilgrimage sites, including moves up or down the hillsides. During previous pilgrimage circuits, Hiroshi had sketched some of the main temples, shrines, statues, and other important cultural markers, and he had noticed that some of the higher Shinto shrines that occupied the original sacred space of this multi-site pilgrimage were largely ignored now in favor of Buddhist sites moved to lower ground during the persecution of Buddhism during Japan's rapid modernization in the late 1860s and early 1870s. While I reset the GPS, Hiroshi, who is an accomplished artist as well as a scholar, made another quick sketch of the beach with rain clouds rolling in. Now we were ready for the temples. I hopped back into the car and then we drove to a parking lot just off the coastal highway less than three kilometers south of Temple #26 (Kongōchōji).

The beginning of our walk was far from spectacular, with small work trucks buzzing by on the highway behind us and a paved road serving both walking pilgrims and northbound auto traffic including cars, minivans, and buses with pilgrims bound for the same temple. Although our surroundings became relatively quiet once we left the parking lot and highway behind, the initial walk through relatively flat agricultural land felt similar to many other parts of Japan, with occasional houses among the irrigation ditches and flooded rice fields. However, once we diverged to the left and abandoned the pavement for the walking pilgrims' winding path up to the temple, the experience changed along with the steeper terrain we moved through on this well-worn footpath. After a few turns, this climb felt more in tune with pilgrims going back for centuries.

We followed the twisting path up the mountain. As we stepped over gnarled roots of ancient trees in the footsteps of generations of pilgrims, the bells on our walking-sticks joined the buzz of insects and croaking of frogs from the fields below. We now felt far away from the highway and from cities – most of Shikoku, in fact much of Japan, is actually quite rural and mountainous – and these noises of nature along with the rare walking pilgrims' rhythmic steps and bells broke through the forest's quiet and calm. I thought about how much this was an experience of the senses. I could smell the lush growth and feel the humidity in which all these plants thrive. My eyes took in the sights of old stones and trees twisted by age. The mountain's contours drove home the characterization of Shinto as animistic – the idea that one's surroundings are animated with gods and spirits.

My mind flitted back and forth between experiencing the beautiful ascent and analyzing what I saw in terms of general ideas about Japanese religion and specific questions driving this research project. How much do the pilgrims know about each site, about the persecution of Buddhism in the early Meiji era, or about changes to the pilgrimage route? Who or what determines their route – the guide or driver for larger tours, guidebooks for pilgrims who drive their own cars, signposts for the walking pilgrims? Do temples and pilgrim associations actively suppress awareness of these changes? Will they be forthcoming with us? This divided attention is an occupational hazard that prevents the scholar from participating in the pilgrimage in the same way as the more typical pilgrims, each admittedly also experiencing the sacred sites and the journey that connects them according to his or her own motivations, encounters, and modes of practicing Shikoku pilgrimage.

When Hiroshi and I arrived at the temple we saw a group of about eight pilgrims. Most of them were women who appeared to be middle-aged or older and who were disembarking from a minibus. The bus driver stood by the door and handed each pilgrim her walking-staff from the umbrella stand as she left the minibus for the last climb up a staircase to Temple #26 (Kongōchōji). Despite the modern mode of transportation, these pilgrims wore variations of traditional garb. Along with the pilgrim's staff, each had the traditional white shirt (*hakui*) with writing down the back that indicated the ongoing presence and centrality of the Daishi (Great Teacher) – one of innumerable references and invocations of Kōbō Daishi throughout all aspects of the pilgrimage. The staff, although seemingly unnecessary for pilgrims who are driven from one site to the next, is essential on account of this same association with Kōbō Daishi; the staff is understood to represent the Daishi, and characters written on it reinforce the idea that the pilgrim is not alone but instead travels with the Great Teacher.

Most in this group wore traditional white leggings, too, and a couple had the traditional conical hat, which is made of woven bamboo or related natural materials, although white sunhats far outnumbered this more traditional head-gear. While the mode of transportation from one temple to the next varied widely among pilgrims, the basic circuit made by this group included the major sites at each temple – including visits to both halls of worship, the hall with Kōbō Daishi's image and the hall with the main image (*honzon*) of worship for that particular temple, Yakushi (the Medicine Buddha) in this case. Unlike most of the Shikoku *honzon*, pilgrims could not actually see this striking gold image of a seated Yakushi in meditation. I was not there at New Year's when the public has access to this image, so I had to recall the serene face from my Japanese book that has the images and background information about the *honzon* at all 88 temples. Even without access to the image, or especially without access as there is sometimes the sense of additional sacrality with a hidden icon, pilgrims still visited the main hall.

Figure 6.1 At left, a group of pilgrims return to their minibus from Temple #26 (Kongōchōji). On the right, the signpost at the next site, Temple #27 (Kōnomineji), indicates that Kōnomineji Shinto shrine is only 0.4 km away, but the temple of the same name (and the bus stop) is now in a different direction.

Most pilgrims chanted the Heart Sūtra, and it appeared that all visited the temple office, where an official provided elegant proof of their visit through a combination of black ink calligraphy written over the top of that temple's red stamps. For most, the temple stamps are gathered in books that open accordion-style to reveal the folded pages with their artful evidence of each participant's progression through the multi-site pilgrimage. Some gather these on a white pilgrim's shirt, which will likely serve as a burial shroud, and others collect stamps on a single, large scroll. Of course, I followed in turn to pay the several hundred yen (about three US dollars) fee to have my book stamped and adorned. The combination of stamps and calligraphy from each temple fill each 7 by 4.5 inch (17.5 by 11.5 centimeter) page. In typical form, the red stamp at the top right corner of my page imprints the *kanji* (Chinese characters) of the temple's number among the *henro* 88 (Shikoku #26, in this case) and the bottom left stamp identifies the temple by name. Here at Kongōchōji, the four *kanji* used for the temple's name are clearly represented in standard form, whereas some other temple's lower left stamp is a very stylized mark that I would be unable to decode on its own. Although each of the completed pages in my accordion-style book is visually striking and usefully informative, the scarcity of stamps in my book reveals the limited scope of this project with its particular focus on several temples in the Kōchi region of Shikoku.

Although the questionnaires we had developed – and the local college students we had hired to seek responses on-site from as many pilgrims as possible – would be deployed at the current reigning Temple #30 (Zenrakuji), we wanted to visit several related temples first to observe patterns and ask questions to gauge the awareness of Meiji persecution and changes to the pilgrimage route. This temple, #26 (Kongōchōji), was reported to have stored cultural treasures for Temple #27 (Kōnomineji) at the beginning of the Meiji era, when the Buddhist cultural markers were forcibly separated from the Shinto shrine at their shared site. We moved on from Temple #26 to Temple #27 to see how this group of pilgrims and others would navigate that divided site.

The Buddhist Temple #27 (Kōnomineji) is located at a significantly higher elevation than the 5 temples before it or the 15 after. However, the Shinto shrine of the same name, as well as the original temple site, is still higher on the hill. We came to the wooden signpost where paths diverge. One of the two pointed boards signaled that the shrine was straight ahead, less than half a kilometer away. Before the Meiji persecution of Buddhism forced out the Buddhist cultural markers – such as temple building and statues – that location had been the original site for Temple #27, too. We walked through the torii gate, which is one of the most recognizable symbols of Shinto and marks an entrance to sacred space, and hiked alone up the older, steeper, stone steps and partially overgrown path toward the quiet shrine above. The tall torii itself appeared to be made of concrete and was contrastingly new and smooth compared to the uneven stone of the much older path. Glancing through the foliage below and to our left, we could see approximately 20 pilgrims in the standard white garb. They had evidently veered slightly to the left at the signpost, climbed the newer stone steps toward the relocated Buddhist temple, and walked through the impressive Buddhist gate to arrive at the flat gravel area where they currently stood and chanted the Heart Sūtra. "Gate" is perhaps a poor term for the large, dark, wooden Buddhist structure that one passes through en route to this temple and many other Buddhist sites in Japan. This was a Niō gate, which refers to the fierce-looking protectors on each side of the gate who are often called Deva Kings. To a Western tourist unfamiliar with Buddhist iconography, these statues would likely appear to be demons; however, their wrathful appearance is understood to be in the service of Buddhism.

In front of the chanting group of pilgrims, I saw one of the ubiquitous signs that look like a cheerful youth whose smile reassures pilgrims that they are on-course. Unlike the older wooden signposts, these signs strike me as mascots of contemporary Japan, where cuteness (*kawai*) is central to marketing as opposed to the frightening (*kowai*) countenance of the Niō guards. The writing on these signs indicates information such as the temple's name, its number among the official 88, and the building, such as the Daishidō (hall for worshipping the Daishi), or other important cultural marker relevant to pilgrims at the site. A metal stand held the pilgrims' walking-staffs so that their hands were free to hold the book from which they chanted the sūtra, though some undoubtedly knew this succinct Perfection of Wisdom text by heart. After exploring the higher, albeit deserted, ground of the shrine above we hiked further up the trail to an observation tower to watch the sun nearly set over the sea below. We hiked back down to Temple #27 to take in the

Figure 6.2 Buddhist gate on the left of the bottom photograph leads to Temple #27 (Kōnomineji) and a group of Shikoku pilgrims (top left). Through the leaves and to the right of the pilgrims' staffs one can just see the signpost of a smiling child's cutout with relevant information for this site. Shinto torii on the right of the bottom photograph leads up a now relatively untraveled path (top right) to the Shinto shrine at the site that used to be part of the official 88-temple circuit but lost visitors when the Buddhist structures were moved to lower ground during the separation and persecution of Buddhism early in the Meiji era.

formidable statue of Kōbō Daishi and the outdoor panels that provided an illustrated account of some of Kōbō Daishi's life and accomplishments. It was clear that this newer site had supplanted the original pilgrimage destination. The older, higher site, once shared by the original Buddhist temple and the Shinto shrine, had shed its Buddhist cultural markers during the persecution. The resulting "purely"

Shinto site, rather than being elevated in status as planned, had been superseded and left to the margins of the pilgrims' path.

The sun had set and little light remained as we quickly hiked down to our rental car and discussed plans for temple visits the next day. At Temple #27 (Kōnomineji), pilgrims' clear preference for the new Buddhist temple site illustrated the perseverance of Buddhism and suggested the importance of Buddhist cultural markers, such as the statue of Kōbō Daishi, for where and how the pilgrimage is actually practiced. We knew our main study of the two Buddhist temples that had competed for and alternately held official designation as Temple #30 would be more complicated as each is a Buddhist site. Moreover, each held one of the two important statues – a statue of Kōbō Daishi and a main temple image (*honzon*) of Amida Buddha in the case of Temple(s) #30. Before conducting interviews at those sites, we wanted to speak to officials at Temple #29 (Kokubunji), where all the important Buddhist cultural markers from the original Temple #30 (Zenrakuji) were first stored to save them from the sudden persecution at the outset of the Meiji period.

The name "Kokubunji" already provides a sign of the temple's history and importance. The name signals that this is an official temple of the country, one of the temples that Emperor Shōmu ordered built in the mid-eighth century C.E. The name "Shikoku" indicates four countries (in this case, a division into four prefectures), and each of the divisions has an official state temple, a Kokubunji. This official status protected Kokubunji from persecution, and its relative proximity (as Temple #29) to Temple #30 made Kokubunji a logical repository for Zenrakuji's treasures before Temple #30 was destroyed. Temple #29 (Kokubunji) proved very valuable for us as well. We had made arrangements in advance to speak with a high-ranking priest at Kokubunji. When we arrived, another Buddhist priest welcomed us into a room bound by sliding doors with a floor of tatami mats and cushions to sit on. I have always enjoyed the feel of these traditional rooms and the smell of the rice straw in the mats. Our hosts brought us green tea and the senior priest came to meet us. We explained our research project and our questions about the competition between two temples to be recognized as the official Temple #30 of the 88-temple *henro*. We indicated interest in the full history of this issue from Meiji persecution to the present.

Although we asked our questions politely, we were concerned that the topic itself may be somewhat offensive as it can suggest calling the authenticity of a site, or the pilgrimage more generally, into question by casting light on more fractious and profane aspects not featured in the pilgrimage association's promotional literature. The senior priest hesitated, and explained that this had indeed been a rather delicate issue. He was also somewhat reluctant to speak about the history of the dispute between the two #30 temples because head priests of his own temple had played an ongoing role in refereeing the dispute long after their original responsibility of protecting Buddhist artifacts from destruction and storing them until they could be reclaimed. In fact, he stated that his father had been involved in earlier attempts at brokering a solution. At the time of our interview – May

2005 – the situation had been more stable for a decade. This may be one reason that he ended up telling us many details we had not read before and may not have discovered without this encounter. I was under the impression that his own advanced age and the passing of his father may have also allowed him to delve more fully into the history, including some of the politics and intrigues likely not evident to most pilgrims through the years. Moving signposts revealed changing locations, names, and designations of official status, but the direction given by this local guide proved invaluable in understanding how and why the contours of the religious landscape of this section of Shikoku pilgrimage had shifted so often in the last 140 years.

Discussion

Our experiences in Shikoku illustrated diverse aspects of religious practice in Japan. Interviews and observations elucidated some dynamics of pilgrimage. Traveling through Shikoku, particularly when walking the pilgrims' path, showcased the natural beauty of mountains and water that continue to foster a religious reading of the landscape in Japan linked to esoteric mandalas perceived in the topographical formations and animistic understanding of extraordinary trees, stones, and waterfalls as sacred. The juxtaposition between "traditional" religious connotations of nature on the one hand and "hyper-modern" secular images of Japan on the other provides one lens for a discussion of religion and change. Another lens could focus on changing patterns in the numbers of pilgrims in relation to their modes of transportation. For example, the short-lived helicopter tours may suggest too extreme a transformation, traveling by bus and car accounts for the vast majority of contemporary Shikoku pilgrims, but the relatively few walking pilgrims remain the enduring symbol of the *henro* as an especially traditional Japanese Buddhist pilgrimage.

However, such contrasts between ancient, natural, and traditional in opposition to contemporary, manufactured, and modern too often exaggerate the antiquity, intrinsic authenticity, and stability of "tradition." While examining any of these aspects could lead to interesting insights, instead I would like to discuss the fluidity and constructed nature of religious tradition by focusing on striking changes in Shikoku pilgrimage rooted in the brief persecution of Buddhism in the nineteenth century with ramifications that continue to the present. In particular, by surveying changes to the sites of temples #27 and #30, this discussion will analyze competition between sacred sites and the perseverance of Buddhist identity in the wake of Meiji persecution.

Although we have evidence of pilgrimage and ascetic religious practices in Shikoku all the way back to Kūkai's time, clear historical records of the full 88-temple pilgrimage circuit are evident only from the seventeenth century onward. Moreover, closer scrutiny reveals signs of changes to the *henro* including competing claims for official status among the 88 temples. By comparing current signposts with older pilgrimage patterns, we discover that some sacred sites have been relocated and that shifting locations are linked to modifications in the relationship between specific sites and the dominant *henro* route. The contrast between the relatively neglected sites off of the main circuit and the wealthy, vital, and bustling temples that benefit from pilgrim traffic suggests profane – as well as sacred – stakes. Changes in the location or status of pilgrimage sites also signal the fluidity of religious "tradition" and the historical, cultural, political, and economic influences that constantly reshape religious landscapes that at first glance might seem constant. Brief, but virulent, persecution of Buddhism in the late 1860s and early 1870s caused the most dramatic – even traumatic – alterations to some *henro* sites and to the religious landscape more generally. Although such conflict between Shinto and Buddhism is unusual in Japan's history – and the anti-Buddhist resentment, political upheaval, and national myth-making that fueled the fire of persecution was primarily a product of that time – the resulting changes still shape the pilgrimage.

The original conflict, later disputes, and modifications to the pilgrimage provide moving signposts of unintentional consequences of Meiji persecution and ongoing issues of the history, complexity, popularity, geography, and management of Shikoku pilgrimage. At the outset of the Meiji era (1868–1912), the restoration of the Meiji Emperor was accompanied by increasingly strident calls among native studies (*kokugaku*) ideologues to revive Shinto by forcibly removing Buddhist elements where the religions were intermingled. This *kokugaku*-inspired directive that Shinto could and should be separated from Buddhism was both practically and theoretically problematic. The allegedly ancient tradition they wanted "restored" was, in part, a Tokugawa and early Meiji-era invention formulated out of incomplete evidence of pre-Buddhist indigenous religious practices and more than a dozen centuries of hybrid forms of Buddhist–Shinto religious development. At many religious sites, fused or complementary and symbiotic expressions of both traditions had been the norm. Because it was so common to have Buddhist and Shinto elements within the same religious complex, the implementation of this separation required violent, and somewhat arbitrary, actions including the destruction of Buddhist cultural markers such as temples and sacred images. In short, the separation of Buddhism from Shinto (*shinbutsu bunri*) entailed the persecution of Buddhism (*haibutsu kishaku*), with disruptive implications for many Japanese religious sites. The persecution lasted for less than a decade, but it was quite aggressive in certain areas, with widespread destruction of Buddhist material culture and forced laicization of monks.

Shikoku's famous pilgrimage sites were not spared. In his insightful book, *Making Pilgrimages: Meaning and Practice in Shikoku*, Ian Reader notes that the Tosa region (now known as Kōchi) witnessed the most extreme persecution and destruction or displacement of Buddhist sites along the pilgrimage circuit. Our study focused on prominent examples near the regional capital of Kōchi that reveal how these early Meiji policies of separation and persecution attempted to displace Buddhist structures, signs, and statues in order to claim Shinto identity for the existing sacred sites. Our research into the histories and current pilgrimage use of specific temples, such as Temple #27 (Kōnomineji) and Temple #30 (Zenrakuji), demonstrates that pilgrims returned to where Buddhist structures and statues were re-established, at times neglecting the original sites that had ostensibly become more purely Shinto. In effect, the separation policies seem to have had the unintended consequence of making the popular pilgrimage sites more purely Buddhist rather than Shinto.

Temple #27 (Kōnomineji) makes for an interesting case study where current pilgrimage patterns so clearly reject the early Meiji attempt to promote a more "pure" Shinto site at the expense of Buddhist elements. Persecution did perform a separation, but it is the relatively new, would-be-marginalized Buddhist site that is visited. The Buddhist site at Temple #27 is replete with Kōbō Daishi references, from a statue to a long display of text and images celebrating his life and accomplishments. In contrast to the groups of pilgrims paying their respects to Kōbō Daishi, the Shinto shrine higher up the mountain was deserted during our observations, with occasional cobwebs crossing the ancient stone stairs. Temple #27 demonstrates that the higher point of the hill, which had been a pilgrimage site for centuries, did not continue to be the main site after Shinto–Buddhist separation. Instead of locating the "sacred site" as a specific geographic place fixed through time and tradition, pilgrims' preference for the newer Buddhist location suggests the importance of cultural markers such as temple buildings and images of revered Buddhist figures.

In the case of Zenrakuji (Temple #30), the contestation of sacred place was complicated by the competition for pilgrims when Anrakuji claimed the status of Temple #30. In fact, the young Japanese laywoman Takamure Itsue lists Anrakuji as Temple #30 in her 1918 newspaper articles reporting her pilgrimage account, which later became the book *Musume Junreki* (*The Pilgrimage Journal of a Young Woman*). Oliver Statler, in *Japanese Pilgrimage*, visits both Anrakuji and Zenrakuji. Moreover, he demonstrates an extensive awareness of the Meiji-era roots of the conflict and relocations as well as more recent temporary victories such as Zenrakuji's winning priority in a 1942 agreement only to lose out to Anrakuji in 1952 negotiations (see pp. 244–48). Ian Reader also addresses this conflict in a paragraph of *Making Pilgrimages*, which was published just before we embarked on our fieldwork. He describes an "uneasy compromise" where both claimed Temple #30 status and issued stamps for several decades before a 1994 resolution in favor of Zenrakuji with Anrakuji "acquiring special status as its *okunoin* (inner sanctum)" (pp. 139–40). Our investigation of the history of each site and the basis of their competing claims bears out this basic characterization. It also reveals a more complex relationship shaped by the confluence of anti-Buddhist persecution, intra-Buddhist politics, and the management of Shikoku pilgrimage by temple priests, pilgrimage societies, and pilgrims' own preferences.

The competing claims for both pilgrimage sites can be understood, in part, as a contest of cultural markers. At first glance, it seems that upon taking possession of the *honzon* (principal image) of Amida Buddha, which had been moved

Figure 6.3 The older stone signpost (right) still proclaims Anrakuji as the main #30 site in the 88-temple Shikoku pilgrimage. However, the new sign (top left) acknowledges that Anrakuji is now a subsidiary *okunoin* (inner shrine) to the main #30 temple. Zenrakuji's signs (bottom left) include the smiling child-like guide signposts of the current officially sanctioned 88-temples of this multisite pilgrimage. This sign marks the location of the Daishidō (Hall for worshipping Kōbō Daishi) at Shikoku #30, Zenrakuji.

away from Zenrakuji when the original Temple #30 was abolished during the early Meiji persecution, officials at Anrakuji claimed to have taken possession of the corresponding status of Temple #30. Anrakuji partisans refused to return the *honzon* to Zenrakuji once it had become re-established. Kokubunji (Temple #29), on the other hand, did return Zenrakuji's statue of Kōbō Daishi, which had been moved from the original site during the same persecution. The re-established Zenrakuji, with its statue of Kōbō Daishi, reclaimed its status as Temple #30. Anrakuji, which did not relinquish its *honzon*, continued to make the same claim. Both temples issued stamps with this designation on the famous and popular Shikoku pilgrimage route, where pilgrim interest and temple income are directly related to being one of the official 88 temples.

A closer examination further complicates the relationship among Zenrakuji, Anrakuji, Kokubunji, and claims of Temple #30 status. Archival research and discussions with a high-ranking priest of Kokubunji (Temple #29) shed more light on shifting identities and their related cultural markers. As early Meiji persecution destroyed both Zenrakuji and Anrakuji, Kokubunji became the repository for Zenrakuji's *honzon* of Amida Buddha, its statue of Kōbō Daishi, and its registry of parishioners, among other important artifacts. Anrakuji, which was rebuilt a half century before Zenrakuji, did successfully petition to adopt Zenrakuji's *honzon* and with it the coveted status of Temple #30. Zenrakuji was later re-established at the request of parishioners from its former location. In the 1930s they regained their statue of Kōbō Daishi from Kokubunji and attempted to reclaim official Temple #30 status from Anrakuji. As noted before, Anrakuji refused to relinquish the *honzon* of Amida Buddha or the status as Temple #30. Kokubunji head priests remained involved in this dispute, sometimes supporting Anrakuji claims and at other times favoring Zenrakuji. Each claimant of Temple #30 status actively recruited pilgrims. In fact, we visited a site on the pilgrims' trail where the path from Temple #29 branched off in the direction of each claimant for Temple #30 status. Rather than leaving this decision to mere inanimate signposts, at certain times proponents of each competing temple met pilgrims here and encouraged them to choose their Temple #30. These competing guides substantiated their claims to authenticity by reference to these two statues that are especially important in Shikoku pilgrimage visits: the *honzon*, in this case a statue of Amida, and the image of Kōbō Daishi, whose presence is inseparable from the pilgrimage.

The current preference for Zenrakuji as the official Temple #30 suggests that the re-established original site with the original Kōbō Daishi statue trumped Anrakuji's claim and image. However, the origins of Anrakuji's current *honzon* further complicate the issue and qualify this assumption. The *honzon* of Amida Buddha at Anrakuji seems not to be the original *honzon* from Zenrakuji after all. Although it is an important cultural property in its own right, it appears to have been brought to Anrakuji from Hiroshima as a later replacement for the original *honzon*, which was purportedly destroyed in a fire at Anrakuji during the Meiji era. Moreover, the layout of each temple site and contemporary concerns of pilgrimage management may come into play. Zenrakuji's location includes several parking lots – even one adequate for several of the large buses of pilgrims to park on-site – unlike Anrakuji, which is more fully in the city of Kōchi and has relatively limited parking. Our fieldwork at Zenrakuji, including a head-count by mode of transportation and a questionnaire eliciting information from willing pilgrims, demonstrated that the vast majority of pilgrims now come by bus, minibus, and car. Issues like parking, which have little religious or traditional significance, cannot be discounted in the management of pilgrimage, including the contest over official status as Temple #30.

The cases of Temple #27 and Temple(s) #30 share Meiji persecution attempts to displace Buddhist images and abolish Buddhist temples. In the case of the two temples #30, the Buddhist sites claiming this status multiplied to two rather than diminished to zero. These cultural responses not only expose the unintended consequences of the Meiji attempt to separate and suppress Buddhism, they call into question larger assumptions about the location and identification of sacred space. Do cultural landscape markers, such as the relocated Buddhist temples, trump the physical location of the sacred site, which was established through centuries of tradition and sanctioned by modern government intervention? Our initial study suggests a short answer – *yes* – modified by a longer and more nuanced response attentive to history, to the significance of cultural markers,

Figure 6.4 Temple #30 (Zenrakuji)—unlike the other contender for #30 status (Anrakuji)—has a large parking lot that can accommodate tour buses along with another lot for cars and other modes of transportation used by contemporary Shikoku pilgrims. Along with Hiroshi (top right) and me, local college students equipped with our questionnaire help interview tour guides, bus drivers, and pilgrims (below).

and to pilgrims' preferences, which are in turn guided by various managers of pilgrimage and facilitated by logistical considerations.

Rather than intuitive expectations of the sacred site for religious pilgrimage as a fixed location where the sense of sacrality has increasingly solidified through tradition, these cases demonstrate that the Temple #30 status and Temple #27 site shifted after Meiji persecution as pilgrims continued their pilgrimage by incorporating new Buddhist locations. Our findings reveal that the expression of pilgrimage, in this case, resists both the naturally prior place – in the sense of the physical location of the original site – along with the artificially enforced state intervention, which attempted to direct people to the old site with a new meaning. We conclude that Meiji policies and dynamics continued to shape Shikoku pilgrimage up to the present, albeit in ways not envisioned during the brief Meiji persecution of Buddhism. Beyond these more local conclusions about Shikoku pilgrimage and Japanese religion, our study may hold larger implications for the study of the persecution, adaptation, and preservation of Buddhism as well as raise more general issues about religion, pilgrimage, and competing claims about sacred space. For any of these complex issues, scholars must rely on careful analysis of shifting signposts and beware of the misdirection of labels such as "tradition" in the ever-changing landscape of religious practice.

Readings

Although the most comprehensive guidebooks and numerous television specials are available only in Japanese, there is no shortage of English-language resources about Shikoku pilgrimage. In addition to two earlier documentaries (Oliver Statler and Masajuzu Ueda's *Japanese Pilgrimage: The Pilgrimage to the Eighty-Eight Sacred Places of Shikoku*, 1983; and Joanne Hershfield and Susan Caperna Lloyd's *Between Two Worlds: A Japanese Pilgrimage*, 1992), a very good 2006 film (Tommi Mendel's *Arukihenro: Walking Pilgrims*) effectively presents pilgrims' perspectives – old and young – along with engaging visual images and useful insights about contemporary Shikoku pilgrimage. Books and articles are better for exposure to the history of the pilgrimage and the importance of miracle tales and the role of the Daishi. Ian Reader's book, *Making Pilgrimages: Meaning and Practice in Shikoku* (Honolulu: University of Hawai'i Press, 2005), provides an excellent and comprehensive study of the pilgrimage. His articles and other book chapters, such as "Legends, Miracles, and Faith in Kōbō Daishi and the Shikoku Pilgrimage," in George Tanabe (ed.), *Religions of Japan in Practice* (Princeton: Princeton University Press, 1999), pp. 360–69, are also useful to highlight key dimensions such as the ongoing importance of miracle tales, folklore, devotion to the Daishi, and various benefits associated with the pilgrimage. With Paul Swanson, Reader also edited a special issue of the *Japanese Journal of Religious Studies* (24[3–4], Fall 1997) devoted to *Pilgrimage in the Japanese Religious Tradition*. Several articles and book chapters by Hiroshi Shimazaki provide unique insights about the geography, cultural markers, and management of the pilgrimage (note that he is named as Hiroshi Tanaka in his 1975 PhD dissertation about Shikoku pilgrimage and early articles, such as "Geographic Expression of Buddhist Pilgrim Places on Shikoku Island, Japan," *Canadian Geographer* 21[2] [1977]).

Bridging academic and more popular readership, the American author and Japanophile Oliver Statler introduced many readers to this practice in *Japanese Pilgrimage* (New York: William Morrow and Co., 1983). This accessible book, which is dedicated to Joseph Kitagawa, the University of Chicago scholar of Japanese religion, was informed by Statler's extensive experience with and research about this pilgrimage in consultation with various scholars and participants. In addition to scholarship about Shikoku pilgrimage, many pilgrims and pilgrimage organizations have written extensively about this famous practice. In the past century, these accounts have ranged in style, content, and the background of the pilgrim. For example, Susan Tennant's translation of *Musume Junreiki* (*The Pilgrimage Journal of a Young Woman*) offers the unique insights of a 24-year-old female Japanese lay pilgrim who later became a well-known author and feminist intellectual; see Tennant's *The 1918 Shikoku Pilgrimage of Takamure Itsue* (Bowen Island, BC: Bowen Publishing, 2010). On the other end of the spectrum, for a quite comprehensive recent account of Shikoku pilgrimage available in English, see *Critical Analysis of the Buddhist 88-Temple Pilgrimage on Shikoku*

Island, Japan (Bloomington, IN: Xlibris, 2010) by the German-born Buddhist monk Ryofu Pussel. To further illustrate the variety of Shikoku pilgrimage accounts, Kōbō Daishi, Shikoku pilgrimage, and the popular folklore account of the practice's origins are even featured in chapter 9 of *Hitching Rides with Buddha* (Toronto: Knopf Canada, 1998) by the Canadian humorist Will Ferguson. Finally, although more than 20 years old, the standard for academic analysis of the early Meiji-era persecution of Buddhism (including the forced separation of Buddhism and Shinto at shared sites) remains James Ketelaar's *Of Heretics and Martyrs in Meiji Japan: Buddhism and Its Persecution* (Princeton: Princeton University Press, 1990).

Author

John S. Harding majored in Asian studies at the University of Puget Sound in Tacoma, Washington, spent a year of graduate study at the University of Cambridge in England, and received his PhD in religious studies at the University of Pennsylvania in Philadelphia. He has conducted research in Japan, North America, and Europe. He is now Associate Professor and Chair of the Religious Studies Department at the University of Lethbridge in Alberta, Canada. His primary areas of interest include Japanese Buddhism and the cross-cultural exchange between Asia and the West that has shaped the development of modern Buddhism worldwide in the past century and a half. His recent books have explored Japanese representations of Buddhism in the Meiji era (*Mahāyāna Phoenix: Japan's Buddhists at the 1893 World's Parliament of Religions*, New York: Peter Lang, 2008), contemporary adaptations of modern and global Buddhism in Canada (*Wild Geese: Buddhism in Canada*, co-edited with Victor Sōgen Hori and Alexander Soucy, Montreal: McGill-Queen's University Press, 2010), and theory and method in the study of religion in the 2008 *Introduction to the Study of Religion* as well as the related 2012 reader (both co-authored with Hillary P. Rodrigues for Routledge).

Chapter 7

From texts to people

Developing new skills

Mavis L. Fenn

Preamble

Buddhist studies, until recently, meant the study of texts. A Buddhologist studied languages, translated texts, and interpreted them from a historical, doctrinal, or literary perspective. It is only within the last 20 years or so that Buddhist studies has incorporated real people into the study of Buddhism. That is not to say that real Buddhists didn't receive any scholarly attention. They did – from scholars in other disciplines. There were anthropologists who primarily focused on the practice of Buddhism in Asia, sociologists who pursued their interests in how Buddhism was being adopted by Western societies, and social psychologists who wondered why so many in the West were adopting this "foreign" religion. But for scholars of the academic study of religion, the area of Buddhist studies was firmly rooted on the page, and not in practice and people, until the 1990s.

And while the study of texts remains central to Buddhist studies, more and more of us traditionally trained scholars have moved to approaches from the social sciences. In my case, several factors contributed to my decision to study Buddhism in the field. First, I taught Buddhism but couldn't direct students to what was going on in the immediate community. Second, I didn't have a good grasp of contemporary Buddhist ritual and practice. Third, I couldn't comfortably answer questions on women in Buddhism. And finally, when I was asked to contribute a piece to a book on the practice of Buddhism in Canada, and our university developed a doctoral program that specialized in the practice of religion in the North American context, I knew the time had come to change my research focus. This chapter is about how a textual scholar learned to work outside her academic comfort zone, developing new skills and meeting new people along the way. By the end, you will see how I learned to navigate in the tricky waters of participant observation, subject interviews, and the shoals of the insider–outsider distinction.

Narrative

Scenario one: the questionnaire

I began to shift my professional focus from texts toward real people about four years ago. I realized that no one was talking specifically to, and about, Canadian Buddhist women. But I had a dilemma. Did I want to talk to Buddhists by culture, Buddhists by choice, nuns, laywomen, and what did I want to talk to them about, specifically? Well, I wanted to do it all. So I produced a preliminary questionnaire that asked a few questions directed at everyone to place them (nun, laywoman, country of origin, education level, and so on) and then followed up with a multitude of sections for each of the categories, ending with a section that asked them to reflect upon their interaction with each other and their thoughts about Buddhist practice cross-culturally. The end result was a substantial survey that I felt would cover every area of women's religious lives and interaction with each other. My project had begun!

The first "glitch" was that carefully crafted survey questionnaire. Most of them went out via email to contacts in various Buddhist communities with requests to circulate the material about the project to anyone they thought might be interested. And many of them came back with just the first section answered and a comment that that was all they had found relevant to themselves. If the second section did not pertain to their specific situation, they assumed that was all there was for them and they never scrolled down farther. Most of the surveys had to be sent out again. In the second sending, I made sure that the participants knew that I was looking for much more information and asked them to please scroll through each section and fill out everything of relevance to their situation. I wanted to know all of their stories and experiences.

Scenario two: doing the interview

Survey in hand, tape recorder loaded, questions and fruit as a gift for the nun I am to interview – I am ready to go. I am nervous, but excited, too. I was certain that I would be great at interviewing. I love meeting new people and talking about Buddhism, and I am very comfortable in social situations. So I make my way, following the directions up the mountain to an older section of "Steeltown" – Hamilton, Ontario (Canada), but I can't find the street address I have been given. I drive around, ask people for help, and get more and more nervous as the time moves on. I am late. I phone, apologize, and clarify the directions. Again I miss the street, and again and again. Finally, I see the "red door" she had told me about, and I park. As soon as "Sister" opens the door, I can see we are off to a rough start. She is not smiling. Things pick up when I bow and offer the fruit with my apologies. We take a tour of the temple and teaching area. A traditional Vietnamese-style altar is set up with icons, incense, and fruit offerings. There are meditation cushions stacked in the corners of the former living and dining area and the room stretches back to a patio door through which I can see a garden and outside meditation area. The atmosphere is calming; I begin to relax. We settle in the upper-floor den area amidst a small library of books, workspace area, and plants, tea in hand. This is nice. Still a bit nervous, I decide there is no need to disrupt things by asking if I can tape the interview. A few notes in my notebook should do. We chat about the interesting life she has led and how she came to be a Buddhist nun. We move on to the questions. I find it hard to concentrate on what she is saying and to write notes at the same time. I need to ask her to repeat herself sometimes and I get caught up in the conversation and forget to take notes. One phrase – "She must think I am an idiot" – keeps running through my mind. Interview over, I think about stopping at the nearby coffee shop I passed three times on my way to the temple to write a few notes and reflections while they are fresh in my mind. But it is getting into rush hour, I have an hour's drive home, and my dog has been alone for much longer than expected. I decide to do it later. But later, I have trouble reconstructing some of the conversation and responses. I realize I will have to make a follow-up phone call or send an email. I feel quite unprofessional and discouraged. Sister's interview produced a wealth of information, but am I up to the task of compiling and interpreting it?

Figure 7.1 Sister Tin Quang

Scenario three: the Simha stone

I am attending the ceremonial opening of a small Theravāda temple in an old manufacturing building situated just off the freeway in a working-class section of Kitchener, Ontario (Canada). The temple caters primarily to the Laotian community, and some people have come a fair distance to attend. Although the temple has been open for some time, today the symbolic stones will be placed around the corners of the temple officially marking the monastic boundaries. I have met one of the monks briefly before when my colleague and I dropped by to see the temple and meet the monks. His English is not good, but he managed to invite us and we managed to accept. He tells me that a very important Thai monk from the United States has come and has agreed to a "Q and A" with us later. I wonder … does everyone get such an opportunity or only special guests? The monk rushes off, leaving us to our own devices. I look around. I knew the temple would be crowded judging by the piles of shoes at the entrance. Women enter and emerge from the kitchen, trailing wonderful smells. There is happy chatter, and the temple is full of children and babies and lots of action. My Scots Presbyterian grandmother would have been shocked by the noise and activity in a "house of worship." I reflect on the first time I went to a temple in India; I remember being surprised at how people were coming and going, children running around, and people chatting during rituals.

Figure 7.2 Theravāda temple, Kitchener, Ontario

On the left at the front is a money tree. I decide to make some merit and clip a bill to the tree. There are very few non-Southeast Asians in the crowd and the few who are there are clearly part of a couple. I am an outsider but feel welcome rather than an object of curiosity. Everyone smiles and an English-speaking man gives us a tour of the temple: he shows us the living quarters for the monks, a reading room, a large room for school and meetings, the kitchen, and the main temple area. We are called to order. We are gently tugged toward an area right in the middle of the second row where we will get a good view. People move over to make room for us, all smiles. In front of us is a row of women clad in white. They are laywomen who have been in the temple for the weekend, having taken temporary vows to mark this special occasion. They have been focusing on their spiritual development, meritorious. The proceedings begin with a familiar chant, "*Buddham saranam gacchami; dhammam saranam gacchami; sangham saranam gacchami,*" words which I know mean "I take refuge in the Buddha; I take refuge in the Dhamma; I take refuge in the Sangha." Every ceremony begins with this chant and each time I hear it I feel a sense of peace and relaxation settle in. Maybe I am a closet Buddhist, I think.

People are attentive but my focus fades as the dhamma talk goes on. I am sitting cross-legged and my left knee is objecting strenuously. I sit with my legs to the side for a while until the right knee complains. I hold each position as long as I can because I don't want to draw attention to myself. I worry about accidently stretching my legs right out. Not good; my feet must never face the teacher – that is just rude. I ponder the fact that I am always going to start meditating on a regular basis. I could use a meditation bench if I cannot manage the half-lotus. They have classes here; maybe it would get better if I committed to a class? I struggle to keep my focus.

After the talk there is food. I love Asian food. I smile inwardly at my own hypocrisy. I say I feel a bit uncomfortable as an honored guest, but when it comes to the food just keep it coming! We meet with the monk in a small room off the kitchen. It is a small mixed group and the monk speaks in English. I recognize him from a book I have read on temples in Chicago and Los Angeles. He is actively engaged in opening up Theravāda Buddhism in the West and has established a retreat center outside Chicago. We talk about the different needs of worshippers, the adaptation of monastic life to North America, and various other related Buddhist topics.

Afterward I go outside and mingle with the crowd, again smiling and speaking to several people about the temple, my experiences of it, and their engagement with it. Too quickly, it is time to go. I seek out the temple monk, bow, and thank him for inviting me. As I walk to my car in the warm fall sunshine I think, "Maybe this fieldwork thing will be okay?"

Scenario four: writing it up

Writing up field research and crafting it into an article for publication has been a real challenge. I have written continuously throughout my life and had already published a few academic, peer-reviewed articles. But this new topic was just that – new – and still felt as if it was not my area. This was social science, and I was using surveys and questionnaires and so felt I should analyze the results with sufficient consideration of method and the limitations of small survey groups and limited representation. Well, I did that and produced an article, which one journal editor referred to as "adequate." That really hurt. I asked a colleague who has published widely in the social sciences to read it over. Her comment was "Boring." Discouraged, but not prepared to abandon all hope, I reread it myself. It *was* boring. It provided no sense of the people with whom I talked, their ideas about the central issues, and my comments contextualizing them. Further, I had spent so much time qualifying what I had to say that I cannot imagine why anyone would care. I rewrote it to better reflect the people I had met as well as the statistics I had generated, had it critiqued, and it was published.

Discussion

Being new to field research, I had imagined a fairly simple process. You have an idea, you talk to people, you write it up. In the broadest sense, that is true, but the process of accomplishing these objectives is fraught with angst and paperwork, lots and lots of paperwork. You cannot just go out and talk to people. You need a detailed proposal for assessment by the university's ethics committee. That proposal must be accompanied by all the materials you will use, permissions, letters for mail and email, phone inquiries, surveys, questionnaires, and sometimes follow-up letters. All of them are carefully reviewed and questioned; sometimes you have to make amendments to the forms. The ethics procedures seem to be based upon medical research, so sometimes the questions you get seem a bit odd. For example, how do you respond when asked about eliminating the risk to your "subjects"? Well, what risk is there in the first place? Some lost time? You can never guarantee that communication between people will be "risk free," especially if some of your questions are sensitive in nature. All you can do is assure the person, in person and in writing with both parties' signatures, that they don't have to answer any questions they do not wish to, and they can withdraw their consent now or later. The negative side of all this is that it is very time-consuming, even when provided with samples. The positive side of having to do all this is that it forces you to really think about what you hope to accomplish. And as my experience in constructing my first survey shows, you need to think about how people will actually use the questionnaire. Lesson learned. If you send out a survey that is too long or segmented, people can't negotiate it very well. It would have been better to have sent out the basic questionnaire and then select a second, relevant section to send.

Several women indicated that they were willing to do a follow-up interview. This is where you sit down with them, phone them, or communicate via email and ask them some ethics-approved "open-ended" questions. These are questions that start the discussion. Then it "opens up" into a deeper or wider discussion or moves into another area according to your mutual interest. As noted above, things didn't go quite the way I expected. Let us go over some of my mistakes. I set up too many appointments in a day. That put stress on me both practically and emotionally. If I got lost – as I did on more than one occasion – I wasn't starting out well with the interview. Second, I was reluctant to use a tape recorder as well as a notebook. In the future, I will always use both. Using both allows you to focus on the person with whom you are speaking. When you use just a notebook, you can become distracted with writing and miss something. I think that the reason why I was initially uncomfortable with the recorder was that it is an indication that this isn't just a social chat. But it isn't. I found myself uncomfortable talking to "subjects" and I felt stressed about "interviewing" people. On the positive side, some of the people who generously gave their time to talk to me about their beliefs and experiences of religion in Canada in the interviews have now become more than "subjects." I made a good friend with whom I have traveled to Mongolia and Vietnam, and several good acquaintances across the country. These friendships serve as one of the many unexpected and underappreciated benefits of the academic life.

Another recommendation is to have two notebooks, one for the interviews and one for your reflections, which I suggest you fill out as soon as possible after an interview (there are coffee shops everywhere and it is worth stopping, even if it is rush hour). These reflections are not just about the interview – context, surroundings, feel, and so on – but they are also about how you see your project taking shape. This is one area that I found was just like working with texts. Scholars always approach a text with some questions and some ideas about what we will find. Sometimes the text pushes back. That is, there are things in a text that may resist your sense of what it is about. You need to reflect on that, and sometimes you must reject or adapt your first interpretation of the material. People sometimes respond to questions in ways you do not anticipate. A reflections journal can help you think about that and what it may mean. It makes you more sensitive in subsequent interviews and may raise issues you need to address.

Sometimes an interview was scheduled after a particular ritual, meditation, or dharma talk. In these cases I was a participant observer. Oddly, this is the area I felt most comfortable with. I say oddly, because I was brought up in a family that was not at all inclined to ritual and felt religious ritual to be "superstitious." When in doubt, I realized I could just follow what others do. I also learned that meditation can be an opportunity to participate in peaceful communion with others and to center yourself for the discussion following, although my knees still object to the half-lotus position. A dharma talk gives you the opportunity to see how well your academic ideas about Buddhism represent Buddhist ideas in practice. Chanting can provide a sense of community solidarity and all of it allows for a quiet smile shared with others that crosses a wide range of language barriers. In addition, questions about the ritual are often a good entry point to establishing a rapport with the person you are to interview. Be observant and try to know and understand.

While I didn't have difficulty with the participant-observation aspect of field research and learned from it that I really have to get out more often, I did have some angst around the insider–outsider aspect of research. I am an outsider: an academic by training, a non-Buddhist, and an agnostic. I am sympathetic to Buddhism as it is close to my personal worldview and, while I have enjoyed and found meaning in talking to Buddhists and participating in their rituals, I am nevertheless an outsider. I feel uncomfortable when people speak to me using insider language. I remind them often that I am a researcher but that makes me feel uncomfortable, too. They are not just "subjects" but people who have been kind enough to share their core values with me, who openly discuss their ideas about the fundamental questions of meaning, often introducing me to family and friends. Still, even if I were an insider, and I never discount that possibility, I would likely continue to feel uncomfortable, as the academic study of religion is different from the practice of it, and academics frequently have a different understanding of things from most practitioners. I think this one aspect of research is just something I have to live with.

Finding time to write is a major problem for academics. We also teach and attend far too many committee meetings. But that is the nature of our careers. You need to create time in your schedule where you will not attend meetings or see students or read books. And you need to hold on to it. When you are writing, remember that it is about the people and the ideas and issues. The statistics and survey results are just there for context.

I will admit that, psychologically, part of my problem with the publishing aspect of academic life has nothing to do with time but with esteem and ego. I don't like making my work public, open to critique. Critique is most often helpful, as the experience recorded above indicates, but sometimes it hurts, and sometimes you feel as if it is directed at you and not the work. The best way to handle this fear is to remember that you are not simply your work: do not make your work your self-identity. Take what is valuable in a critique and leave the rest; consider the message and not the messenger. Finally, a word of wisdom gained from the study of Buddhism: life is a series of ups and downs, successes and failures. Deal with them equally and never lose your sense of humor.

My current project is on Buddhism and Canadian multiculturalism. I look forward to meeting – tape recorder and notebook in hand – Buddhist Canadians from coast to coast and talking about their vision of Buddhism in Canada.

Readings

There follow several suggestions for books I wish I had read before engaging in field research. These include Howard Becker's *Tricks of the Trade: How to Think about Your Research While You're Doing It* (Chicago: University of Chicago Press, 1998); James V. Spickard, J. Shawn Landres, and B. McGuire's edited volume *Personal Knowledge and Beyond: Reshaping the Ethnography of Religion* (New York: New York University Press, 2002); Scott Grills' edited volume *Doing Ethnographic Research: Fieldwork Settings* (Thousand Oaks, CA: Sage Publications, 1998); and Margaret Diane LeCompte and Jean J. Schensul's Ethnographer's Toolkit series (Walnut Creek, CA: AltaMira Press, 1999). To read more about my own experiences in the field, consult my articles "Buddhism in Southern Ontario" (with Kay Koppedrayer) in *Buddhism in Canada*, which was edited by Bruce Matthews (Abingdon: RoutledgeCurzon, 2006), and "Buddhist Women in Canada: Researching Identity and Influence," which appears in Karma Lekshe Tsomo (ed.), *Ninth Sakyadhita International Conference* (Kuala Lumpur: Suki Hotu Publications, 2008), pp. 171–78. My article (with Kay Koppedrayer) on Sakyadhita represents our work on the International Association of Buddhist Women, an organization that was established in 1987: "Sakyadhita: A Transnational Gathering Place for Buddhist Women", *Journal of Global Buddhism* 9 (2008), pp. 45–79. (online at http://www.globalbuddhism.org/9/fenn08.htm). I am currently working on two additional articles on Buddhism and multiculturalism.

Author

Mavis L. Fenn is an Associate Professor in the Department of Religious Studies at St. Paul's University College, University of Waterloo, Canada. She was trained to read Buddhist texts at McMaster University, Hamilton, Ontario (Canada). Her forte was Sanskrit, Pāli, and the application of narrative approaches to texts, unlocking the complex interplay between story and religious doctrine. Then she was asked to co-author a chapter on Buddhism in Ontario. Her mandate was to talk to a range of Buddhists, teachers, and practitioners, to augment the statistics and demographics. She would have to talk to real Buddhists about their lives, beliefs, and practices. While she had not been trained in fieldwork, she enjoyed the experience tremendously and plans to pursue other kinds of research in the field in the future.

Chapter 8

Merit, gender, and Theravāda Buddhist practices in times of crisis

Monica Lindberg Falk

Preamble

This narrative is from a long-term anthropological research project carried out in coastal villages in the south of Thailand. The aim of this study is to explore how Thai Buddhist survivors use Buddhism in the recovery process after the tsunami catastrophe in 2004. On December 26, 2004, the Indian Ocean tsunami hit the shores of 13 countries, and almost 230,000 people lost their lives. In Thailand, about 10,000 people died or went missing, and approximately 8,500 people were injured. Six provinces in Thailand were hit by the tsunami. My research project concentrates on Phang Nga province, where 69 villages were directly affected by the tsunami, which totally destroyed some of them.

The anthropological fieldwork for this project was conducted between 2005 and 2009. I have followed ethical standards and masked the informants' identities; the names in the narrative are fictitious. Because of the sensitive nature of working with traumatized informants, it was necessary to utilize a number of different research techniques. The main methods involved were participant observation, semi-structured in-depth interviews, life stories, and narratives. One strategy for obtaining detailed interviews was through social networks, and this involved spending long periods of time in the field.

Theravāda Buddhism is the dominant religion in Thailand, and about 95 percent of the population identify themselves as Buddhists. There are, however, more Muslims in the south of Thailand than in other parts of the country. In Phang Nga, approximately 60 percent of people are Buddhists and about 40 percent are Muslims. After the tsunami, the intact Buddhist temples became important places of refuge and the focal points around which everything functioned. Religion has played an important role in the survivors' recovery process. Buddhists believe in *karma*/*kamma*, which means that people's intentional actions directly affect their life. It is a moral cause-and-effect relation, and every person's individual *kamma* is believed to determine his or her life here and now as well as in future existences. Thai Buddhists emphasize the importance of being generous, following the Buddhist precepts, and, if possible, receiving Buddhist ordination to make religious merit and thereby offset undesirable *kamma*. Lack of religious merit is considered to result in an increase of suffering and difficulties in this life and to risk experiencing future existences in one of the realms of hell. The tsunami happened suddenly and nobody was prepared to die. Therefore, it is very important for the Thai Buddhist survivors to make as much merit as possible and transfer the merit to their deceased family members and relatives to mitigate their suffering. In this chapter, I have chosen to give examples of how Buddhism is practiced on a local level after a crisis situation and show how Buddhism is entwined in people's lives.

Narrative

Transferring religious merit

It is morning, the sun is shining, and it is going to be another hot day. I am on the west coast in the south of Thailand, not far from Burma. I am sitting on the floor in a room without walls. The roof is made of dry blades of grass, which rattle in the breeze. The room is packed with people – mostly women but there are also men and children. The floor is covered with a blue patterned oilcloth and I find it rather uncomfortable to sit on the floor with my legs in the mermaid position. I know that it is important to make sure that my feet do not point to the Buddha statues or towards other people. The Buddhist ceremony is coming to an end and a man wearing a yellow T-shirt and an orange wristband with the text "*rak nai luang*" (I love the King) takes the clay pot from the monks' platform. A string of white thread has been tied around the pot and the thread has been held in the folded hands of the monk while he chants Buddhist texts. There is only one monk present. When I look at him, I think he looks serious and sad. His fellow monks at the temple died in the tsunami, and he was the only monk who survived. The pot is filled with sheets of white paper inscribed with the names of villagers, family members, relatives, and friends who lost their lives in the tsunami. The man in the yellow T-shirt lights the papers and people concentrate on the open fire. More sheets of white paper with names are added to the fire and the smoke makes my eyes smart. I have visited several ceremonies at the small temples in the tsunami-stricken area and, apart from burning paper, the ceremonies conducted here follow the same pattern as commonly carried out at Thai Buddhist temples and nunneries.

This small Buddhist abode is located on the mainland in northern Phang Nga province. It was set up after the tsunami on the outskirts of a new settlement built for survivors from one of the stricken islands. It is a rural area and very far away from the more affluent parts of Thailand that have large, shiny temples with modern facilities. I was introduced to this temple by a family that I met at a temple in the small town of Takuapa. After the tsunami, the temple in Takuapa was one of the main sites for storing dead bodies and accommodating the forensic teams from Bangkok and abroad. I have frequently visited the temples in Phang Nga, and after months of busy activity, most of the temple grounds were now left in peace. However, many of the buildings bore traces of the tremendous strain inflicted by the tsunami on the temples, such as broken interior fixtures and bathrooms that were not working because of over-use.

I am standing in the shade outside a building where a family and relatives have gathered for a cremation ceremony that is going to take place later that day. The family is sitting in an open room, *sala*, at the temple site and the coffin is kept in the same room. The weather is hot and Khun Siriporn, the deceased woman's daughter, asks if I want some water to drink. We talk and she tells me that she used to be a teacher on an island that was partly wiped out by the tsunami. The tsunami hit on a Sunday so all the schools were closed and Khun Siriporn had gone to her permanent home on the mainland. Her husband, who had recently accepted a government offer of early retirement from his occupation as a teacher in a government school, was on the island when the waves hit. He had opened a shrimp farm on the island, and he survived the tsunami by clinging to a tree. Since then he has suffered from post-traumatic stress disorder and has severe symptoms.

There were two small Buddhist temples on the island located in two villages which each had a few resident monks. The village where Khun Siriporn taught was the worst hit. She said that before the tsunami the school and the temple co-operated and the teachers and the monks worked together. As mentioned above, the temple had three resident monks and two of them died in the tsunami. The monk who survived returned to the island shortly after the tsunami had hit and he, the villagers, and the rescue workers collected the dead bodies and transported them to a temple on the mainland.

The monk is important in helping the villagers cope with what has happened and he comforts them and gives them hope for the future. The villagers who survived the tsunami sought safer ground in the Buddhist temples on the mainland. In the beginning, they lived in temporary shelters but have now moved to new villages built by the Thai government and non-governmental organizations (NGOs). The new village that is close to where this small Buddhist temple is located was built by a Thai organization from Bangkok. They thought it was for a Muslim community and, therefore, did not include a Buddhist temple in the plans for the village. The Buddhist temple and the monk are very important to the villagers and they struggle to find a suitable place for the temple. None of the villagers own any land, but they have found a provisional solution by setting up a temporary temple on land owned by a Muslim man. He is kindly helping out in this difficult situation and lets them borrow the land until they find a place to build a permanent temple.

Khun Siriporn admires the monk and she wants to support his activities. She invites me to visit him. The monk has organized temporary ordination for a group of young boys with the main purpose of transferring religious merits to deceased family members and relatives. The following Sunday, Khun Siriporn, her husband, and I travel to the temple. It is about one and a half hours' drive by car to the new village. We depart in the early morning and stop at the market close to the bus station to buy fruit and useful items that we later donate to the group of novice monks. Khun Siriporn has prepared food that she offers to the small monastic community. The temporary temple is located on the outskirts of the new village in a grove filled with young trees. When we arrive, the novices help the monk prepare for the daily morning ceremony.

Khun Siriporn talks with some of the villagers who have arrived at the temple and I walk around the small temple area. It is a truly simple Buddhist abode constructed mainly from grass and leaves. The novices washed their robes in the morning and the ochre garments are now hanging to dry in the sun. Outside one of the buildings, 13 yellow plastic bowls, commonly used for scooping water from a large water basin while washing oneself, are lined up. I feel happy to see how well and with what small means the monk and the laypeople have organized this temporary temple and seem to keep everything in impeccable order.

The ceremony is about to begin and the laypeople gather in the *sala*. They have brought food in special containers and have placed them beneath the monks' platform. They are chatting while waiting for the monk and novices to arrive. Food for the monks must be given before noon, in time for their last meal of the day. Khun Siriporn donates the food and other items that we have brought before the ceremony begins.

The lighting of two candles placed on either side of the Buddha statue marks the opening of the ceremony. The monk, the novices, and the laypeople bow three times. The monk leads the laypeople in the recitation about taking refuge in the Buddha, the Dhamma, and the Sangha. The entire ceremony is conducted in the Pāli language. Thereafter, a layman asks the monk in Pāli for the five Buddhist precepts. The monk holds his religious fan in front of his face and the laypeople recite after the monk, who gives the precepts one by one. The five Buddhist precepts are: to abstain from killing, stealing, sexual misconduct, lying, and taking intoxicants. The religious fan is here used to de-emphasize the personality of the individual monk and instead stress that the relation is with the Sangha as an institution. The fan is of oval shape and attached to a long staff. Originally the monks' fans were made from palm leaves but today they can be elaborately decorated and are a symbol of authority and high ecclesiastical position. In ceremonies, the monk holds the fan with one hand in a fixed position in front of his face while reciting or chanting and keeps the round-handled staff resting on the floor. After giving the precepts, the monk puts the fan in its stand and the ceremony proceeds with the monk giving a Buddhist talk in Thai about life and death and how to lead a happy life.

Today is Wan Phraa, the Buddhist holy day, and the villagers have, as mentioned above, brought food to the temple. Every day, except on Wan Phraa, the monks walk an alms round in the village early in the morning. Theravāda Buddhist tradition follows the lunar calendar and Wan Phraa occurs four times a month. On Wan Phraa it is common for Thai villagers to adopt a stricter regime, staying at temples the whole day and sometimes also spending the night there. When they stay overnight they wear white clothes and adhere to the eight Buddhist precepts of abstaining from killing, stealing, sexual activity, lying, taking intoxicants, eating after noon, beautification, or entertainment, and they sleep on thick mattresses.

The sets of five and eight precepts are lay precepts; ordained monks and novices have more precepts to follow. Theravāda novice monks receive 10 precepts; fully ordained male Theravāda monks, *bhikkhu*, receive 227 precepts; and Theravāda female monks, *bhikkhuni*, receive 311 precepts.

The monk at this temple takes only one meal a day but the novices are allowed to have two meals – breakfast and lunch, both before noon. The monk and the novices take some food from all the containers that the villagers have brought. The laypeople transfer the merit earned by their generosity by using water. They pour water from one small container to another and dedicate merit to the deceased persons. The laypeople wait until the monastics have finished the meal and then they return home with their food containers. Most of the villagers walk or ride on motorbikes, while a few stay to help with practical matters at the temple. The monk is willing to give an interview while we sit on the floor in the *sala*. The people around us are welcome to listen if they wish. The monk's mobile rings several times and one of the novices assists him by answering the phone.

I have interviewed many monks and nuns over the years and I lived more than a year at a Buddhist "nunnery" in Thailand when I was conducting fieldwork about Buddhist female ascetics. I feel comfortable and enjoy talking with Buddhist ascetics. What is different about this interview is that the monk has experienced personal loss and is carrying the great burden of leading the laypeople through this time of extreme suffering. This is the first interview I conduct with him and I do not want to ask questions that would make him recall traumatic memories that might affect his recovery process.

The monk is 32 years old and he has been a monk for 11 years. He is from Phuket province and he was studying at the university when he decided to leave the lay life and become a Buddhist monk. He was ordained in the north of Thailand and lived there for seven years before he chose to return to the south. He has lived at the small temple on the island since 2002. A villager had donated land with the purpose of establishing a temple in the village, which had long been a wish of the villagers. Before 2002 there was no Buddhist temple on the island, and the monk said that it was strange that two small temples were established almost simultaneously. He tells me that the school did not have enough teachers, so he helped out by teaching mathematics and other subjects in the school. He went on an alms round every morning and he came to know the villagers' situation quite well. He organized temporary ordination for the villagers at their request because they wanted to make merit. The monk says that some of them were anxious because they were fishermen and they knew that it was against the Buddhist precepts to kill and that killing created *baap*, demerit. The monk supports the community, and he says that he helps the villagers to develop their minds. He explains that the villagers were born Buddhists but have not had a close relationship with a temple. The monk remembers that when he first came to the island the villagers were very keen to talk with him and they sought explanations from him and discussions as well as participation in Buddhist ceremonies and activities at the temple. Some villagers ceased to fish on Wan Phraa.

On the day the tsunami hit, the monk had left the island to collect a Buddha statue that had been donated to the temple. When he returned everything had been wiped out by the waves: the small temple, the school, and the houses in the village were all gone. The monk worked side by side with the survivors and the volunteers to collect dead bodies and to transport them to a temple on the mainland. The monk says that he applies the Buddhist way of being in the present moment; he emphasizes the importance of encouraging the villagers and he wants to make them happy. I find it a pleasant experience to talk with him. He is very calm and relaxed, and he appears to be very kind. He is a scholarly monk and knows how to explain Buddhism clearly.

At this and other temples, Buddhist ceremonies have become very important to those who survived the tsunami. The people carry photos of the deceased to the temple ceremonies, and the religious merits that they accumulate through various acts of generosity are dedicated to those who died in the catastrophe.

I find it interesting to observe how crucial the monks and temples seem to be to the recovery process after the tsunami. When Khun Siriporn, her husband, and I are about to leave the small temple, a family from the new village invite us to visit. All of the houses are the same and are made of white concrete and stand on stilts. We sit in the shade under the house and talk. They tell us about their loss and how strange it is for them to live on the mainland where everything costs money and they find it hard to make ends meet. The family have deep respect for the monk and describe how important he is to them as a leader. When they speak I can clearly see that the novice ordination offers them encouragement. The woman tells us that she wakes up early every morning and prepares food for the monk and the novices.

I decide to stay for a period of time in a village with several small temples. It takes me a couple of hours to go there on the local bus. I travel through a beautiful landscape that attracts many so-called eco-tourists. The road is curvy and I enjoy the scenery and talk with some of the passengers, who are going to work as day laborers. They are from Burma and we communicate in broken Thai. The village where I will stay is approximately 30 minutes' drive from the temporary temple mentioned above. In the village a larger temple with about 15 resident monks became a hub for many aid projects after the tsunami. It is not located close to the sea and was not, therefore, directly affected by the waves. A temporary shelter was set up in the temple grounds and I visit the temple frequently, finding the head monk's leadership skills to be extraordinary. This temple became a safe place and the source of guidance and hope for the future for many survivors. I am amazed by the resident monks' ability to run so many projects and at the same time carry out their usual activities.

Many people that I talk with say that religion has become more important to them after the tsunami. They want to learn more about Buddhism and, most importantly, they want to make religious merit. In Thailand it is common for temples to organize temporary ordination for schoolboys during the summer vacation. The abbot at the temple mentioned above told me that after the tsunami, more boys than ever before have enrolled in the temporary ordination that the temple has arranged.

The ordination ceremonies take two days and the families and the villagers are involved in the activities. In the afternoon of the first day, the boys arrive at the temple with their families. I stroll around the temple area talking with some laypeople from the village who have volunteered to prepare food. They are busy cooking large quantities for the boys, who will tonight have their last dinner for almost three weeks. As novices they will not eat after noon. Theravāda Buddhist ascetics are strict about having only one or two meals a day. They can only eat between 7.00 a.m. and noon. The rest of the day they are only allowed to drink.

The first phase of the ceremony is held in the *sala* building. The parents or relatives are sitting on the floor in a row and the boys are seated in front of them. All sit with their legs folded under them. The sons bow to their parents and ask forgiveness for any wrongdoings. The monks arrive and sit on the platform in the *sala*. The boys walk to the platform and sit in front of the monks. They bow three times and then sit on their knees with folded hands and receive the five Buddhist precepts from the monks, who use the religious fan in front of their faces. Ordination is a meritorious act for all the participants. The monks hold a white thread in their hands while reciting a Buddhist text and the abbot sprinkles blessed water over the boys and their families and any family member who wants a white thread has one tied around his or her wrist.

The boys are given a large green leaf shaped into a cone and the family members each cut a strand of hair and place it in the cone. The boys line up in front up the abbot with the leaves in their hands. They walk on their knees and the monk cuts some hair from each boy and places it in the leaf. The boys' heads and eyebrows will now be shaved and many fathers and some monks help to do this. After being shaved the boys' heads are whitened with talcum powder and they put on white clothes. Many wear a white T-shirt with a red heart and red text in Thai which reads "We love the King." All boys wear a length of white folded fabric that looks like a traditional skirt secured with a belt. The boys are now in an intermediate state between the lay and the ordained state. The parents and relatives will return home, and the boys will spend their first night in the temple and the ceremonies will continue the following day.

It is already dark when I walk on the roadside with trucks passing me at high speed. I am renting a room not far from the market. I stop at one of the small restaurants to have something to eat before I type up the day's field notes. The next morning I wake up early and have rice soup and an old-style Thai coffee at the market before I walk to the temple. A woman on a motorbike offers me a ride there. The temple is busy and many villagers are preparing for the ceremony. We are offered water and soft drinks while waiting for the ceremonies to begin. The ceremony commences with a procession. First come a group of musicians and villagers who dance on the way to the ordination hall, *bot*. After them a group of men arrive, carrying Thai and Buddhist flags. One man carries a large photograph of the Thai king. The boys, with their heads shaved and dressed in white, walk

Figure 8.1 The monk cuts some hair from each boy

after them. Each boy has three white lotus flowers, three incense sticks, and a candle in his folded hands in front of him. The families and relatives follow at the end of the procession, carrying monks' robes, monks' bowls, thermoses, plastic bowls, soap, and other necessary and useful things.

The ordination hall is beautiful, with a soft, dark-blue wall-to-wall carpet. The walls are decorated with colorful drawings depicting episodes from the Buddha's life. The white-clad novices-to-be and their parents take their places on the floor and the monks sit close to the Buddha statues.

Figure 8.2 The boys, now shaven and dressed in white, face their families

Figure 8.3 After receiving robes from their relatives, the boys walk on their knees to the monks

The boys are positioned in front of their parents and relatives and receive the ochre robes from them. The boys walk on their knees to the monks with the folded robes resting on their outstretched arms. The monks take one item from among the robes and place it around the boys' necks. The boys disappear through the back entrance and outside the ordination hall they change into the ochre robes, assisted by some laypeople. When the boys come back inside the hall wearing the robes they sit in front of the monks. The abbot gives them the ten Buddhist novice precepts and the novices repeat the precepts after the abbot. The parents and relatives witness the ceremony and the novices once again take their positions in front of their parents. By receiving ordination, the novices no longer belong to the lay realm. Their relationship with laypeople such as their parents has changed, and they will, for example, cease to bow to their parents. The families hand over the monks' bowls to the novices and the last phase of the ceremony takes place outside the ordination hall. The laypeople are standing on each side of the pathway that leads from the ordination hall, and the novices walk down the stairs from the ordination hall with their alms bowls in front of them, while the laypeople along the pathway place food in the bowls.

I have asked permission to take photos of the ordination ceremony, and the boys and their families seem to be proud and happy about the event. Some laypeople have brought cameras and the temple will receive photos of the occasion. This is an important time for the boys and their families and they appreciate having their photos taken. While photographing and taking notes of the ordination procedure, I cannot avoid comparing boys' and girls' ordination ceremonies that I have observed. I find that the most striking difference is the large attendance at this ceremony, which is a manifestation of the considerably greater support for the boys' ordination ceremony.

Discussion

Gender, merit, and ordination

This group of novices will be ordained for 20 days. During that time they will experience life at the monastery. They will have a lot of fun, but they will also learn to control themselves and learn about the Buddhist approach to life. The religious merit that they earn by being ordained will be transferred to those family members and/or relatives who lost their lives in the tsunami.

Experiencing a natural disaster and the loss of close family and relatives has changed the lives of the people involved forever. Religion is of essential importance in the recovery process, and religious practices provide ways to cope with difficult situations. The number of merit-making ceremonies to transfer religious merit to the deceased family members and relatives increased tremendously after the tsunami. Receiving temporary ordination after a family member has died is practiced widely in Thailand. Ordination is the ultimate act to make merit, and in

Figure 8.4 The novices, now in ochre robes, receive monks' bowls

Thailand it is only men who formally belong to the Thai Sangha and have access to ordination.

Although ordination was something that women had access to during the Buddha's time and still have in several Mahāyāna Buddhist countries, girls do not have the same opportunity as boys to be ordained in Thailand. There have always been female ascetics in Thailand; however, women are not eligible to enter into the Thai Buddhist Sangha and women's ordinations are not recognized. Nonetheless, a few temples in the tsunami-affected area organize temporary ordination for girls and women, and there is an increasing interest among Thai girls and women in receiving Buddhist ordination.

Over the years I have asked many novices why they have been ordained and the most common answer is that they are doing so for their mothers. Motherhood is highly esteemed in Thai society, and children are always in debt to their parents in general and to their mothers in particular. Traditionally, Thai sons are expected to become novice monks for at least one period of their lives out of gratitude to their parents. Through ordination, a young man's parents are perceived to acquire merit, and this is particularly important to the mother, who gains much merit primarily through her son's ordination.

After the tsunami, the ordination of men, women, and children has been organized with the specific purpose of transferring merit not to the parents but to those who died in the disaster. A few temples have arranged temporary ordination for women. The Buddhist "nuns" in Thailand are called *mae chii*. They shave their heads and eyebrows and adopt similar precepts to the monks, even though they formally receive only the eight Buddhist precepts mentioned above. It is uncontested that religion is particularly important in times of crisis, and both male and female ascetics are needed. A few weeks after the tsunami, I went to the affected area with a small group of *mae chii*s. The female survivors especially were very eager to talk with the *mae chii*s and they appreciated conversing with female Buddhist specialists. The *mae chii*s explained that this appreciation of their presence stems from the fact that women feel they can talk about certain things with the *mae chii*s that they cannot talk about with monks and they believe that the *mae chii*s understand them.

The Buddha founded the female monks' order, the *bhikkhuni* order, a few years after establishing the male monks' order, the *bhikkhu* order. The *bhikkhuni* order existed in India and Sri Lanka for about 1,300 years before it was disbanded. The *bhikkhuni* order did not spread to Thailand; however, the *mae chii*s have long existed in the country and the international *bhikkhuni* movement has been successful in reviving women's access to *bhikkhuni* ordination, which is currently possible in Sri Lanka. The Thai Sangha does not recognize the *bhikkhuni*s' ordination, and Thai *mae chii*s usually do not want to receive ordination as *bhikkhuni*s and instead strive for recognition in their religious role as Thai *mae chii*s.

The intention of this chapter is to illustrate how Buddhism can be of practical importance in times of crisis. It strives to give a glimpse of how Buddhism is woven into the daily life of Thai women and men. By studying how religion is practiced we learn also about how beliefs affect the wider society. By understanding how local Thai Buddhist people comprehend the doctrine of *kamma* and rebirth we get a better understanding of why rituals and ceremonies play such a vital part in local Buddhist practices and how these doctrines and rituals create order in society.

Readings

Writings on the tsunami catastrophe in 2004 have so far mainly been about aspects of aid management, tsunami warning systems, and how to rebuild houses and infrastructure after the tsunami. Religion's role in the recovery process after the tsunami is addressed in *Religions, Natural Hazards, and Disasters*, a special issue of the journal *Religion*. I have contributed an article to that special issue: "Recovery and Buddhist Practices in the Aftermath of the Tsunami in Southern Thailand," *Religion* 40(2) (2010), pp. 96–103. The volume edited by L. Woodhead, H. Kawanami, and C. Partridge, *Religions in the Modern World: Traditions and Transformations* (New York: Routledge, 2009), has a very insightful section on contemporary Buddhism. D. K. Swearer's book *The Buddhist World of Southeast Asia* (Albany: State University of New York Press, 2010) gives an introduction to how Buddhism is practiced in Southeast Asia. P. Harvey's *An Introduction to Buddhist Ethics: Foundations, Values and Issues* (Cambridge: Cambridge University Press, 2003) explains in an accessible way core Buddhist values and how Buddhist ethics should be performed. Buddhism's engagement with society has been debated, and various examples of socially engaged Buddhist leaders and movements are described in C. S. Queen and S. B. King (eds.), *Engaged Buddhism: Buddhist Liberation Movements in Asia* (Albany: State University of New York Press, 1996). S. B. King's *Socially Engaged Buddhism* (Honolulu: University of Hawai'i Press, 2009) is an interesting book on contemporary socially engaged Buddhists' thoughts and activities.

In 1993 R. M. Gross published *Buddhism after Patriarchy: A Feminist History, Analysis, and Reconstruction of Buddhism* (Albany: State University of New York Press), which was groundbreaking in addressing women's role in Buddhism. The first and very important volume on Thai women in Buddhism was written by C. Kabilsingh, *Thai Women in Buddhism* (Berkeley, CA: Parallax Press, 1991). Two interesting edited volumes with articles on women in Buddhism in different traditions and countries are E. B. Findly (ed.), *Women's Buddhism, Buddhism's Women: Tradition, Revision, Renewal* (Boston: Wisdom Publications, 2000), and L. K. Tsomo (ed.), *Innovative Buddhist Women: Swimming against the Stream* (Richmond, Surrey: Curzon Press, 2000). S. Brown, *The Journey of One Buddhist Nun: Even against the Wind* (Albany: State University of New York Press, 2001), focuses on meditation and women's limited access to an ordained life in Thailand. I have published a monograph that describes the Thai Buddhist "nuns'" lives and their circumstances in Thai society and how they achieve religious authority: M. Lindberg Falk, *Making Fields of Merit: Buddhist Female Ascetics and Gendered Orders in Thailand* (Seattle: University of Washington Press; Copenhagen: NIAS Press, 2007).

Author

Monica Lindberg Falk is a social anthropologist and vice director at the Centre for East and South-East Asian Studies, Lund University, Sweden. Her research interests include gender, Buddhism, anthropology of disaster, religious movements, development, and social change in Southeast Asia. Her scholarship includes extensive fieldwork in Thailand. She has published a monograph and several articles on themes related to gender and Buddhism, socially engaged Buddhism, and Buddhism and crises. One of her current research projects is gender and Buddhism's role in the recovery process after the 2004 tsunami catastrophe in Thailand. That project, which also is the source of research for this chapter, is supported financially by the Swedish Research Council, VR. Another of her current research projects is on gender, religion and education mobility within Asia. That project is also financially supported by the Swedish Research Council, VR.

Chapter 9

Encounters with Jizō-san in an aging Japan

Jason A. Danely

Preamble

Most cultural anthropologists, even those who have detailed and structured methodological strategies, will engage in what is called "convenience-based sampling" during fieldwork research. At its best, this method simply entails engaging with the variety of individuals who might cross your path as you go about your everyday affairs and conduct research. It involves an openness towards those so-called "chance encounters" that may not directly relate to the topic of study outlined in your formal research proposal, and it reminds you never to leave home without a notebook, or a camera. Sometimes a casual chat with a stranger at a café can yield just as much insight as that semi-structured interview at the religious service you are studying. Even if, like me, you are studying the lives of older adults, it's always wise to talk with the often convenient sample of neighborhood children as well.

One outcome of convenience-based sampling and perhaps of long-term ethnographic fieldwork in general is that it will almost inevitably draw out the eager self-appointed informant as well. At times such informants can be inimitable resources, providing an in-depth look at one individual's life in his or her social and cultural context. At other times, however, the self-appointed informant seems to show up far too often, stealing the show from others who are perhaps more directly related to the research project at hand. During my research in Kyoto, Japan, from 2005 to 2007, this self-appointed informant happened to be a bodhisattva named Jizō (Sanskrit *Kṣitigarbha*); I would see him everywhere I went, carved into thousands of stone monuments placed on every city block, standing stoically in temples and cemeteries no matter how remote, or with his Mona Lisa smile in the middle of a busy downtown shopping arcade.

How could Jizō, a figure I had known primarily as a guardian of children and travelers, be directly related to my studies on aging and memorializing ancestors? If there is a relationship, what does this say about the way Buddhism shapes people's understandings of the generational life cycle?

In this chapter, I describe an improvised ritual centered on a carved stone image of Jizō and led by two older adults. Both the ritual and the Jizō image itself illustrate the fluid boundary between public and private, the sacred and the everyday, and formal and informal religious practice. It also gives yet another pertinent example of how personal relationships, if nurtured over long-term fieldwork, can yield unexpected and sometimes profound insight.

Narrative

I had come to Japan in 2005 as a visiting researcher at Kyoto University to study aging and memorializing ancestors in contemporary urban Japan. Although I was aware that Buddhism has an important role in Japanese society through performing funerals and memorials for the dead, and that it had also had deep historical and symbolic influence on cultural attitudes towards death and the life cycle, I was cautious about presuming that my informants would identify their own beliefs and practices as essentially "Buddhist" in nature. In some of my initial interviews I found that when I explained my research to people using terms like "Buddhism" or "religion" it would generate confusion rather than elaboration: "Oh, I'm not an expert on Buddhism," or "Maybe you should talk to some Buddhist monks about that? People like me don't really know about religion" were common responses.

I quickly learned to adjust my language to talk about specific events or practices and to gently prompt further elaboration when a topic regarding Buddhism came up. This technique seemed to work well, since what I was interested in was how average people framed their religious beliefs in ways that might even be thought to contradict conventional Buddhist doctrine, or that drew on alternate understandings of spirituality gathered from other religions, folk traditions, or even popular media. Talking about offerings made at graves or memorials performed at the home altar often led to invitations to observe or participate in these activities, and over the course of 18 months I gradually became more immersed in a world full of spirits and buddhas, deities, and ghosts.

What I saw as more standard representations of Buddhist figures like Jizō Bodhisattva seemed far too entrenched in the kind of formalized understandings that I wanted to avoid, and as a result, I was generally satisfied to relegate his frequent appearances to the general landscape of Buddhist iconography along with the others like Kannon-sama (Sanskrit *Avalokiteśvara*) or Shaka-sama (Sanskrit *Śākyamuni*).

This is not to say that I was ready to dismiss Jizō's importance entirely. Like other buddhas and bodhisattvas, Jizō's power to intercede for those suffering in all six realms of existence and his role as a source of aid in this-worldly affairs were widely revered. Moreover, the abundance of Jizō images tended to localize and personalize his power, almost like a tutelary deity. The most common representations of Jizō were as a simple tonsured monk, either seated or standing and holding a mendicant's staff – a sharp contrast to other popular Buddhist figures like the fierce Fudō-Myō, who holds a sword and is surrounded by flames. The intimacy felt towards Jizō was often expressed in offerings of handmade hats and

Figure 9.1 Votive statues of Jizō Bodhisattva at a temple in Kyoto. Each is dedicated to the protection of a child's spirit and may be presented with offerings of food, drink, and incense or decorated with handmade bibs.

bibs, sometimes bearing the name of a soul in need. In my research, however, "O-Jizō-san," as he was usually referred to by Kyotoites, rarely came up as a topic of conversation, and for the most part, I was happy to let him be the focus of someone else's study.

In September of 2007, I returned to Kyoto after more than a year's absence to conduct follow-up research. At the time my wife, Robin, was pregnant with our first child. Robin had accompanied me during my initial research period, but at that time we were still in our first years of marriage, a status that was regularly acknowledged by our friends as "shinkon," or "newlyweds" (with all of the expectations of dreamy idealism and romance that went along with it). Most of the older adults I spoke with had met their spouses through formal family introductions and arranged meetings (*omiai*), with the resulting pattern of courtship, compromise, and contract. Being a young, newly married American, I sometimes felt my confidence drain as I tried to relate to my informants' experiences, and I did my best to avoid falling into the scripted role of grandchild. Now, I thought, things might be different, and I was excited to spread the news.

Knowing that our expectant parenthood would signal at the very least a new kind of legitimacy as adults, we dashed off as many postcard announcements as we could in the weeks before we arrived in Kyoto. As a result, our reunions in Japan were more than mere follow-up research, but also occasions for celebration.

In several instances Robin was given small red brocaded protective amulets purchased from Shinto shrines promising a safe and easy childbirth. She also received frequent admonitions to keep her swelling belly warm, and to be careful doing anything strenuous or requiring balance, like riding a bicycle or walking down stairs. At first these comments seemed exaggerated, or even invasive, but as time went by, we felt that they were perhaps simply a way of voicing concern; they were signs of attention, but not genuine worry.

One of our last visits was to a woman I will call Nishida-san, who at 87 still worked whenever she could for her small family silk-weaving business in Kyoto's Nishijin neighborhood. Because of her age and physical frailty, I hadn't expected that Nishida-san would become one of my most generous informants, sitting for nearly 50 hours of interviews over the course of our year together. Not only this, but Nishida-san also participated in numerous parish activities, such as regular meetings of the local Women's Buddhist Association, and had served for 30 years as a member of her neighborhood social welfare association, caring for older adults and helping to arrange funeral ceremonies for those who died unexpectedly.

Nishida-san, who had met Robin only once during our previous stay, beamed when she saw her again. She immediately noticed that Robin was pregnant, and asked her how far along she was. When Robin replied "six months," Nishida-san looked surprised, "You don't look six months! Maybe it is because you're taller? Usually women get a lot bigger that that!" she said, pointing at her own stomach and giggling. We all settled down in the middle room of the house, and after some tea and light conversation, I began the interview.

Soon we were again talking about familiar topics of growing old and caring for the dead. Nishida-san's sister-in-law had passed away only a couple of weeks prior, the result of advanced age and diabetes, which made her prone to fainting spells. One day, as she sat under the warmth of a *kotatsu* (a covered table with a recess underneath containing a heating device), her feet slid down too close to the heating coils, burning them severely and resulting in the amputation of her leg at the knee. Although the procedure itself was successful, she died a few weeks later. Without pausing in her story, Nishida-san continued, "I thought, how should we send her off? There is the 49 days memorial, right? I thought she'd be so lonely, since she didn't have anyone to do that for her."

Since there were no descendants available to perform the expected funerary or memorial rituals, Nishida-san took it upon herself to see that these things were properly attended to. After I had finished jotting down the story in my notepad, I looked up to find Nishida-san smiling and leaning forward, staring directly into my eyes.

> So I petitioned Jizō-san. There's a person in the neighborhood who has a Jizō [shrine] in the back of his house, so I prayed there and offered chants. I can't do it here (gestures to her family altar), since our family names are different. Jizō-san is the guardian Bodhisattva of children, but I thought, well this should be good enough!

There he was again. Although I had frequently seen Jizō statues in cemeteries, often in groups of six to represent his power to help beings in all six realms of existence, I'd never thought of him accompanying old and frail spirits crossing into the other world. I was more familiar with another popular genre of art known as Raigō that depicts Amida Buddha and his entourage floating down to the deceased on wisps of clouds to take the spirit to the brilliantly luminous Pure Land.

When I ask why she prays to Jizō-san, Nishida-san responds quite matter-of-factly, "The other world is a dark place. Don't you think it would be hard to walk with only one leg? So I pray for Jizō-san to guide her."

In Nishida-san's mind, Jizō seemed to be a kind of guide for lost or abandoned old people. I imagined Jizō almost as kind of bibbed Boy Scout, leading old women safely across the dark street, one hand gently lending support and the other carrying a grocery bag. It was hard for me to get this image out of my head.

After our conversation, I thanked Nishida-san and told her that Robin and I needed to be leaving soon. Before we could stand, however, she stopped us saying, "Well then, why don't we at least make a short visit to Jizō? It's very close to here! We can go [make offerings] before Jizō for your child!" I answered, "We would love that! Would that be alright?", remembering that it is never a good idea to decline an invitation during time in the field. "Oh of course it is! If you have a little time, we can go quickly and pray for your baby's health. Just let me go get my purse!" replied Nishida-san as she carefully stepped down from the room and onto the cold stone floor of the kitchen corridor.

I explain what is happening to Robin, who has been patiently listening during the interview, trying to piece together the occasional Japanese that she recognizes, and Nishida-san fetched her things. We packed up our own belongings and Nishida-san returned, and slipped on a pair of soft tan shoes shorter than the length of my hand. She quickly drank a glass of water and then, grabbing her cane, led us out the front entrance into the street.

Although I had attended many religious ceremonies during my time in Japan, this was the first time that I had ever been taken so spontaneously to one. It was especially unusual for me, since it was in honor of my wife and our unborn child. The thought of this aroused feelings of expectation which merged with the adventure of the ceremony we were about to perform. It also struck me as strange that we were going to the same Jizō shrine where Nishida-san told me she had been conducting memorial services for her deceased sister-in-law. What about the standard pollution taboos? What about the fact that Jizō is also commonly associated with stillborn, miscarried, or aborted fetuses? As we hurried out, there was little time to consider the specifics, and, as so often in any fieldwork, we just let ourselves go along with the flow of things.

Robin and I unlocked our bicycles parked in front of the house and walked them beside us. Nishida-san walked ahead of us, looking very much like any other older Japanese woman bent over her cane, not much taller than a child. She led us to the small shopping arcade around the corner, and then stopped to greet her

Figure 9.2 A typical roadside Jizō shrine (left of the vending machine). Shrines such as these are located on each city block unit (*chō*) and are the focal point for the annual Jizō Bon activities and are cared for by members of the community.

neighbors in a small converted open-front house selling women's clothing. As she stepped inside Robin and I waited in front, not sure if we should follow or if this was only a side-trip on the way to the Jizō shrine. I had expected the shrine to be one of the frequently seen structures tucked between vending machines along public streets or on a quiet corner surrounded by houses. Nishida-san soon motioned excitedly for us to come inside, and as we wove through the racks of sweaters and blouses, we awkwardly exchanged greetings with the shopkeepers. Nishida-san led us through a door at the rear of the shop and into the home of the owners. The inner room was dimly lit and lined with several wooden cabinets and shelves. On one wall I noticed two elaborate and brightly colored hanging scrolls depicting various Buddhist figures associated with the esoteric sects of Buddhism, such as the Buddha Dainichi (Sanskrit *Mahavairocana*). This surprised me, since Nishida-san's family belong to the Pure Land (Jōdo) sect, which is known for its more austere images of Amida Buddha.

Still unsure of where we were or what to expect, we followed Nishida-san through another door and into the courtyard, where two rough and weathered bas-relief statues of Jizō had been placed in a small alcove. In front of them was a wooden table with a stand for flowers, candles, and a small pot for burning incense. It seemed as though the whole house had been built to accommodate these statues, which, in comparison, seem ancient. When I first spotted the statues I remembered a visit I made a few days earlier to a nearby temple dedicated to Enma-Daiō, the fearsome red-faced bureaucrat sometimes referred to as the "King of Hell," who judges the deeds of the dead and delivers their sentences. Because of their shared prominence in hell, Jizō has long been associated with Enma Daiō, so it was not surprising that in the rear of this temple there was a large pool in which hundreds of Jizō statues gathered from the area had been placed. Perhaps the two Jizōs of this house were once abandoned in the area as well, I thought. Given the abundance of these images, dating back centuries perhaps, how many other houses in the city might have similar shrines?

Just as we were brought to the alcove, a door in the courtyard opened and a man came out of the bathroom greeting us enthusiastically, still buttoning his trousers. He too was older, perhaps in his seventies, and wore thick plastic-framed glasses. I gathered that Nishida-san had already spoken with this man while we were waiting in front, and he had decided to quickly use the toilet before we began. After brief introductions he appeared eager to begin the ceremony, and ushered us in front of the two statues. Nishida-san sat behind us in a chair.

Figure 9.3 Stone bas-relief carvings of Jizō at the entrance of a Buddhist temple in Kyoto. The two on the right roughly resemble the images that were enshrined in the house where I performed the ceremony described here.

The man retrieved a lighter from his pocket and lit the candles. Then, handing me the lighter and three sticks of incense, he instructed me to light them and place them at the altar. As I did this, I knelt in front of the Jizōs, reflexively placing my hands together in the respectful gesture of *gassho* when I was done. When I finished, Robin too was given incense and directed to follow the same procedure. She followed my example, gently stabbing the incense in the burner, and putting her hands together with her eyes closed. Nishida-san leaned forward and gently rubbed Robin's back in encouragement.

After a short pause, we all sat upright again as the courtyard began to fill with the aroma of the incense. The man leading the ceremony stood in front of us beside the altar where he made a short dedication in honor of us and the spirit of our child, stating our names and our reasons for coming to Jizō. He then produced a thin accordion-fold sūtra book and began to chant the Heart Sūtra. The "Heart Sūtra" or "Great Heart of Perfect Wisdom Sūtra" is one of the most popular and widely distributed Buddhist sūtras in Japan, extolling the philosophy of non-attachment as the means to liberation from suffering. I had heard this sūtra and recited it myself on countless previous occasions, as it is used in all of the major Japanese Buddhist sects. The previous month, for example, as I traveled a portion of the 88-temple Shikoku pilgrimage route, I had chanted with other pilgrims at each stop, many of which, I was reminded later, were devoted to Jizō or had an area for dedicating votive statues of him somewhere on the grounds. I joined softly from what I could remember, my hands pressed together again. As the man read, Robin knelt directly in front of the statues with her head down, and Nishida-san continued to gently rub her back.

The sūtra took only a couple of minutes to chant, and although he did not rush it, it seemed to be over quickly. When the last syllable trailed off, I bowed once more and the ceremony was finished. When I looked over to Robin, I noticed that she was flushed with tears. We helped her to stand and Nishida-san touched her comfortingly and consolingly. As she led Robin out of the house I trailed behind them, thanking the man repeatedly in my most polite Japanese. Behind me I could hear Robin still crying and Nishida-san gently reassuring her. As I approached the threshold between the house and the shop, the man who conducted the ceremony brought the sūtra book over to me, telling me to take it along. I protested out of courtesy, but I was cut off by an intense and direct look as he said, "It is not for me, it's because Jizō-san told me to give this to you." Once he saw that I'd understood, he continued, saying, "This [the book] is a deity (*kami*), and you should take it with you and place it under her pillow when she gives birth." He went to one of the many drawers and found a square of plain white paper which he folded around the book in an angular fashion I'd seen used to wrap gifts at department stores. When he handed it to me, he told me, "Your boy is going to be healthy and strong." I took the small package with both hands, bowing, bewildered and grateful.

When I left the shop, I saw that Nishida-san was standing close to Robin with one hand on her arm. She spoke in a hush, so I only caught part of what she was saying, but from what I did hear, I gathered that Nishida-san was telling Robin about the child she herself had lost. Nishida-san told me this story on one of our first meetings, about how she had a difficult birth that rendered her comatose for nearly a month, and how the child, who had initially survived, subsequently died in the hospital months later. At that time it was considered inappropriate for parents to attend their child's funeral, since it was considered inauspicious for a child to precede their parents in death. A small lacquered memorial tablet was created for the child and placed on the home altar for remembrance and offerings to placate the spirit. Near the end of World War II, Nishida-san gave birth to two boys, and the grief and survivor guilt over the first child began to mend. Nishida-san never mentioned participating in any *mizuko-kuyō* ceremonies or other special rituals for the spirits of deceased children, but the memory seemed to strongly affect her sensitivity to others and feelings about the sanctity of life.

I reached my arm around Robin's shoulders, and thanked Nishida-san for arranging the ceremony. Nishida-san told us, "I know how difficult it is to have a baby, and I want your baby to be safe and healthy." Robin's face was wet with tears, but she managed to smile and nod, even if she could only understand half what was being said. Satisfied with this, Nishida-san then turned to me, taking my wrist with her small hand. Her back half-turned to Robin, she lowered her voice slightly, saying, "Be sure to take care of her." I told her that I'd do my best and thanked her again. As we mounted our bicycles to leave, she called out, "Come back and visit again while I'm still alive!" We waved goodbye to her until we had turned the corner and were out of sight.

Discussion

Like most Kyotoites, Nishida-san refers to Jizō Bodhisattva as "Jizō-san" or "O-Jizō-san," the honorific addition of "O" and "-san" indicating a level of both respect and intimacy accorded to other public figures like pilgrims (Ohenro-san), policemen (Omawari-san), or even others' children (Oko-san). In the Japanese cultural context, this honorific has the effect of inclusion rather than separation; it is as if to say "I respect you as one of us." In the case of Jizō, this inclusion makes his power available at any time and for any number of purposes, be they directed towards care of the dead or those yet to be born. While the spirits of the ancestors are similar in this respect, they are typically believed to be able to exert influence only on their family, hence Nishida-san's reluctance to conduct final rites for her sister-in-law at her own family's home altar, despite the fact that a representation of Amida Buddha was enshrined there as well. This also helps to explain why it might be an appropriate place for the ceremony for our child. Still, the association of Jizō with dead children made me wonder. Was it possible to separate Jizō's efficacy in death and his guardianship of children? To see them, perhaps, as distinct points in the life cycle that only rarely overlap? If this is the case, what role might older adults have?

In Kyoto, a Jizō shrine is erected in each *chō* unit, usually resembling a small wooden house atop a stone pedestal in which a statue is kept. Each shrine is cared for by the members of the block unit, whether a residential area or a business district, and has no official administrative relationship with a Buddhist temple. These local altars are the center of the festival of Jizō-bon, which follows the more widespread August holiday of Obon, during which the spirits of the dead are said to return to the world of the living to enjoy their family's company and partake of offerings.

The Jizō-bon festival is believed to have originated in Kyoto and then spread to other parts of Japan. During the festival, the local Jizō shrine is decorated and presented with offerings, and neighborhood children enjoy gifts of candy and games. When I asked older Kyotoites to tell me about the most enjoyable moments in their childhood, several recalled Jizō-bon – not only eating sweets and playing with their friends, but also having the chance to fully participate in a religious ritual. If you grew up in Kyoto, Jizō-san would likely be the first Buddhist figure that you would learn to care for and depend upon, to merge the Buddhist concept of compassion with the cultural concept of *amae*, or "passive dependence."

It is this distinctly Japanese sense of dependence that links children to older adults under the care of Jizō, and it is this inter-generational narrative of the life cycle that made the ceremony described above not only logical, but also emotionally powerful. In popular Japanese belief, the spirits of children come from the same "other world" (*ano yo*) that spirits return to after death. Neither journey, however, is easily made without assistance, and just as it would be arduous for an old, one-legged woman to go into the other world alone, newborns also need protection and assurance as they enter this world. At both ends of the life course, then, comfort can be found in dependence, whether it is in the form of mourning or blessing.

Folk-tales about the miracles of Jizō underline the narrative of his simple and selfless dedication, especially towards older adults. Only a few weeks before the ceremony with Nishida-san, when I accompanied a friend to a pharmacy, I noticed among the magazines a dog-eared children's book about Jizō and the hats (Kasa Jizō). In the story, a poor but hard-working elderly couple make hats to sell in town, but the husband has bad luck selling them and so on his way home through the snow, he places the unsold hats on several Jizō statues. The next morning is New Year's Day, and the old couple wake to find that an enormous bag of rice has appeared at their door. Other such tales abound, such as those where Jizō secretly cuts and piles wood for an old woman (Kotsumi Jizō) or shovels snow for an old man (Yukikaki Jizō). And although images of Jizō surrounded by children are much more prevalent, in recent years his compassion for those at the other end of life is evidenced by the appearance of "anti-senility" Jizōs with older people kneeling at his feet.

Despite my familiarity with Jizō, I had overlooked not only the parallels of *amae* and dependence at the ends of the life course, but I had underestimated the power of the inter-generational cycle. The fact that Nishida-san and the man leading the ceremony were older adults allowed us as participants to take on a passive-dependent role, to relieve ourselves of some of the burden of asserting our autonomy and accept the benevolence of the bodhisattva. More than ever I was grateful that Robin was there with me, because it was in her emotions that I understood this. While I was busy committing the ceremony and everything said to memory in order to write up my field notes later, I had distanced myself from fully entering the ritual.

Later, as I asked Robin about her experience, she told me that although she didn't have a clear explanation of why she began to cry during the ceremony, she did think that the reading of the Heart Sūtra had something to do with it. When I asked what she meant, she told me that when she taught English at a Buddhist kindergarten during our first stay in Kyoto, all of the students would be led in a recitation of the Heart Sūtra every morning. Hearing that familiar chant cut through an otherwise incomprehensible situation; with the mysterious Jizō statues in front of her veiled in incense and Nishida-san gently rubbing her back, there was an overwhelming sense that everything had come together.

Things do come together in sometimes unexpected ways during fieldwork, whether it is in a chance meeting with an informant or a spontaneous ceremony at a hidden Buddhist shrine. After nearly two years of immersion I was finally beginning to feel as if I had enough information to understand connections, contexts, and nuance that had escaped my attention before, and suddenly the taken-for-granted landscape of everyday Buddhism materialized in sūtras and statues, in mourning and blessing. In the fullness of this, the generational life cycle began to make a little more sense.

Four months after the ceremony, almost to the day, our son was born at a small birth center in San Diego. It was dawn by the time he finally arrived, safe and screaming, into our world; weeks of tense anticipation dissolved into the glow of new parenthood. As I unzipped the labor bag we had brought along looking for fresh clothes, I noticed the small sūtra booklet we'd received in Kyoto, still swaddled in its paper wrapping. It hadn't made it under the pillow, but I felt relieved to see that it was at least there in the room. When we returned home later that morning, I set the booklet next to a statue of the Buddha, placed my hands together, and thanked Jizō-san and Nishida-san once again.

Readings

While much has been written on the role of Jizō Bodhisattva in *mizuko-kuyō* ceremonies (in particular William R. LaFleur's *Liquid Life: Abortion and Buddhism in Japan* [Princeton: Princeton University Press, 1994]), there are few book-length treatments of Jizō available in English. A nice general introduction to understanding Jizō Bodhisattva and his history, symbols, and place in Japanese Buddhism is Jan Chozen Bays' *Jizō Bodhisattva: Guardian of Children, Travelers, and Other Voyagers* (Boston: Shambhala Publications, 2003). More on the role of Buddhist and other religious practices for older Japanese adults can be found in

John W. Traphagan's *The Practice of Concern: Ritual, Well-Being, and Aging in Rural Japan* (Durham, NC: Carolina Academic Press, 2004). An excellent analysis of personalization in the worship of Jizō and other Japanese religious figures appears throughout Ian Reader and George J. Tanabe, Jr.'s *Practically Religious: Worldly Benefits and the Common Religion of Japan* (Honolulu: University of Hawai'i Press, 1998).

Author

Jason Danely received his PhD in Anthropology from the University of California, San Diego. He is Assistant Professor of Anthropology at Rhode Island College and an Assistant Researcher at the Center on Age & Community at University of Wisconsin, Milwaukee. He is currently writing a book based on his research in Japan entitled *Departure and Return: Mourning, Memorial and Aging in Japan*.

Chapter 10

Amitābha's birthday and liberation of life

Paul Crowe

Preamble

Popular notions of the nature of Buddhism and Buddhist practice tend to focus on the figure of a solitary meditating Buddha. Solitary practice is an important part of what Buddhist monastics and lay practitioners do but most of what happens on a daily basis in a monastery or temple is communal. Large, energetic gatherings of monks, nuns, and lay supporters involving music, movement, and often food are the fabric of a rich and varied practice shared by Buddhist communities. Activities follow a cycle of more than two dozen ritual celebrations of significant dates such as the date Śākyamuni Buddha entered *nirvāṇa*, or the date Bodhisattva Guanyin, "she who hears the cries of the world," attained enlightenment. Recounted here is my visit to Gold Buddha Monastery in Vancouver, British Columbia, to join a celebration of Amitābha Buddha's birthday. A second part of the proceedings included a ceremony known as the "Liberation of Life." This retelling, based on my notes, video recordings, and photographs, provides a window onto ritual practice at a Chinese Buddhist temple and the community that comes together to enact the Buddha's teachings concerning reverence for life.

Narrative

The ritual celebration of Amitābha Buddha's birthday was to take place over a five-day period commencing on December 27, 2009. This posed a challenge because extended family would be visiting and I had our 11-year-old son to take care of until school resumed. I chose to attend the first day, which would also provide an opportunity to witness not only the opening of the birthday rites but also a Liberation of Life ceremony. Having previously interviewed the monastery's head nun, I tried contacting her, but she was on the Australian Gold Coast teaching Buddhist philosophy at a university. After a first email to her, several days passed and the day of the celebration drew closer. I was reluctant to simply appear on the scene as it is important to conduct oneself with propriety and respect. I was relieved to receive a call from another nun at the temple who had been informed of my request and who offered me a warm invitation to attend the proceedings.

I set my alarm as I was planning to walk 20 blocks to the temple in the morning. However, the volume on my iPod was turned down and I awoke just 20 minutes before the ceremony was to start. After quickly dressing I skipped breakfast, grabbed an apple, my camera, a notebook, and a pencil and ran for the car. Checking the dashboard display, I saw the temperature was hovering just above 0°C; there was frost on the grass, and the blue sky was clear. Driving down Centre Street, which runs through the heart of Vancouver and terminates in Chinatown, I found parking and ran the rest of the way. Pausing at the front door I caught my breath, composed myself, and entered the lobby at five past eight. A stickler for punctuality, I felt bad at being late. The sounds of chanting were already coming from the Buddha Hall to my left.

A smiling volunteer greeted me at the door and told me to remove my shoes. The Buddha Hall is a pure place, and the removal of shoes is an important acknowledgment of this fact. I nodded and smiled and after removing my shoes and coat moved uncertainly into the hall. To my right as I entered I could see the main altar on which were three large statues: Śākyamuni Buddha (*Shijia mouni* 釋迦牟尼) in the center, Universal Worthy Bodhisattva Samantabhadra (*Puxian pusa* 普賢菩薩) representing practice and meditation on his right astride a white elephant, and Mañjuśrī Bodhisattva (*Wenshu pusa* 文殊菩薩) representing the ideal of wisdom on his left, riding a lion. The entrance, located as it was midway

Figure 10.1 The main Buddha Hall at Gold Buddha Monastery

down the ranks of kneelers, made it impossible to slip into the hall discreetly. Heads turned as I made my way to a row of chairs at the rear of the hall and opened my notebook prepared to watch passively and record what details I could. Having missed the beginning of the ceremony I did not want to disturb the participants. An elderly gentleman, whom I recognized from a previous visit, firmly and politely guided me to a music stand in front of one of the kneelers, where I joined the rows of lay chanters. A chanting-book was placed on the stand and opened to the correct page; my guide kindly pointed to the line currently being recited. Smiling, I nodded appreciation.

My attention immediately split: I was supposed to record the proceedings but what were we chanting? Would I remember the page numbers for later reference? Would I be able to examine the book of chants or would they all be collected and stored away? Oh no! – look at the phonetics – *Yi yi jin, yin, lyou, li, bwo li, che jiu, chr ju, ma nau, er yan shr jr*. This was clearly a book produced in Taiwan, where they pride themselves on not subscribing to the People's Republic of China's Pinyin phonetic system. At the brisk pace being set I would have trouble relying on the Chinese characters. The first line was: "adorned with gold, silver, lapis lazuli, crystal, mother of pearl, red pearls, and carnelian" – this was not going to roll off my tongue in Mandarin Chinese. My guide brought me back to my senses as his finger on another page firmly updated me on where everyone else was in the chant and I was not. Relying on the Chinese characters, I approximated the pronunciation of those I did not immediately recognize. I had a feel for what we were intoning. This was a description of the wondrous Pure Land of "ultimate bliss" where those with sufficient faith can go at the moment they depart this life, the place where they can join the compassionate Amitābha Buddha. Conscious of the need to keep up with the chant I tried to scan the room to estimate the number of participants. Three groups were present and distinguishable by their clothing. At the front, seven nuns in yellow robes led the chanting. One, standing at a microphone, provided a clear tone to follow. Another nun struck a large "wood fish" to keep time. To my left and across the center aisle, the women were assembled while the right side of the hall was reserved for men. The separation of men and women reflected a concern for proper conduct in the temple, and I had noted a concern to maintain this arrangement in some centers dedicated to Chinese popular religious practice of various forms. Roughly 30 participants were wearing brown and black robes indicating that these lay followers had taken the five basic vows to refrain from harming living creatures, stealing, sexual misconduct, telling lies, and misusing intoxicants. They would also have taken refuge in the Buddha, Dharma (teachings of the Buddha), and Sangha (Buddhist community). Another group wore pale blue robes whose significance remains unclear.

The chant drew to a conclusion and I looked around to see what would now follow. The nuns began to move up the center aisle away from the main altar and each row of women followed. The men then joined the procession, which moved clockwise around the hall as we chanted *namo Amitofo*. I fell in behind the man in front of me and settled into the rhythm of the pace, intoning the name of Amitābha as I moved. After several circumambulations we moved back to our places at the kneelers.

Once we returned to our places continuing the chant, people on the outer aisles began taking cushions from cupboards and distributing them to the group. My helpful friend provided me with a cushion and indicated that I should sit. With a quick glance around I confirmed that we were now moving into a phase of the proceedings that would require seated meditation, though I had no idea how long it would last. Given that the Liberation of Life ceremony was scheduled for 10:20 a.m. we could not have more than an hour left. Sitting comfortably in a half-lotus posture, I straightened my spine and relaxed into the posture as I do on most evenings at home. The recitation of the six-syllable phrase continued and I allowed myself to sink more deeply into the experience. This was a conscious decision to give up on my observations and to simply participate. After a time the chanting stopped and the group became silent. There was no way I could now keep track of time or anything else for that matter. I do not recall how the meditation session stopped but it was probably with the sounding of a small bell, which is customary in Buddhist temples I have visited. We returned the cushions to their cupboards and resumed the chanting and circumambulation of the Buddha Hall.

Having returned to our seats, the participants began a series of five groups of prostrations. The first set was to the Buddha Śākyamuni, the second to Amitābha, the third to Guanyin 觀音, the female bodhisattva of compassion, the fourth to the "Great Strength" Bodhisattva, and the last to the Great Pure Sea of Bodhisattvas. The prostrations required dropping to my right and then left knees while placing my palms on the edge of the kneeler. I lowered my forehead to the kneeler and then turned the palms of my hands up. The recitations alternated, with one side standing and chanting while the other side prostrated in contemplation. It occurred to me as I moved through the kneeling, rising, and chanting that this was good exercise. The formal celebrations now drew to a close with a final recitation declaring the intention of all to return for refuge to the Buddha, Dharma, and Sangha.

As the birthday ceremony concluded, I noticed a considerable number of lay devotees entering the hall and taking their places next to those of us who had gathered earlier in the morning. Attendees were adding extra kneelers, music stands, and chanting-books for the newcomers. The transition to the brief ceremony dedicated to the Liberation of Life was evidently now taking place and went very smoothly, considering that the number of people in the room appeared to have doubled. There must now have been well over 200 people in the Buddha Hall. Obviously, this was a very popular part of the monastery's liturgical calendar. The main part of the ceremony was to take place outdoors, but the opening had to be performed in the Buddha Hall. Many had come that morning for the specific purpose of supporting this rite to demonstrate their reverence for life.

Once again my book was opened to the correct page and the chanting commenced with a brief recitation titled "Praise for Purifying the Water." We then chanted the "Great Compassion Mantra," the "Heart Sutra," and the "Spirit Mantra for Rebirth in the Pure Land." On behalf of those gathered, the nun in charge of the proceedings then recited in Mandarin a verse invoking Śākyamuni Buddha and the bodhisattvas and requesting their compassion for the creatures who were to be released and thus spared the death for which they had been destined in the kitchens of Lower Mainland restaurants. Following this declaration we offered repentance for our wrongdoings. Next, everyone declared that they took refuge in the Buddha, Dharma, and Sangha and offered homage to the Buddha. We concluded with a statement of hope that the creatures soon to be released would be saved from their torment and receive a more favorable rebirth.

The next stage in the proceedings involved releasing the creatures that had been purchased with donations from the participants. We moved out of the Buddha Hall into the crowded lobby of the monastery. I had parked some distance from the monastery, and even if I had time to get to my car, I had no clear idea of where we were supposed to go. I waited patiently and hoped this would not conclude my participation. Part of my reason for attending these proceedings was to see a Liberation of Life ceremony for the first time and to describe it in this chapter. To my relief one of the participants noted my hesitation and offered me a ride to the harbor. Through the rear entrance of the monastery we went out to the parking lot and climbed into a chilled, well-used, and tired-looking Japanese sedan.

Deciding to break the ice, I turned to the fellow in the back and introduced myself as a professor who taught at Simon Fraser University. He grinned; he was a fourth-year psychology student at the same university. I asked the driver if he had lived in Vancouver very long. He had come from Hong Kong three years ago. As we pulled out onto Main Street the driver got straight to the point: "Do you believe in the Pure Land?" Such questions can prove challenging. As a professor who teaches the academic study of religion, I am inclined to avoid discussing my own position concerning religion, preferring to keep myself out of the conversation as much as possible. However, refusal to answer may result in bad feelings and hinder the process of learning more about the ceremony and community. I decided to be as honest as possible, and said: "Well, perhaps a Pure Land on earth." The driver looked skeptical, and said: "The Pure Land is real, you know." He began to tell me a story about a woman who was a regular participant at the monastery who had experienced something remarkable. One night her elderly mother, who lived with her, had gone to bed but later came out of her room saying, "What should I do? What should I do?" The daughter was very puzzled by the question and did not understand what her mother was asking or why. The daughter reassured her mother and sent her back to bed. Thirty minutes later she died. The driver told me that the mother had been visited by Guanyin on the night of her death and the bodhisattva had beckoned her to come to the Pure Land. Uncertain, she had come out of her room pondering how she should respond; hence the question, "What should I do?" I asked the driver how the daughter knew that Guanyin had visited her mother that night and was told that during her meditation she had visited the Pure Land, where she was able to speak with her mother and learn

Figure 10.2 Temple members gather at the dock at Canada Place to release the sea creatures

more about the moments before her death. Thus, the existence of the Pure Land could not be doubted. Clearly the driver was absolutely convinced of the veracity of the story and its implications for belief. I nodded and expressed appreciation for his willingness to share the story with me. Shortly afterwards, we arrived at Canada Place, where the fish and crab would be released.

The asphalt had a slippery glazing of frost; I watched nervously as the elderly devotees walked from their cars toward the ramp leading down to the water. A small truck from an East Vancouver Chinese seafood and meat company had already arrived on the scene and was being unloaded with the help of several volunteers as a senior nun in her yellow and brown robes and a brown stocking hat moved toward the ramp accompanied by two women. I had envisioned something on a smaller scale, with perhaps a couple of temple members bringing containers of fish in their own cars or trucks. This was a much bigger and better-organized affair than I had anticipated. I walked through the gate which had been opened by a security guard and down the ramp to the dock to join roughly 30 people of mixed ages, including some children, who had come to assist in releasing the assorted sea-life. Large plastic tubs were brought down from the truck and set down near the edge of the dock. As people chanted *namo Amitofo*, the nun tapped a small bell to keep time and people began carefully scooping up the larger fish and placing them into the water as I filmed the proceedings. The security guard approached me and asked whether I was with the monastery. It seemed the group had special privileges in being permitted to access the water from this secured area. I assured him I was with the group and he left me to continue participating and filming. More than one person approached me to point out how the fish, once placed into the water, did not swim away immediately. I filmed some of them as they swam away and then turned around and returned to look up at the people on the dock. The fish, I was told, were returning to offer thanks, aware that they had been spared. They were reaping the rewards of the merit that had been transferred to them through the ritual performed earlier at the monastery. With all of the creatures returned to the sea, the tubs were gathered up and the groups moved back to the parking lot for the short drive back to the monastery, where a Buddhist vegetarian lunch had been prepared. I thanked the monastery member who drove me back, both for the ride and for the story he had shared with me. Before going in to lunch, I went out to the front of the building and found two volunteers packing up plastic tubs and a complex array of tubing. I helped them put things away and asked what this was for. It seems the fish had been kept outside in front of the monastery while the ceremony had been taking place inside. The tubes had provided oxygen for the sea creatures while they awaited their liberation. Great care was given to ensure the good health of the fish and crab before the release, making it more likely that they would survive once freed.

Back inside I walked into the crowded dining area to be greeted by wonderful smells. Long narrow tables had been set up in rows with stools placed at intervals along the tables. The gentleman who had been so helpful during the ceremonies now took me over to the vegetarian buffet to get my food. All the while I could hear a voice preaching in Mandarin over the PA system. I assumed it was the voice of revered Buddhist teacher Hsuan Hua, who had provided the motivation to found the monastery in Vancouver. I knew he had passed away in 1995 but the monastery continued to make his sermons available to members and monthly memorials of his passing into *nirvāṇa* were still part of the ritual calendar. After filling my plate with food and taking a bowl of soup, I returned to a seat near the entrance. Shortly after I began my meal the master's voice stopped and a devotee from Cambodia was introduced. It seemed he was going to share an inspirational story during the remainder of the meal. He was going to speak in mandarin but I was quite sure I would not be able to follow the details, as a clear Beijing accent seemed unlikely. It appeared this eventuality had been anticipated for just as I considered how unfortunate it would be not to have a record of what was said another gentleman sat down next to me and said he would provide a translation. I had kept my notebook and pencil with me and took notes between mouthfuls of food. The speaker, who sat at a table at the other end of the room near where the nuns were eating together, recounted a period of illness in his late teens and explained that visits to doctors had not yielded a cure. At some point he became inspired to try reciting the name of Amitābha Buddha (Amitofo), which had occupied much of our time earlier that morning. After beginning this practice he noticed that he became more patient with others and felt more peaceful. As a result his life gradually became happier. He said that some people wonder where the "dharma gate" (*fa men* 法門) is; that is, the entrance or way into the true teaching of the Buddha. He explained that some say it is in the heart or mind but he thought that the dharma gate was actually the mouth. Disciplined speech is the way; by chanting the name of Amitābha Buddha throughout the day, the mouth is kept too busy for angry, deceiving, or destructive words. Keeping an eye on what we say requires careful attention and that can be difficult. He compared it to driving after drinking, when lack of focus can have disastrous consequences. Through recitation of Amitābha Buddha's name these dangers can be avoided and we are led into a more tranquil way of life. The speaker concluded by explaining how his life had become simpler, as had his desires and his diet. He no longer uses salt and has removed sugar from his diet and has now regained his health and feels happier. As the speaker's story concluded so did the lunch, and after the plates and bowls had been collected everyone filed out of the dining area into the lobby.

A Christmas tree had been set up and people were invited to write down their wishes on slips of paper and to hang them on the tree. I was given a piece of paper and composed my wish, which I then hung on the tree. Seated on a bench out of the way of the people coming and going, I jotted down some notes and then turned my attention to the display of books for sale in the hope that the book of chants and ritual instruction might be among them and it was. I also found a copy of *A Biographical Sketch of the Venerable Master Hsuan Hua* (*Xuan hua shangren jianzhuan* 宣化上人簡傳). As the crowd thinned out I moved across the lobby to the reception desk, where people could make donations and purchases. The woman behind the desk welcomed me to the monastery and asked if I had been there before. I told her that I had visited three or four times. I noticed that people were making donations and asked what they were for. She told me that people offer donations to support the purchase of fish for release at future ceremonies. Hearing this, I elected to make a donation at the same time as purchasing my two books. She asked whether I was a vegetarian. I said no, as seafood (the irony and contradiction was not lost on me) was still a part of my diet and, occasionally, if meat was on the menu at a host's house I would not refuse to eat it. I asked the same question and was told that she had not eaten meat for many years. This change came about after she met and spent several days with Master Hsuan Hua in San Francisco. I asked about the rest of her family and was told that they continued to eat meat and she prepared it for them. Circumstances were not yet right for her family to adopt this way of life and she was not going to force them to accommodate her own preferences. I handed over my donation and was told that a third of it would go to the temple while the rest went to the purchase of fish.

Before leaving I was fortunate to have a chance to speak briefly with the senior nun, who I assumed was currently in charge of the monastery. I thanked her for graciously allowing me to participate in the day's events. She asked me what I taught, and I told her that I was a professor in the Department of Humanities at Simon Fraser University and that my department was very text-oriented. I mentioned that whenever possible the students and I tried to read through whole texts rather than relying on short excerpts in textbooks. She was pleased to hear this and said that was the best way to approach Buddhist teachings presented in sūtras. I mentioned also the concern I felt in teaching texts that were often based on experience by way of disciplined daily practice and on insights derived from meditation. In the academy, we focus almost exclusively on abstraction and conceptualization. There seemed, I said, to be a fundamental disconnect between rationalist, Enlightenment-based European traditions of philosophy and the mode of teaching assumed by compilers of Buddhist texts. I mentioned an earlier visit to one of my classes on Buddhist history by two nuns from the Buddhist association of which this institution was a part and recounted the interest of the students. It had been helpful to hear directly about the daily experience of Buddhist nuns, and the students were genuinely surprised at the level of personal discipline observed. Once again I expressed thanks and was invited to come back any time.

Discussion

Throughout the year at Gold Buddha Monastery, a series of 39 anniversary dates are celebrated with public ceremonies, including the birthday of Amitābha Buddha, on the seventeenth day of the eleventh lunar month. The number of ceremonies in a given month varies from only one in the fifth month to six in the seventh and ninth months. In addition numerous sūtras and mantras are recited on fixed dates throughout the year and other major celebrations, including an entire week devoted to the Chinese lunar New Year. The Liberation of Life ceremony is performed every month.

Amitābha is said to preside over a Pure Land of bliss known as Sukhāvatī. In the Mahāyāna Buddhist text titled *Sukhāvatīvyūha-sutra*, he is described as a monk named Dharmākara who renounced his kingship and took up the quest for awakening. Through the power of merit achieved as a result of his determination to achieve Buddhahood, he was able to create a Pure Land. Much of the sutra is dedicated to describing the beauty of this land, recounting its trees and flowers with golden leaves and silver fruit, its perfumed rivers, wondrous birds, and countless gems. In the text *Sagely City of 10,000 Buddhas Daily Recitation Handbook* (Wanfo shengcheng risong yigui 萬佛聖城日誦儀規), which was chanted during the celebrations, the Buddha offered the following description of this land:

> Passing from here through hundreds of thousands of millions of Buddhalands to the west, there is a world called ultimate bliss.
> In this land a Buddha called Amitābha right now teaches the Dharma.
> Shariputra, for what reason is this land called ultimate bliss?
> All living beings of this country endure none of the sufferings, but enjoy every bliss. Therefore it is called ultimate bliss.
> ...
> Moreover, Shariputra, the land of ultimate bliss has pools of seven jewels,
> Filled with the eight waters of merit and virtue. The bottom of each pool is pure, spread with golden sand.
> On the four sides are stairs of gold, silver, lapis lazuli and crystal; above are raised pavilions
> Adorned with gold, silver, lapis lazuli, crystal, mother of pearl, red pearls and carnelian.

Following his initial commitment, Dharmākara made a series of 48 vows worded in such a way that if his Pure Land did not aid, in numerous ways, the salvation of those with faith in him then he would not become enlightened. In this way he linked, inextricably, his own salvation to the salvation of all those with faith in him and his Pure Land. Thus, the two key themes of this text and the central focus of participants at the monastery are the accumulation of merit through good deeds and the selfless compassion that supports such deeds.

The eighteenth, nineteenth, and twentieth vows of Dharmākara indicate that those who practice good deeds, accumulate merit, and call upon him with complete faith as few as ten times will, at the moment of their death, be assured rebirth in the Pure Land. Once there, conditions are so perfect that eventual enlightenment is guaranteed. Thus, fear of death and a painful rebirth are eliminated and eventual salvation assured. This depends upon faith and practicing good deeds.

It was clear that the second part of the day's proceedings, the Liberation of Life, accorded well with the general orientation of Pure Land praxis. Throughout the ceremony the focus was on the transference of merit, earned by the participants, to the halibut, ling cod, rockfish, crab, shrimp, clam, oyster, and other sea creatures that were to be released. It was hoped that they would achieve a much better rebirth and find their way to eventual rebirth in the Pure Land and enlightenment. The compassionate service rendered by the devotees also yielded rewards for them: they avoided the "three disasters" (*san zai* 三災) of war, disease, and hunger, and they were rewarded, for example, by longevity, children, freedom from worry, and good health. The ceremony opened with the ritual purification of water accompanied by recitation of the *Great Compassion Mantra* (*Dabei zhou* 大悲咒) and the *Heart of the Perfection of Wisdom Sūtra* (*Banruo boluomiduo xinjing* 般若波羅蜜多心經), the content of which served as a reminder that the sea creatures, the people performing the liberation, and the location of the liberation were all ultimately empty. Reflection on this fact was intended to free everyone from attachment to the deeds they were performing. The sacred water was sprinkled on the creatures in the storage containers prior to departure for the harbor. As the ceremony progressed, the presiding Dharma Master called upon the compassionate bodhisattvas to use their powers of virtue to assist the creatures and declared that those who donated funds to purchase their freedom will now repent of all wrongdoings for their sake and transmit to them the three refuges of Buddha, Dharma, and Sangha. The creatures needed this valuable assistance as they were unable to make such repentances or to pledge to adopt the Buddha and scriptures as teachers for the sake of progress in future lives. During the conclusion of the proceedings, the Dharma Master declared the hope that participants would join all creatures in a rebirth in the "land of ultimate bliss," the Pure Land, and as they were placed into the water the participants continuously chanted "homage to Amitābha Buddha."

Readings

An excellent way to gain insights into the Pure Land approach to practice is to read the three principal texts recited by practitioners, which include the doctrinal foundations and general assumptions that inform that practice. A translation and analysis of these texts is Hisao Inagaki's *The Three Pure Land Sutras: A Study and Translation from Chinese* (Kyoto: Nagata Bunshodo, 1995). An overview of Buddhist practice in relation to ecology is Mary Evelyn Tucker and Duncan Ryuken Williams (eds.), *Buddhism and Ecology: The Interconnection of Dharma and Deeds*, Religions of the World and Ecology (Cambridge, MA: Harvard University Press, 1997). A useful volume of articles referring to the history and practice of Pure Land in Tibet, Japan, Nepal, and on Taiwan is Richard K. Payne and Kenneth K. Tanaka (eds.), *Approaching the Land of Bliss: Religious Praxis in the Cult of Amitābha*, Kuroda Institute, Studies in East Asian Buddhism 17 (Honolulu: University of Hawai'i Press, 2004).

Author

Paul Crowe is an Associate Professor in the Department of Humanities at Simon Fraser University (Canada) and Director of the David See-Chai Lam Centre for International Communication. His research is focused on eleventh- to fourteenth-century Daoist cultivation practice and Chinese intellectual history and on contemporary Chinese religions. In addition to articles and chapters on these subjects he has recently edited, with Philip Clart, *The People and the Dao. New Studies in Chinese Religions in Honour of Daniel L. Overmyer*, Sankt Augustin: Monumenta Serica Institute and Nettetal: Steyler Verlag, 2009.

Chapter 11

Preaching as performance

Notes on a secretive Shin Buddhist sermon

Clark Chilson

Preamble

On a cool November afternoon I arrived at an old wooden Buddhist temple nestled in an urban residential area of Kyoto, Japan. The priest and others at the temple were performing an annual memorial service for the temple's founder, Kūya, who is widely known as a tenth-century holy man. The temple was dimly lit, with about a hundred people sitting pressed shoulder to shoulder on tatami mats. Although I had come that day to learn about Kūya, I met people who would teach me about a religious tradition that had little to do with Kūya and which scholars assumed had died out long ago – secretive Shin Buddhism.

During the service, in addition to observing recitations of Buddhist scriptures, ritual dancing, and a tea ceremony, I asked those in attendance about Kūya and their interests in him. Many told me about his historical significance, but one man said he went to a Kūya-related temple in a city about an hour from where I lived. None of the published sources on Kūya mentioned the temple, so I was eager to see it. But when I expressed my desire to visit it and asked where it was, he became evasive. With curiosity overpowering polite impulses, I pushed to get an exact location. He consulted with some men he was with about my request, and then gave me his phone number. He said I could visit if I called him first.

Later that week I telephoned him and was told a time at which to go to the temple. I expected that the temple was old and would need to be opened for guests. I was therefore surprised to find a newer temple with about 30 or so people already inside listening to a sermon. Upon arrival, I was led to a back room to meet an old man, who was referred to as *sensei* (teacher) and *zenchishiki* (good friend). After talking for a while about Kūya and my research, the old man told me that for him and the others at the temple Shinran was more important than Kūya. I indicated I knew about Shinran, the founder of Shin, one of the most popular forms of Buddhism in Japan for centuries. The old man, whom I shall call K-sensei, said that his group, unlike Shin priests, followed Shinran's ultimate teachings called Urahōmon (secret dharma). These teachings, he said, were entrusted to the laity and were kept secret to protect against corruption by priests and others who might try to use them to make money. Intrigued, I asked for permission to return

Figure 11.1 Statue of Kūya

and was allowed to do so. After visiting the temple for a while, I learned that the association with Kūya was primarily a façade to protect the group from being seen as a nefarious secret society. Eventually K-sensei invited me to be initiated, but I declined for ethical reasons after he told me the rite should not be done for research purposes. Because I still wanted to study the group, an agreement was worked out by which K-sensei would let me visit on days when there were no secret initiation rites, during which the most secret doctrines were taught. On the basis of this agreement, I studied these people's practices, their secrecy, and their ideas on the "real" Shin. Most of my fieldwork was done between 1998 and 2001, with a follow-up visit in 2008. During my fieldwork I took detailed notes and was allowed to make audio recordings of some sermons and interviews. Among the many things I learned from secretive Shin Buddhists is that the deeper we look the more we can see.

Narrative

Urahōmon practice and practitioners

Throughout Japan the secretive Shin Buddhist tradition of Urahōmon has some 10,000 members who belong to one of perhaps a couple of hundred groups. Each group is autonomous and led by a *zenchishiki* who is the highest authority; there is no larger organizational structure in Urahōmon beyond the individual group. They are secretive in that they hide their religion and its activities from outsiders – they do not reveal where they meet, they do not allow those without the *zenchishiki*'s permission to participate in any of their services or rites, and only the initiated are given in-depth instruction in the secret teachings.

Followers of Urahōmon refer to themselves as "practitioners" or *gyōja*. As practitioners they practice more than just their secretive tradition – they practice *shinjin*. The term *shinjin* is central in Shin Buddhist doctrine in general, not just Urahōmon. Priests at public Shin Buddhist temples teach that it refers to a heart that trusts Amida Buddha, or more simply to an entrusting heart. For Urahōmon *gyōja*, it means this and more. For them, *shinjin* also refers to what they received in the secret initiation rite.

Although I did not witness this rite, over time the *gyōja* did talk about it with me. Shin Buddhists who were able to infiltrate groups and who wanted to expose them also have published details of the rite. During this rite, called *ichinen kimyō* (one-thought moment of entrusting), an initiate bows up and down repeatedly while earnestly asking Amida for help by saying over and over again "*tasuketamae, tasuketamae, tasuketamae*" ("save me! save me! save me!"). At some point, perhaps after about 20 minutes or so, the *zenchishiki* who is watching the initiate do this shouts "*yoshi*" ("good"), indicating the sudden moment when Amida endows the initiate with *shinjin*. When a person receives *shinjin* from Amida, he or she is said to experience great happiness and to become like a buddha. As those who have received *shinjin* from Amida, they then practice it in their lives.

One way they practice it is by attending an Urahōmon place of worship. The place where the *gyōja* I came to know best meet is a privately owned chapel that is quite inconspicuous. On the outside it resembles in architectural style and size a middle-class home. On the inside, it looks similar to many Shin temples. It has a large tatami-mat room where people sit for religious services. The furnishings in the front of this room are similar to a Shin temple's sanctuary: gold-colored shrines about four feet tall house statues of Amida and Shinran; in front of the statues, flowers are placed and incense and candles are burned; there is a platform upon which the head teacher sits to recite Buddhist texts; and next to the platform sits a bell in the shape of a large bowl used to announce the beginning and end of services. In the back of the room is an offertory box the size of a storage chest, into which people occasionally drop coins.

Gyōja gather at the chapel several times a month for services that last from 10 a.m. to about 3 p.m., with a break for lunch. About once a month, there is a secret initiation rite or a ceremony open to non-initiates such as a memorial service for the deceased (*eitaikyō*). The most common type of service, however, is called *sōzoku* ("succession") and consists of three or four different sermons, each given by a different man. The *zenchishiki* always gives his sermon right after lunch. The sermons before lunch and the last sermon are given by ministers who have the authority to preach but who, unlike the *zenchishiki*, do not possess the secret text or have special training in the secret teachings.

A sermon by K-sensei

December 16, 2000: 15 or so people are in attendance this day; all except a few appear to be over 60 years old. It is almost 1 p.m. We have just left the kitchen, where we ate a light lunch consisting of miso, rice, and vegetables. Some men are sitting around a brazier in the hallway smoking cigarettes, while some women chat in front of the sanctuary. A faint scent of incense fills the air. Few have left or arrived since 10 a.m., when the service started. During the morning everyone recited the *Amidakyō*, a sūtra that describes Amida Buddha's Pure Land, and then everyone listened to two different ministers give two sermons: one on attaining *shinjin* and the other on a Buddhist hymn written by Shinran.

At 1 p.m., a minister strikes a gong with a mallet to indicate that K-sensei's sermon is about to begin. Everyone moves to the main hall and sits on the floor. The ministers and K-sensei walk in through a side door and sit facing the image of Amida. Although K-sensei and the Urahōmon ministers say they are lay Buddhists, while giving sermons they wear the vestments of Shin priests, consisting of a stole and of black robes over a white gown that go down to their ankles.

K-sensei begins by ringing the large bowl-shaped bell twice, after which everyone presses their palms together in a gesture of reverence and recites several times "*namu amida butsu*." (This recitation, called *nenbutsu*, can be translated as "I take refuge in Amida Buddha," or "In Amida Buddha I trust.") Some are holding prayer beads (*nenju*). He then turns around to face the congregation, and sits on a chair behind a desk that is brought to the center of the room by the ministers. K-sensei is an affable man who at almost six feet is remarkably tall for a Japanese man approaching the age of 80. He laughs often and easily. Before becoming a *zenchishiki* a few years earlier, he ran a medical supplies business that he owned. His son, he proudly once told me, is a physician. No one knows what his sermon will be about today, but the expectation is that compared to the ones given in the morning, which were mostly read and delivered with much archaic language, his sermon will be easier to understand.

K-sensei again recites "*namu amida butsu*" several times and, without greeting the audience, starts reading a phrase from a text. He begins as follows:

> [Reading] "*Ichinen to iu wa hongan o shin'gyō suru gokusoku o sashite mōsunari.*" [Speaking] These are the words of Shinran. The word *ichinen* is one that Shinran explains the meaning of at length. If I may convey what he said, there is *ichinen* and *tanen*. What is *ichinen*? Shinran said it is *hongan wa shin'gyō suru gokusoku o sashite mōsunari. Hongan* refers to the eighteenth vow of Amida.
>
> [K-sensei then says as if quoting a scripture passage from memory] "By concentrating on the three aspects of faith – sincere mind, entrusting, and aspiring to be born [in Amida's Pure Land] – one receives from Amida the Buddha wisdom of *shinjin*." This is *hongan*.
>
> *Shin'gyō* means to rejoice and to put into action. That is *shin'gyō*. Then there is *gokusoku*. This indicates not the gradual, or something that happens while unaware. Rather it means "immediately" or "in an instant" to receive from Amida wisdom, Buddhist wisdom. That is what Shinran is teaching.
>
> This all, however, on the surface makes no sense. It would not be normally understood. If the person is not one who has been led to practice, he will not understand. If one is not a practitioner [*gyōja*], it will convey no meaning. Thus even if *ichinen to iu wa hongan o shin'gyō suru gokusoku o sashite mōsunari* is written, what that means will not be understood; but if a person asks Amida to receive *shinjin*, and thereby Buddha wisdom, he will have the intelligence to understand.

Following the above explanation of K-sensei, we might translate the reoccurring sentence attributed to Shinran as "*Ichinen* indicates the instance when Amida, in accordance with his eighteenth vow, brings a person to happiness and to practice." This passage, K-sensei is telling them here, can only be understood by those like themselves who have participated in the secret *ichinen kimyō* rite of which most Shin Buddhists, including Shin priests, are ignorant. He thus relates this first part of the sermon to the initiation experience of his audience.

Using a mix of formal honorific language when referring to Amida and Shinran and informal language when addressing the audience, he next explains *tanen* in a similar manner.

> [Reading] "*Tannen to iu wa shin no ue ni mōsu shōmyō o tanen no gyō to iu nari.*"[Speaking] What does *tanen* mean? It means numerous sayings of the *nenbutsu*. With the phrases *shin no ue* ("with faith") and "saying *nenbutsu* numerous times," Shinran is teaching that the recitation of *namu amida butsu* comes after the receiving of *shinjin* from Amida.
>
> There are, as I always teach, three types of *namu amida butsu*. *Shōmyō* is to recite. Then there is the *nenbutsu* that is contemplation on Amida. That is *nenbutsu*. Then there is *myōgō*. *Myōgō* is also *nenbutsu* but it is that which is practiced, the thing which ... it is the practicing of. *Myō* is ... well ... the origin. *Gō* is what we call the result of that origin. Because we ask Amida for help with complete concentration and are vitalized by him, we understand the origin by which we are moved. We can understand the feelings of the Buddha. That is *butsugō* or the result of the Buddha. Because of this we recite the *nenbutsu*. Without *shinjin* the *nenbutsu* would not come out [of our mouths]; that is what this means. Reciting the *nenbutsu* with faith is called the "*gyō* of numerous recitations of the *nenbutsu*." What is called *gyō* is the happiness due to Amida's merit and our receiving of *shinjin*.
>
> "Ahhh ... Thank you for that." You have some food or something and feelings of gratitude arise. You say "Ahhh my stomach is full. My stomach's full." You must take the action. If you don't eat your stomach won't be full. It is with this type of gratitude in mind that we can understand *tanen*. It is the *nenbutsu* of gratitude. When we repeatedly say the *nenbutsu* with gratitude; we call that *tanen*. Our recitations of the *nenbutsu* become numerous. Shinran is teaching that the *nenbutsu* will not come out of those who don't practice. He is teaching many things simply.

Over the next 30 minutes or so, the sermon continues in this way, with K-sensei reading phrases by Shinran and explaining the words in those phrases. He explains other ideas related to *ichinen* and *tanen*. He relates *ichinen* to *tasuketamae* ("save me!"), which they said during the initiation rite. He preaches that Shinran taught that what is most important is to receive *shinjin*. He also talks more about joy and gratitude. At the end he concludes by simply saying, "That is *ichinen* and *tanen*." He then turns to face the image of Amida, rings the bell, and says the *nenbutsu* while all in the congregation press their palms together in prayer, some wrapping their hands in prayer beads. He exits through the side door by which he entered to return to his private room. After a break of about 10 to 15 minutes, a minister gives a final sermon, after which people say the *nenbutsu* a few times. With that, the services for the day end. People leave while the ministers clean up and change back into their regular clothing.

Discussion

The sermon as a pedagogical performance with multiple messages

The above description is the only one published of a contemporary secretive Shin sermon. It is also the only text to include a transcription of the oral language of an Urahōmon sermon or that includes translations into English of what is said. Although the description indicates that K-sensei's sermon is distinctive, we can read it as representing something common. Depending on the context in which we situate the sermon, we can see how it is similar to (as well as different from) other religious practices. To show how this is the case, I will mention just two contexts.

The first is that of Shin Buddhism's dharma talks (*hōwa*). Although dharma talks are not as central to the liturgy of Shin temples in Japan as sermons are to Christian churches in North America, they are frequently given. At large Shin temples, priests give sermons daily. Those who attend commonly bring prayer beads (*nenju*) and sūtra books. Some people might bring a donation for the temple. As with the Urahōmon sermon above, *hōwa* often include recitations of the *nenbutsu* and readings of Shin texts, which are then explained in depth. One key difference is that sermons at temples often include stories and end with a song or with the recitation of the Shin text *Gaikemon* ("Confessional Statement"). By situating K-sensei's sermon in this context, we can learn how it both reflects and refracts from public Shin sermons to understand Urahōmon's unique doctrine and how its sermons differ from those of mainstream Shin to better understand both.

Another much wider context in which we can situate it – and the one I will focus on here – is that of performance. To view the sermon as a performance is not to suggest that it is theatrical or entertaining; rather it is to say that it makes a presentation to an audience with actions at a particular place and time. By examining it as a performance, we can notice what we might miss if we were to simply focus on the words of the sermon. Examining it as a performance can also show how actions and the setting of the sermon can complement the spoken words. Furthermore, it can reveal how multiple messages are presented, only some of which may be intended by the preacher or consciously understood by the audience. It is worth emphasizing that all the messages a sermon presents and potentially conveys are not limited to the intentions of the preacher or what the audience notices, any more than the potential multiple meanings of a novel or short story are limited to their authors' intentions or what a particular reader understands.

As a performance, K-sensei's actions would most likely be recognized by many people as a sermon, even if they did not understand Japanese and knew little about Shin Buddhism. The reason for this is that it resembles performative patterns and elements of sermons found elsewhere, beyond Shin Buddhism: a man in distinctive clothing speaks to a group of people who sit lower than him; there is no dialogue between speaker and audience; hands are put together in a gesture of reverence or prayer at the beginning and end of the event; there is formulaic recitation; candles and incense are burned; and icons are displayed that distinguish the site from a classroom or lecture hall. But to understand how the specific sermon event under investigation communicates different particular messages, rather than just how it is similar to other sermons, we can analyze it by identifying major and minor parts of it, examine how those parts interact with each other, and then highlight some of the messages they present. The three major parts I will focus on are the framing elements, the actors, and the articulated words.

Framing elements are boundary markers that set the sermon apart and help distinguish it from ordinary speech and other activities. The subparts that make up the framing elements are the site of the performance, the objects at that site, and the formalistic actions performed at the start and conclusion of the sermon. The site of the sermon is a large room in a building which only those invited are allowed to enter. This building and its restrictive access help distinguish it from the open, public realm. The exclusivity of the site also serves to valorize the activity in it. The objects in general associate the place with Shin Buddhism. The statues of Amida and Shinran are particularly important because they evoke their presence and serve as symbols that connect the actions in the room with Shin history and scripture. Like the *mise-en-scène* of a theatrical production or the set of a film, they create an atmosphere of expectancy about the type of activity that will be performed and shape perceptions.

In addition to the site and inanimate objects in it, symmetrical actions also frame the event. The main actions that do this are the ringing of bells and the recitations of the *nenbutsu*. These formalistic actions at the beginning and end of the sermon serve to punctuate it and set it apart from the other activities before and after it.

The actors in the sermon performance are K-sensei and the audience. They are actors because they perform actions – not because they pretend to be what they are not.

K-sensei's main act is speaking. As a preacher, he is the leader of the sermon while the audience acts as listeners and as supporters of K-sensei in framing the sermon with recitations. As the main actor, K-sensei delivers the sermon in a voice that is eager to share knowledge but is not dramatic. K-sensei's style is didactic. His exegesis of Shinran's words is that of an instructor rather than an entertainer. This is proper, because the audience does not expect to be entertained; in fact, a sermon that is too entertaining would probably be seen as inappropriate, less than profound, and more about the messenger than the explicit message. His clothing also distinguishes him from the audience.

The audience members perform fewer actions, but without them there listening, K-sensei would be performing a soliloquy rather than a sermon. The audience also influences what he says. As he formulates his speech, he does so with knowledge of its members. He knows he can speak to them as insiders, that is, as people who have received *shinjin*. Their presence also creates a communal experience of the sermon that is shared by all in attendance.

We can understand *the articulated words* of the sermon more deeply by looking beyond just what is said and asking a basic socio-linguistic question: what types of language are used during the social event? In K-sensei's sermon performance, we can identify three types of language. First, there are the formulaic sacred utterances of the *nenbutsu*. In addition to helping frame the preaching event, they are distinctive in that they are addressed to Amida, are said repeatedly, and are recited, more or less, in unison by all the actors. Unlike other speech during the sermon, the *nenbutsu* is not didactic; rather, it expresses reverence and gratitude. Second, there are words that are read out loud by the preacher. These are words attributed to Shinran found in texts that could be referred to again at a later time. They are the source and focus of K-sensei's speech throughout the sermon. By speaking them, he orally re-presents them. Third, there is the spontaneous expository speech of K-sensei. Although K-sensei no doubt thought about what he would say in advance, his speech is primarily spontaneous in that it is neither read nor recited completely from memory. This gives the words a greater sense of immediacy. As unwritten speech, it is also ephemeral. It was only the intrusion of a recording device that kept all tangible evidence of what he said from disappearing. His use of honorific language for Amida and Shinran, furthermore, makes the sermon not only sound more formal, but also indicates their relational distance and higher status.

With the framing elements, the actors, and the articulated words of the sermon performance delineated, we can now turn to how the sermon presents multiple messages by clarifying one of its explicit messages and three of its tacit ones.

Explicitly the sermon is a pedagogical performance that presents knowledge of Shinran's conception of *ichinen* versus *tanen*, or the one-thought of Amida (or recitation of the *nenbutsu*) versus repeated thoughts or recitations. K-sensei says as much at the end of the sermon. On the surface, it thus deals with the problem of how we can understand the terms *ichinen* and *tanen*. It is, in effect, explicitly about Shin Buddhist vocabulary.

This explicit message teaches us about basic Urahōmon doctrine and a *zenchishiki*'s interpretations of Shinran's writings, but the sermon as a whole communicates much more. While actions in the sermon might speak with greater subtlety than the explicit words articulated, they do tacitly make important statements. A few of the tacit messages presented are: a method for engaging with Shinran's writings, the authority of K-sensei, and the identity of the actors.

In presenting a method for reading, it is not just what is said but how it is said. The way K-sensei presents the words provides an example of a method for grappling with Shinran's statements. He models this method by the manner and structure in which he presents Shinran's teachings. This method involves contemplating and examining in depth specific words and phrases, how they relate to each other, and how they relate to personal experience, such as the gratitude you might feel after eating. K-sensei models this method in his preaching when he meticulously explains key words in each sentence attributed to Shinran. He presents each word as having importance and a rich array of meanings. This manner of presentation demonstrates for members of the audience how they too can come to better understand and read the writings of Shinran.

The way K-sensei preaches is also conducive to enhancing his authority. Although this is not obvious from observing the event alone, his style of instruction imitates Shinran's. K-sensei does not mention it during his sermon, but there is a well-known text by Shinran on *ichinen* and *tanen* titled *Ichinen tanen mon'i* (Notes on Once-Calling and Many-Calling). Members of his audience, or at least some of them, are almost certainly familiar with it. In this text, Shinran presents words individually and then explains them. Here is an example from Shinran's text: "*Soku* also mean to ascend to and become established in a certain rank. *Attain* means to have attained to what one shall attain. … 'To grasp' (*sesshu*) means to take in (*setsu*) and to receive and to hold (*shu*)" (*Collected Works of Shinran*, vol. 1, p. 474). K-sensei imitates Shinran in this manner of explanation. This mimesis, common in many performances, has the rhetorical effect of closely associating the preaching of K-sensei with that of Shinran. This enhances his authority because it shows him to be following the example of the founder, Shinran.

K-sensei's style of preaching, moreover, indicates that he is not teaching his own ideas so much as those of Shinran. His words of explanation are spontaneous, but by reading the words of Shinran he presents the teachings as rooted in the authority of Shinran, not in any way in his own authority. To emphasize this he frequently repeats Shinran's words. K-sensei thus presents himself as a conduit for Shinran; he is merely passing on Shinran's teachings. By articulating the teachings and explaining what they mean, however, he gives the words a vitality that would be lost if they were simply read from a prepared script.

K-sensei finally enhances his authority by the way he physically presents himself during the sermon. This is most obvious in his distinctive clothing, which imitates that of a Shin priest. Despite his claims that he is simply a layman, his use of clerical vestments has the effect of associating him with clerical authority.

The third tacitly conveyed message relates to identity as *gyōja*, literally "practice people." In the sermon K-sensei is implicitly addressing a basic question related to identity formation: "Who are we?" He answers this question in at least three ways. First, he defines who they are by contrasting them with others. When he says while explaining a sentence by Shinran "If one is not a practitioner (*gyōja*), it will convey no meaning," he is emphasizing how they as a people who can understand Shinran's teachings are distinct from most other people. K-sensei knows that his audience consists almost exclusively of people who received the *shinjin* in the *ichinen kimyō* rite, which he tells them during the sermon endows them with Buddha wisdom to understand. This supposedly gives them the intelligence to comprehend what those outside Urahōmon, who are not *gyōja*, cannot. Second, he clarifies their identity by alluding to their sameness or what they have in common with each other. He does this when he interprets the words of Shinran in a way that summons to mind the *ichinen kimyō* rite that they experienced. When he explains "*gokusoku*" as "'in an instant' to receive from Amida wisdom," he is reminding them of the moment in the rite when he as *zenchishiki* says "*yoshi*," indicating the moment they received *shinjin*. He also does this when he says "if a person asks Amida to receive *shinjin*." With these words he is suggesting the part of the rite in which they "ask" Amida for *shinjin* by repeatedly reciting "save me!" (K-sensei has explained on other occasions that the word "ask" [*tanomu*] is one that Shin priests misunderstand as "to rely on.") A third way K-sensei answers the question "Who are we?" for the audience of *gyōja* is by explaining why they are a people who do what they do. At the beginning and end of the sermon event, and on many other occasions, *gyōja* recite the *nenbutsu.* K-sensei's sermon tells them why with his explanation of *tanen.* He does this when he preaches that Shinran taught that "the recitation of *namu amida butsu* comes after the receiving of *shinjin* from Amida." He further adds that it is because of *shinjin* they recite the *nenbutsu* and because they asked "Amida for help" they understand that Amida is the origin "by which they are moved" to recite the *nenbutsu*. K-sensei, in his exegesis of Shinran's writings, is thus giving the *gyōja* an understanding of why they recited *nenbutsu* before the sermon and why they will recite it after. In effect, he is telling them that as *gyōja* they recite the *nenbutsu* because of who they are and because of their relationship with Amida, who has led them to practice it.

Concluding remarks

If we were to examine the sermon further, we could no doubt find more messages. Viewing sermons as performances opens rich interpretive possibilities. I expect others examining the sermon will see things I missed and have insights I did not. In fact, I hope they will, because this can increase our knowledge of both Urahōmon sermons and the performance of sermons more generally.

We have all learned that scholarship should be critical. Yet, once we have done the critical analysis, we can synthesize the elements found in our analysis to gain new appreciation for what on the surface may seem mundane. To a simple onlooker, much of Buddhist activity can appear boring. At the same time, if we labor to cultivate our ability to observe, to formulate and to ask illuminating questions, and to place an activity in a new context or view it from a unique perspective, we are rewarded with the pleasure of discovery. Persistent ethnographic work, in short, possesses the power to reveal that our world is indeed a fascinating place.

Readings

A wide variety of ideas on how to view performance can be found in Richard Schechner's *Performance Studies: An Introduction* (London: Routledge, 2002). Those interested in exploring speech in particular as a performative act would do well to search in the fields of socio-linguistics and anthropological linguistics. On sermons specifically, the reader can consult Rosaleen Howard-Malverde's "Words for Our Lord of Huanca: Discursive Strategies in a Quechua Sermon from Southern Peru," *Anthropological Linguistics* 40 (1998), pp. 570–95, and Mahinda Deegalle's *Popularizing Buddhism: Preaching as Performance in Sri Lanka* (Albany: State University of New York Press, 2006).

On Shin Buddhism, secondary sources in English are plentiful, but most of them deal with historical and doctrinal issues. The best historical overview of Shin Buddhism up to the sixteenth century, which gives particular emphasis to its doctrinal development, is *Jōdo Shinshū: Shin Buddhism in Medieval Japan* by James Dobbins (Honolulu: University of Hawai'i Press, 2002). For translations of primary sources, see *The Collected Works of Shinran*, 2 vols. (Kyoto: Jōdo Shinshū Hongwanji-ha, 1997) and Ebsen Andreasen's *Popular Buddhism in Japan: Shin Buddhist Religion and Culture* (Richmond, Surrey: Curzon Press, 1998). The most in-depth study in English on Shin sermons is Elizabeth Harrison's doctoral dissertation "Encountering Amida: Jōdo Shinshū Sermons in Eighteenth-Century Japan" (University of Chicago, 1992).

On secretive Shin Buddhism, there are very few studies in English. Most scholars of Shin Buddhism have treated secretive Shin as heretical. This can be seen in Chiba Jōryu's "Orthodoxy and Heterodoxy in Early Modern Shinshū: Kakushi nenbutsu and Kakure nenbutsu," in James Foard, Michael Solomon, and Richard Payne (eds.), *The Pure Land Tradition: History and Development* (Berkeley: Regents of the University of California, 1996), pp. 463–96. Although Chiba's chapter privileges the perspective of Shin priests, it provides a useful introduction to the history of two types of secretive Shin. For ethnographic-based studies, the reader can refer to two articles by me: "Religion Concealed and Revealed: The Uses of History by a Secretive Shinshū Leader," *Japanese Religions* 27 (2002), pp. 195–206; and "A Religion in Death Throes: How Secrecy Undermines the Survival of a Crypto Shin Buddhist Tradition in Japan Today," *Religion Compass* 4(4) (2010), pp. 202–10.

Author

Clark Chilson is an Assistant Professor in the Department of Religious Studies at the University of Pittsburgh. He is the co-editor of two books: *Shamans in Asia* (with Peter Knecht, London: RoutledgeCurzon, 2003) and the *Nanzan Guide to Japanese Religions* (with Paul Swanson, Honolulu: University of Hawai'i Press, 2005), which was recognized by *Choice* magazine in 2007 as an "Outstanding Academic Title." He has published scholarly articles on the tenth-century Buddhist holy man Kūya and on secretive Shin Pure Land Buddhists. He is currently writing on the consequences of concealment for secretive Shin Buddhists. He is also researching the life and religious leadership of Ikeda Daisaku, president of Sōka Gakkai International.

Chapter 12

The insides and outsides of a Tibetan Buddhist ritual on the outskirts of Sujātā village

James B. Apple

Preamble

Tibetan Buddhists engage in a number of ritual activities for various reasons including, among others, to generate merit, to purify negativities, or to protect against malevolent forces. In this chapter I describe a ritual that I participated in outside Sujātā village in late 2000. I relate the narrative to the study of ritual in Buddhist traditions and to the insider/outsider relation in the study of Buddhism(s).

Narrative

I had been in Bodh Gayā, India, staying at the Burmese *vihāra* for the past five months as a faculty member of the Antioch Buddhist Study Abroad program. It was late December and the tropical air of northeast India was beginning to cool and become frigid by Indian standards. Bodh Gayā, located in the present-day northeastern Indian state of Bihar, is the most celebrated of locations for Buddhists around the world. Buddhist traditions hold that around 2,400 years ago, just outside this small village, a young, wandering, disenfranchised prince named Siddhārtha sat underneath a large tree, and, with diligence, sustained energetic focus, and concentration, became a Buddha, an awakened being. Since that event, cultures in Asia have conceptualized this location as being the navel of the earth, the middle country, and even the center of the universe. According to tradition, Bodh Gayā is a *vajrāsana*, "a diamond seat," of great cosmological significance, the very place where Buddhas of the past were awakened, where the Buddha of the present, namely the young prince who became Śākyamuni, became awakened, and where all Buddhas of the future will attain awakening. The exact location of the diamond seat is on the eastern side of the fabled Bodhi tree under which the young Siddhārtha sat; underneath that spot, a double-looped intersecting diamond (*vajra*) marks the universal spot where all Buddhas become awakened. About a kilometer and a half north of this fabled spot is where the Burmese *vihāra*, a Theravāda Buddhist monastery, is located. This monastery accepts a number of guest and pilgrims from various places around Asia, but mostly religious pilgrims from Theravāda Buddhist areas. Other pilgrims are welcome as well, including Tibetan and American students.

One morning I was informed that a Tibetan monk from Sikkim, Lama Kunsang Dorjee, was staying at the *vihāra* and that he was planning an expedition to Sujātā village. I knew of Sujātā from legends of Siddhārtha's life. She was the young woman who offered milk-rice to the future Buddha Siddhārtha after he had practiced six years of ascetic practices and before his awakening. Lama Kunsang inquired if anybody from the Antioch program would like to accompany him on the expedition, and since I was the faculty member of the program who specialized in Tibetan Buddhism, colleagues encouraged me to travel along. Sujātā was just two kilometers away from Bodh Gayā and we would be travelling in rented jeeps. A small group of around ten people loaded into two jeeps and we set off on our way to Sujātā village. About a kilometer northeast from Bodh Gayā, we crossed the Nairañjanā River, a western tributary of the Phalgu River, and entered the village of present-day Bakraur, known in ancient times as the village of Senānigama. On the north side of this village are the archeological remains of a *stūpa*, or reliquary, that is traditionally known by various names – Sujātā Kuti, Sujātāgarh, and Sujātā Quila. The site commemorates, at least from the ninth century C.E., what is thought to be Sujātā's residence. Our two-jeep caravan did not initially stop in the village of Sujātā. We actually drove two kilometers east of Bakraur to the much smaller village of Silaunja on the bank of the Mohane River, an eastern tributary of the Phalgu River, to a location known as the Dharmāranya Temple.

According to the Pāli Buddhist tradition, it was at this location on the outskirts of Bodh Gayā where Sujātā offered milk-rice to Prince Siddhārtha, who had decided to abandon the path of asceticism following six years of extreme austerities. Sujātā, a daughter of a landowner from the nearby village of Senānigama, pledged that she would offer milk-rice to the spirit of a tree if she gave birth to a son; once her wish was fulfilled, she asked her maid Punna to visit the tree and prepare the place for offering. When Punna visited the place, she saw that Siddhārtha was sitting under the tree in meditation. Mistaking him for a tree-*deva*, she quickly returned home and reported the matter to Sujātā, who in great joy reached the spot and offered Siddhārtha the milk-rice in a golden bowl. Receiving the milk-rice from Sujātā helped to restore the strength of the emaciated Buddha-to-be and to prepare his mental concentration for awakening under the Bodhi tree. According to a tradition followed by Tibetan Buddhists, the location commemorates the place where Siddhārtha performed austerities for six years under a Banyan tree.

The jeeps finally arrived at this commemorative location, which consisted of a run-down temple complex slightly beyond the impoverished grass huts of Silaunja village. A crippled young man immediately came running towards us, except that he was running without any legs. He was using his arms, a clear indication of the poverty within the area. Soon local people of the temple seeking handouts swarmed us. Lama Kunsang and a Hindi-speaking colleague informed the people who seemed to be in charge of the area that we would give donations after we performed a ritual.

Making our way beyond the crowd of villagers who greeted us and walking along a path through the ancient and worn temple buildings, we came upon a square platform made of stone. One end of the platform had elevated flat-topped layered blocks built upon it that were painted red and blue. Slightly behind this end of the platform was a huge Banyan tree whose split trunk and elongated branches towered over the platform. An inscription in Tibetan and English, engraved on top of one of the layered blocks, commemorated the occasion of a visit by the fourteenth Dalai Lama, Tenzin Gyatso, and proclaimed that here was where Siddhārtha Gautama performed the six years of austerities.

As soon as we arrived, Lama Kunsang's two young monk attendants, assisted by several North Americans in our group, began placing offerings of dozens of small white candles and incense on top of the flat-topped blocks. They also spread *kata*s (Tibetan *kha btags*), long pieces of white silk cloth often used for ceremonies, across the blocks. Swiftly, the ancient stone platform was transformed into a place for Tibetan Buddhist ritual activity.

Lama Kunsang asked me if I would like to participate in the activities. Thinking it might be rude to refuse an invitation in this situation, I readily agreed. So Lama Kunsang sat down in the center of the platform with his attendants in a row beside him and I sat next to the attendants, on the right end of the row. Two women in our group sat behind us. An American couple who had also come along stood behind us, off the main platform. Several local Indians sat on the platform with us, indifferent to whatever activities we were up to. A picture of this setting, taken by a colleague just as the ritual was about to begin, is reproduced here as Figure 12.1.

Lama Kunsang and the monk attendants began to chant offering prayers in Tibetan. I was familiar with several of the prayers and chanted along with them. The chants consisted of a well-established liturgical format representing or invoking a sequence of spiritual moods through which a ritual participant is drawn through processes of veneration and purification. This included invoking the three jewels of the Buddha (teacher), Dharma (teaching), and Saṃgha (community), cultivating the aspiration to achieve Buddhahood, and then giving praises, making offerings, reciting confessions of faults, rejoicing in merit, requesting the teaching, begging the Buddhas to not abandon beings, and dedicating the merit of the performance. As a group sitting together in our particular formation and cross-legged posture, we were emulating the ideals of Buddhist mindful awareness. The offerings of candles and *kata*s, as well as the prayers, were not exactly acts of *giving to* a divine being, but were rather acts of *giving up* in emulation of the renunciate acts that the Buddha-to-be Siddhārtha, for the Tibetan tradition, had performed at this very spot 2,500 years ago.

At one point the monks began chanting Tibetan prayers that I was not familiar with and I became silent. One of the young monk attendants then handed me a prayer book and pointed out where they were in the recitation. The prayers at this point in the recitation included visualizations of Buddhist deities as well as

Figure 12.1 A Tibetan Buddhist ritual outside Sujātā village

Tibetan Buddhist lineage figures. I did my best to follow along in the reciting of the prayers. But as it was getting late in the afternoon and the sun was beginning to set, the monks began reciting prayers at a very fast pace and I could no longer keep up. The monks were reciting from memory and in their native Tibetan, and my American vocal capacities were unable to enunciate the Tibetan at the pace they were going. I remember being impressed during the ritual at the speed of the recitation of the Tibetan prayers. I had heard and recited Tibetan before but never at this pace.

Did I experience visions of Buddhas, special blessings, or have any other religious experience during the recitation? I cannot speak for the experience of the other members of the group, but for me, at least, the memory is of peace from all the turbulence of hectic daily life found in India. The villagers in the area left us to perform the ritual commemoration and there was a certain stillness all around the stone platform as we chanted. When the ritual was over, the attendant monks removed the pieces of white silk cloth and candles from the stone blocks. Everyone in the group packed up his or her belongings and we made our way back to the jeeps. Before loading into the jeeps, Lama Kunsang and a Hindi-speaking colleague negotiated the sum to be donated to the local attendants of the weathered and time-worn temple complex. As the sun was setting, our group drove homeward in the falling darkness to the Burmese *vihāra*.

Discussion

The preceding brief ethnographic description I have provided contains a great deal of data to be explained in the study of Buddhist traditions. The picture, in both its description and depiction, evokes questions concerning Tibetan Buddhist ritual practices, sacred places, the range of forms of Tibetan Buddhist worship and devotion, and the relations between monastics and lay practitioners, among others. But the picture also provokes the question: what is my role (practitioner, scholar, both, or neither) in this picture? Am I a Buddhist practitioner, as the picture seems to depict? If I am a practitioner of Buddhism in this picture, how can I be a detached and so-called objective scholar? In what follows I would like to relate these questions to a foundational issue in the study of religion, as well as for the study of Buddhism, to what the eminent scholar of religion J. Z. Smith has described in his book *Relating Religion* as "that cluster of urgent and complex methodological and theoretical issues gathered under the label, 'the insider/outsider problem'" (p. 201).

The insider/outsider issue in the study of religion

The intellectual issue of the insider/outsider in the study of religion, as well as in other areas of the human sciences, is one that is complex and multiform. In the following few pages I will analyze some of this complexity, and while not necessarily resolving the problems this issue presents, I hope to evoke how students studying Buddhist traditions may think about the insider/outsider problem in the study of religion.

It is important to initially establish that "insider/outsider" is a relative term applied by humans in speaking about humans. As J. Z. Smith explains in *Relating Religion*, we are not dealing here with humans and Martians. Smith continues to discuss how the term "insider/outsider" often invites misunderstanding, as it suggests a fundamental state of being rather than an anthropological distinction. As I will argue below, from an anthropocentric angle, the distinction is not an absolute one but is rather a classification shaped by relations. On a more general precautionary note, one of the problems with the language of being an "insider" or "outsider" is the apparent "presence-ness" the terms evoke. The use of this set of terms presumes a strict homogeneity to subjects across time and space. If one considers things in a different manner, the past (and, for that matter, the future) is all outside. No one is able to dwell either back in time or out in the future. In this respect, one can affirm that you, the readers, and I, the author of this essay, are equidistant from the ritual event described above that occurred slightly outside Sujātā village late in the year 2000. The scholar's use of the present tense in writing ethnographic descriptions can hide this fact – what Smith calls the "zero-time fiction" in *Relating Religion* (p. 261). The question then becomes one of the strategies undertaken to negotiate this difference of time and space, including interests and accompanying representations and interpretations in order to do so.

Along these lines, J. Z. Smith, in a lecture, "The Insider/Outsider Problem in the Study of Religion," given at the University of Alabama in 2003, has suggested that the phrase "insider/outsider" may be applied in at least four distinct ways in modern Euro-American discourse. In his analysis, there are four quite distinct ways of thinking about the issue and they ought not to be homogenized: cultural or social identity; religious identity; representation; and academic formulations. I will follow these four ways in order to disassemble and then reassemble how we may think about the phrase "insider/outsider."

In terms of cultural or social identity, the insider is one who belongs as a member of a group and who shares a sense of cultural or social identity with the group; this identity is often expressed in contrastive and comparative terms such as "us and them." This is to share somebody's worldview; it is to share somebody's language; it is to share in a whole set of cultural markers. Obviously that is what is inside. "Outside" in this instance simply negates these shared characteristics. To be outside is to not belong to a group and it is to not share various cultural traits. In this way of thinking, the words "inside" and "outside" convey a sort of social understanding and are based on a set of cultural features that are construed in terms of ethnic or social identity. The humans depicted in Figure 12.1 may be classified into three groups in terms of shared cultural identity through language and social customs: North American, South Asian (Indian), and Inner Asian (Tibetan). As the ritual is taking place in South Asia, we could say that the insiders are the Indians sitting on the edge of the platform as well as the Tibetans in the center row, as they are from the Indian state of Sikkim. I, as a North American, would be considered an outsider from this point of view, perhaps as a guest from a rich and powerful country invited to sit in an open space near a tree with other guests.

Along with socio-cultural identity, another sense of insider and outsider is one that often focuses on, or is limited to, questions of religious identity. And questions of religious identity, particularly in modern North American discourse, are not phrased in terms of "sharing in" but rather in terms of those tricky words "believe in." In this sense, to be an insider is to believe and to be an outsider is not to believe; and then there is a third option, which Smith proposed in his 2003 lecture and which people do not explore very much, and that is to be indifferent to an aspect of or some totality of a group's worldview. The distinction between "believe in" and "sharing in" is slippery and often people treat them as if they were the same, but there is a difference. What is the difference? "Sharing in" is often practiced in popular North American culture through visiting the residence of a person from another culture, having a native meal, or even borrowing a native outfit and trying it on for a few minutes. Afterwards, you go home. So, to put it briefly, this is what it means to be with or share with someone of a different culture. On the other hand, from a North American popular culture viewpoint, if you meet or visit someone of different beliefs and you like what they have to say, you "join up" or convert. Here we have an astonishing choice: tourist or convert with nothing in-between.

This brief portrayal of North American culture reflects the weight that the question of insider and outsider seems to carry for North Americans when we talk about the insides and outsides of a social or cultural event as opposed to when we talk about the insides and outsides of a religious event. In terms of religious identity, the insider is often thought to control the understanding of belief while other components that might be of interest for the study of religion, such as ritual, power relations, gender, history, are not given as much weight. It is often the case that someone challenges less the outsider's interpretation of social or cultural matters than the outsider's understanding of religious matters.

However, beliefs are not limited to just religion. As Malory Nye argues in *Religion: The Basics*, when belief is considered a central element in religion, the concept carries a lot of ideological assumptions in that it may often apply a predominantly Protestant Christian concept to a non-Christian context, such as the Tibetan Buddhist ritual on the outskirts of Sujātā village that I described. It is not clear from this description what role *belief* had in the *practice* of this ritual. I did not interview all the participants as to what their beliefs were in regard to this ritual or think much about my own beliefs while the ritual was being performed. Nor did all the ritual participants recite a common creedal statement. However, what does seems to unite the participants in this ritual is the embodied activity, in thought and action, of sitting cross-legged while facing a tree and reciting prayers, postures that represent the socio-cultural dispositions and interests found in Tibetan Buddhist culture.

A third sense of insider and outsider is in terms of representation and is a reformulation of the above two categories of social and religious identity, as Smith explained in his 2003 lecture. Rather than talking about the insider and the outsider who believes "this" or "that" or shares "this" or "that," one might talk about representing the "insider" and "outsider." That is, we put a little gap in-between who they are and how we represent them to ourselves and to each other. In this sense, language represents the insider or thinks of the insider as somebody who is near, with whose views we are familiar and comfortable; we do not necessarily insist on sharing those views, but we are comfortable being around them. Outsiders are represented as if they were far away, as if they were exotic and strange, and the thought or the term provides an evaluation of their cultural configuration. In brief, an "insider" is represented as one who is near, whose views are similar to our own culture, and the "outsider" is represented as totally other and exotic.

The fourth way Smith suggests we consider the insider/outsider issue is in terms of academic formulations, which see insider and outsider as two roles that one can play with respect to the same object. In this formulation, insides and outsides are not permanent fixtures of the world but rather ways of representing to ourselves the near as if it were far, a technique known as defamiliarization, and representing the far as if it were near, a technique known as familiarization. Throughout this essay I have described, in English, a ritual event that occurred far away in India in a different culture, familiarizing readers with events of that day utilizing descriptive interpretations. Yet, I have also tried to analyze and represent my participation in this ritual in a way that is not so obvious. I have tried to defamiliarize the reader as to my status in relation to this ritual.

What such techniques do is critically suggest that near and far are neither states of being nor locations in which one stands. Rather, inside and outside are ways of approaching cultural goods, beliefs, needs, actions, and linguistic formulations. An approach through academic formulation therefore suggests a critique of the substantive understanding of "insider" and "outsider" as well as the question of whether any set of simple binary formulations are in fact useful for describing the complexity of how human beings, as human beings, relate to each other.

The dichotomy of either/or, either one is an "insider" or one is an "outsider," is a binary that is perhaps inadequate, perhaps too simplistic, that needs more relativity. The issue is one of scale – how close you are or how far away you are. And the scales may shift depending on the angle of analysis. In terms of language, I was in the center of this ritual taking place in India and the ritual was performed in the Tibetan language, and since I was chanting Tibetan and have some knowledge of the Tibetan language, I was inside with regard to the ritual on that occasion. But what of the seven other people in the picture attending this ritual who did not know Tibetan? They are spatially close but linguistically far away. Alternatively, as previously suggested, six people including myself who are sitting in a cross-legged posture seem to be spatially inside in relation to the ritual while the three Indians and two North Americans not sitting cross-legged seem to be outside. Yet, the two non-sitting North Americans considered themselves a part of the ritual occasion, while the three Indians, seemingly indifferent, were, at least, hanging around for the occasion.

The question of insider and outsider is thus a tricky sort of matter that is not so easily demarcated. There can also be an inside/outside dichotomy within a tradition, rather than between traditions. Likewise, people are not always so concerned with those outside a tradition – Buddhists are not so historically concerned or troubled with Jews. On the other hand, as J. Z. Smith has aptly pointed out in chapters 11 and 12 of *Relating Religion*, within the scale of near/far relations it is the "proximate other" of traditions that often presents the profound problems of inside and outside. In some ways this may be more of an "intra-cultural" problem than an "inter-cultural" one. Here it may be the proximate other that seems to most capture one's interest, either inviting us to erase differences or emphasize them. For example, within "Buddhist" traditions there are a number of different groups and classifications – Mahāyāna, Tibetan, Japanese, Chinese, Theravāda, etc. Theravādin Buddhists may not follow, agree with, or have an interest in what Tibetan Buddhists are doing. Or even within Tibetan Buddhist communities, there is a whole spectrum of different identities and relations. Put in this way, the inside/outside distinction is not a category between folk but a category within folk. As Smith observes in his 2003 lecture, "the far that is within is often seen as more troubling than the far without."

The trajectory of this type of analysis might lead to the acknowledgment that any one individual or group does not really have a single identity. Humans are made up of a complex of multiple belongings, have a number of identities, and have a whole set of markers that do not add up to a single thing, making our lives a shifting kaleidoscope of relations to each other. The insider/outsider problem, rather than being something about stable locations, is in fact about complex and ever-changing positions. No one is an "insider" or "outsider," Smith suggests in his 2003 lecture, rather they are "only inside or outside with respect to 'something' or 'other' and at a particular point with respect to 'someone' or 'other' at a particular point in time with respect to 'someone' or 'other'." Inside and outside are "situational or relational categories, mobile boundaries which shift according to the map being employed." More interesting is if you write the terms as "insider/outsider." Here it is the slash that turns out to be the most interesting part of the expression. Why? In some way the slash connects what look like two oppositional sorts of categories and indicates interaction and interrelation, as well as implying shifting temporality and relative modes of relationship (for this see Smith's *Relating Religion*, especially p. 256).

So what is underneath the question of insider and outsider? It is in a way an epistemological question, an epistemological question of how we know something about someone else, a question of knowledge. This is a much larger question that has to do with things like truth, which leads to much stronger combative stances in Euro-North American intellectual history. And this relates to what many would consider the nub, the real problem of the inside/outside issue that comes at the level of understanding, at the level of interpretation. As Russell T. McCutcheon writes in his 1999 book *The Insider/Outsider Problem in the Study of Religion*, "the problem is whether, and to what extent, someone can study, understand, or explain the beliefs, words, or actions of another." And perhaps a further related question would be how much we could ever really know of ourselves. In the intellectual history of interpretation, one may find utterly counterintuitive Immanuel Kant's claim in the *Critique of Pure Reason* (p. 370) that "he knows Plato better than Plato knew himself." This is quite an extraordinary statement that relates to what the insider/outsider issue is largely all about: the question of whose interpretation is privileged. Not whose fact and whose reality is privileged but whose interpretation of matters is to be privileged and whose is not. Kant's claim seems especially counterintuitive to most people, in that they are quite sure that no one knows them better than they know themselves. In recent politicized discourse this has become the counterintuitive expression of the phrase "you have to be one to know one," "you have to be one to understand one," "you have to be one to interpret one." Such claims, as José Cabezón has recently illustrated in his 2004 article "Identity and the Work of the Scholar of Religion", are not at all necessary for cogent and adequate scholarship. But maybe Kant was not actually making such a strange claim. Perhaps what he was saying is, look, I know what has happened to Plato over the last 1,500 years and I know that things that Plato wrote kind of carelessly have become in fact terribly central, and I know that things Plato thought were terribly central sort of drifted out of discussion. Kant has the advantage of hindsight, being what fans of football in the United States call the "Monday morning quarterback" or what Canadian fans of hockey call the "armchair general manager." Kant could look back and see what happened to Plato in a way that Plato could never have known. We could use more fancy language and say that Kant could see certain aspects of thought that were latent or even unconscious in Plato, which have become terribly significant since. His claim is really not quite so dramatic a claim as it initially sounds.

With regard to the topic at hand in relation to the study of religion, I want to reformulate Kant and say that we can know Plato in a different way than he knew himself. And I want to insist that there is an advantage to having that difference. I want to claim that the James Apple of 2010 can know and relate to the ritual events in Silaunja, India, in a different way from the James Apple of 2000. This is not now a claim that garbles the insider/outsider question. Nor am I claiming that the outsider in some sense is objective and the insider in some sense is subjective. I am not claiming that an outsider by being uninterested and indifferent has objectivity. Such claims to objectivity are false and pernicious. As Smith notes in his 1990 book *Drudgery Divine: On the Comparison of Early Christianities and the Religions of Late Antiquity*, one must be aware of what Nietzsche wittily called "the myth of the immaculate perception." This is the idea that we have access to pure data or straightforward truths of observation. And we must refute the claim that somehow one guarantees objectivity merely by virtue of being outside. We could retranslate such a claim in other terms and you would see how silly it is. "Merely because I am utterly ignorant of Tibetan Buddhist culture, I am therefore utterly objective in my interpretation of it, and …" – such a claim really does not make a lot sense after all. And so the claim is not about an outsider's objectivity, it is the claim of the cognitive advantage, or the interpretative advantage, of seeing things otherwise. The nature of language and cultural observations is that we never deal directly with presences. While insiders will often claim that they have direct access to presences, I would say that we always work with re-presentations. We always deal with representations of things; we do not deal with the unmediated presence of things. This is because humans grapple with things through the medium of language and language-like things that are mediated and necessarily indirect (see Smith's *Relating Religion*, pp. 207 and 366). Ethnographies are written representations, embedded within culturally postulated experiences, within culturally postulated contexts and expectations, that a student of religion, from collegiate to professional level, needs to be reflexively aware of. This includes the representation of my presence at this ritual.

So, where does the preceding discussion lead in terms of my place in this ritual at Sujātā ten years ago? Was I an insider or outsider? Perhaps this is not an adequately formed question to answer. Rather, I would say that I was obviously inside with respect to the performance of this ritual and yet, in terms of the analysis of the ritual's occurrence and my place within it, I am outside. I have tried reflexively, with self-awareness, to come to terms with the particularity and historical context of the social formation of this ritual in its time and place. I have tried to disassemble the apparent dichotomy of "insider" and "outsider" following

Smith and reassemble an understanding of insider/outsider in terms of reciprocal relations that are constantly shifting through time and place. This is to suggest that the study of Buddhism in its practice(s) must be described and explained with an awareness of language and its representation of things, and a translation that restrains from a substantive understanding of binary structures. This suggests as well an ongoing conscientious struggle to negotiate between relations through language with an aim toward intelligibility in both understanding and explanation.

Readings

This essay brings together several issues that are of critical importance in the academic study of religion. For basic methodological principles in the study of religion, students should consult the introductory text by Malory Nye, *Religion: The Basics* (London: Routledge, 2007). In addition to the issues of accurate descriptive ethnography and ritual in the study of Buddhism, the essay addresses the theoretical controversy and debate centered on the "insider/outsider problem." This crucial theoretical and methodological issue has, until recently, been unacknowledged in mainstream academic discourse in the study of religion. Two of the foremost scholars to confront the insider/outsider problem are Jonathan Z. Smith and Russell T. McCutcheon. Smith analyzes the insider/outsider problem in a number of his books and essays in relation to discourse on the "other" in the study of religion. Smith's books that discuss the insider/outsider problem are *Drudgery Divine: On the Comparison of Early Christianities and the Religions of Late Antiquity* (Chicago: University of Chicago Press, 1990) and *Relating Religion: Essays in the Study of Religion* (Chicago: University of Chicago, 2004). Smith presented an unpublished lecture, "The Insider/Outsider Problem in the Study of Religion," at the University of Alabama, Tuscaloosa, AL on September 24, 2003 in which he addressed fundamental points of analysis that are given in the present essay. Russell T. McCutcheon has published a reader on the insider/outsider problem, *The Insider/Outsider Problem in the Study of Religion: A Reader* (New York: Cassell, 1999), which is the foremost current study and set of essays to confront this issue in the academic study of religion. McCutcheon has also published a collection of essays, *Critics Not Caretakers: Redescribing the Public Study of Religion*, Issues in the Study of Religion (Albany: State University of New York Press, 2001), which discusses this issue, as well as an essay, "'It's a Lie. There's No Truth in It! It's a Sin!': On the Limits of the Humanistic Study of Religion and the Costs of Saving Others from Themselves," *Journal of the American Academy of Religion* 74(3) (2006), pp. 720–50.

Other recent works on the insider/outsider problem in the study of religion include an essay by Gladys Ganiel and Claire Mitchell, "Turning the Categories Inside-Out: Complex Identifications and Multiple Interactions in Religious Ethnography," *Sociology of Religion* 67(1) (2006), pp. 3–21; essays by Kim Knott, "Insider/Outsider Perspectives," in John R. Hinnells (ed.), *The Routledge Companion to the Study of Religion* (London: Routledge, 2005), pp. 243–58, and "Inside, Outside and the Space In-Between: Territories and Boundaries in the Study of Religion," *Temenos* 44(1) (2008), pp. 41–66; and Faydra Shapiro "Autobiography and Ethnography: Falling in Love with the Inner Other," *Method & Theory in the Study of Religion* 15(2) (2003), pp. 187–202. Sources related to the insider/outsider issue in the study of Buddhism include an essay by José Ignacio Cabezón, "Identity and the Work of the Scholar of Religion," in José Ignacio Cabezón and Sheila Greeve Davaney (eds.), *Identity and the Politics of Scholarship in the Study of Religion* (New York: Routledge, 2004), pp. 43–59; and Oliver Freiberger, "The Disciplines of Buddhist Studies: Notes on Religious Commitment as Boundary-Marker," *Journal of the International Association of Buddhist Studies* 30 (2007) [2009], pp. 299–318. Studies related to the issues of ethnography, fieldwork, and anthropological discourse in the study of religion include Robert A. Orsi, *Between Heaven and Earth: The Religious Worlds People Make and the Scholars Who Study Them* (Princeton: Princeton University Press, 2005); Dan Sperber's "Interpretative Ethnography and Theoretical Anthropology," in *On Anthropological Knowledge: Three Essays*, Cambridge Studies in Social Anthropology 54 (Cambridge: Cambridge University Press, 1985), pp. 9–34; John Van Maanen's important book *Tales of the Field: On Writing Ethnography* (Chicago: University of Chicago Press, 1988); and George E. Marcus and Michael M. J. Fischer, *Anthropology as Cultural Critique: An Experimental Moment in the Human Sciences* (Chicago: University of Chicago Press, 1999). Important studies on Buddhism related to the subject matter in this essay include Hajime Nakamura's *Gotama Buddha: A Biography Based on the Most Reliable Texts*, trans. Gaynor Sekimori (Tokyo: Kosei Publishing Co., 2000); Ria Kloppenborg, *The Sūtra on the Foundation of the Buddhist Order (Catuṣpariṣatsūtra)* (Leiden: E. J. Brill, 1973); and Martin A. Mills, *Identity, Ritual and State in Tibetan Buddhism: The Foundations of Authority in Gelukpa Monasticism* (London: RoutledgeCurzon, 2003). Finally, a study that articulates the issues of ritual in the study of Asian religion is Lawrence A. Babb's well-received analysis "Ritual Culture and the Distinctiveness of Jainism," in John E. Cort (ed.), *Open Boundaries: Jain Communities and Cultures in Indian History* (Albany: State University of New York Press, 1998), pp. 139–62.

Author

James B. Apple is an Assistant Professor of Buddhist Studies at the University of Calgary, Alberta (Canada). His recent publications include *Stairway to Nirvāṇa* (Albany: State University of New York Press, 2008) and "Redescribing Maṇḍalas: A Test Case in Bodh Gayā, India," in Willi Braun and Russell T. McCutcheon (eds.), *Introducing Religion: Essays in Honor of Jonathan Z. Smith* (Sheffield: Equinox, 2008).

Chapter 13

Practicing the study of Buddhism

Cross-cultural journeys and renewed humanism in the history of religions

William R. LaFleur

William R. LaFleur, a distinguished professor of Japanese religion, culture, and intellectual history at the University of Pennsylvania, was working on a chapter for this volume when he passed away suddenly on February 26, 2010. Although he had not finished that essay, it later became apparent that he had recently drafted a more retrospective account of his academic career that dovetails appropriately with this volume's focus on the practice of the study of religion. The format of this chapter will necessarily depart from that of the others, with his reflections appearing in a combined narrative and discussion section. I have written this preamble and the title, which lacks LaFleur's characteristic poetry, as well as the "further readings" and "about the author" sections. The inclusion of this essay is gratifying to me as the editor of *Studying Buddhism in Practice* and as a scholar who admires LaFleur's work, but also as a friend and former PhD student of Bill LaFleur's in religious studies at the University of Pennsylvania.

William LaFleur was an exemplary mentor to generations of graduate students through his teaching and research at Princeton University, the University of California at Los Angeles (UCLA), and Sophia University in Tokyo before consecutively holding two endowed chairs at the University of Pennsylvania – most recently serving as the E. Dale Saunders Professor of Japanese Studies in the Department of East Asian Languages and Civilizations as well as a professor in the Religious Studies Graduate Group and a Senior Fellow at the Center for Bioethics. These various roles illustrate his unique range of expertise and interests. LaFleur's interdisciplinarity explored the relationships between Buddhism and Japanese culture, ranging from medieval literature and his translation and analysis of the poet-monk Saigyō to intellectual history and contemporary bioethics. Remarkably, his depth of scholarship did not suffer from this breadth of interest. Instead, his work fostered insightful synergies that culminated in groundbreaking books and international recognition including being the first non-Japanese recipient of the Watsuji Tetsurō Prize in 1989.

Representative of the diversity of William LaFleur's scholarship, former students and colleagues organized three different panels in his honor for the 2010 annual meeting of the American Academy of Religion (AAR). Jacqueline Stone, a former student of LaFleur's and an eminent scholar at Princeton University, spearheaded one of these, "The Karma of Words Remains": A Tribute to William R. LaFleur (1936–2010). I presided over this panel, which also included a presentation by Richard A. Gardner, a friend of Bill's and a fellow religious studies scholar trained at the University of Chicago who now serves as Dean of the Faculty of Liberal Arts, Sophia University in Japan. A version of the following essay by William LaFleur came to light in preparation for this commemorative panel courtesy of Richard Gardner. I am grateful to Dr. Gardner and to Mariko LaFleur, who granted permission for the posthumous use of this essay for *Studying Buddhism in Practice*. It is our hope that this chapter provides some sense of William LaFleur's impressive legacy and unique academic journey from studying under Joseph Kitagawa and Mircea Eliade to mentoring his own students, influencing several disciplines, and insightfully challenging torpid ideas or categories with fluidity and flourish. This volume would not be complete without the reflections of our friend, William LaFleur.

John S. Harding

Figure 13.1 William R. LaFleur

Narrative / discussion

by William R. LaFleur

When a scholar reaches a certain age he or she will, when being asked to write an essay, with increasing frequency be told that it would be acceptable, even maybe preferred, to prepare something "autobiographical." This is an implicit recognition that the scholar in question has already lived long enough to find it easier to be retrospective than prospective. But the invitation to be somewhat autobiographical here is one I happily accept. And I do so with an added degree of pleasure because it is accompanied by the request for some exploration of how the study of religion, especially in the mode we have often called "History of Religions" or *Religionswissenschaft*, has been an important part of my own life and work. Because I have not reflected on this in print before and because I think it an important matter – not just for me but for all of us – I am happy to do what has been requested.

I am a historian of religions. But since I am also an Asianist, I will try to connect the two. Although I was already curious about Asia during my early teenage years, my own interest in studying Japan grew greatly when I was an undergraduate student in Michigan in the mid-1950s. And that was largely because the professor I then most admired, a scholar of English literature, at times mentioned Japan during the course of his superb lectures, even when discussing Shakespeare. His experience had been that of an ordinary soldier who, having just completed his doctorate in literature at Harvard, was drafted into the American Army and in the early fall of 1945 entered a just-defeated Japan. In a letter he had written to his wife from Japan in December of that same year, one later published, Henry Zylstra expressed admiration for the people he and others had met upon entering Kyoto:

> They handed us the key to the country on a lacquered plate, and gave it with a smile. I do not know what they were thinking as they did it. But that they did it argues for an accomplishment. The reports come in: no deaths, no violence, no riots, no subversive activities, everything according to plan, hardly an incident to keep us alert.
>
> Neither the word *civilization*, nor its adjective, *civilized*, comprehends all that can be valuable in a people. But the Japanese are civilized. Japan is a civilization; it is full of human achievement as contrasted with natural wealth.

And in subsequent paragraphs Zylstra implied that, by comparison, the United States might be somewhat *less* civilized – still more dependent on its natural wealth than on its human achievement.

It was probably about 15 years later that I read Mircea Eliade's essay "History of Religions and a New Humanism," but it immediately resonated in my mind with what my earlier teacher had said and written about Japan. The "old" humanism, by re-introducing modern Europe to its own classics, had willy-nilly reinforced the notion of a "West" that dared think of itself as being incomparable in its artistic and religious creations. But Eliade, decades before the word "globalize" would become popular, wrote that serious students of humankind's religions were already uncovering a wider range of impressive human creativity, one far beyond those of the traditional "West." Surely based in part on his own experience in India in 1961 he wrote:

> Westerners are being increasingly led to study, reflect on, and understand the spiritualities of Asia and the archaic world. These discoveries and contacts must be extended through dialogues. … A true dialogue must deal with the central values in the cultures of the participants. Now, to understand these values rightly, it is necessary to know their religious sources.

My initial graduate work at the University of Michigan was in comparative literature, and it was in that context that I felt the desire to study medieval Japanese verse. But I could sense that some of the finest poetry and the Noh plays of that epoch had been profoundly shaped by the religious sensibility of their time and culture. Eliade's essay and what I had been hearing about unusual vitality in the study of religion at the University of Chicago pulled me there.

Arriving in Chicago in 1968 I found that the late Michio Araki was already there and well ahead of me in the study of religion in Japan. We were together as students in a seminar with Professor Eliade on the topic of prehistoric religions. Although I found the materials fascinating, midway through the seminar I must have begun to wonder how what I was reading about burial practices in Jōmon Japan could connect with the medieval Buddhist poet-monk Saigyō I had already chosen as the focus of my dissertation research. (Professor Joseph Mitsuo Kitagawa, my esteemed mentor at Chicago, had already approved research on Saigyō as a way in which I could combine my interest in both religion and literature.) Worried that it was a long way from Jōmon burial pottery to my poet of the twelfth century, I expressed my anxiety about this to Michio Araki one day over coffee, saying I perhaps should have trained to become a "Buddhologist." Araki's seniority to me justified what was slightly sardonic in his response. "Do you," he suggested, "really want to trade what you have here at Chicago to become a 'Buddhologist' by going somewhere else to study?"

I knew right off that Araki was right. Even though at Chicago too I would have to invest heavily in language study and scrutinize the texts relevant to my topic of study, the Chicago approach to the study of religions would never be satisfied with a narrow textual scholarship that might ignore attention to a religious or literary text's *meaning*. Studies that merely compare document A with document B will miss the value of both – and, more importantly, that of the human spiritual situation to which both are responding. "[B]y attempting to understand," wrote Eliade, "the existential situations expressed by the documents he is studying, the historian of religions will inevitably attain to a deeper knowledge of man."

This sounds right. But it was also a severe challenge. I was to discover that problem very soon when trying from my context in twentieth-century America to understand the "existential situation" of Saigyō in twelfth-century Japan. Very soon after I got into the studies by Japanese scholars who had researched Saigyō I found references to there being something "inexplicable" (*fukakai*) or "unfathomable" in the life and religious sensibility of this poet. And, I had to conclude, if Saigyō was inexplicable to the Japanese experts, he would be even more so to me! And even now after many years of study and a good deal of guidance from scholars in Japan, something in the life and religious sensibility of Saigyō remains a profound mystery to me. Even after publishing one small book on Saigyō early in my career and a larger one much later, I have a sense that something important and valuable may be eluding my grasp and I will need, if I can, to go on studying and trying to fathom the depths of this poet for the remainder of my life. My studies of Saigyō have, I know, greatly benefited not only from the mentoring by Professor Kitagawa but also from subsequent guidance by the late Kitayama Masamichi and by what in 1990 was a wonderful six-month seminar on Saigyō at the Kokubungaku shiryōkan hosted by Koyama Hiroshi. My gracious guide then was Matsuno Yōichi.

In 1983 I published a book exploring the multiple ways in which Buddhism had an impact on the literature of medieval Japan. Perhaps because that book was relatively well received, I was fortunate thereafter to have working with me a superb group of graduate students both at UCLA and the University of Pennsylvania – some focusing on religion and others on literature in medieval Japan. We who are scholars are very lucky when privileged to have excellent students.

What, however, was at work within me or in my situation that caused me to strike out in a different direction sometime in the late 1980s? I can't be sure, but know that my interest in religion in *modern and contemporary* Japan intensified around then. And at the same time I became very interested in comparing the religious sensibilities and concerns of today's Japanese with their counterparts in America – especially in areas of life where religion has an impact on ethical views and societal practices.

At that time Americans were much involved in discussing, sometimes very heatedly, the morality of abortion. And, in truth, those debates are still rather intense in the USA. I wondered to myself then how this problem was being dealt with in Japan. To my surprise at that time I could not find even a single book in Japanese on abortion and religion. So I began my own study by asking people there about it and delving into the history of how children, fetuses, and what are called *mizuko* were treated in Japan. Realizing that in America we had nothing comparable to a rite to memorialize and apologize to a *mizuko* [*mizuko-kuyō*], I recognized that, although there is something extremely sad when their life circumstances make individuals feel the need to discontinue a pregnancy, the rituals in Japan, ones often with the Bodhisattva Jizō as their focus, may provide a very humane and spiritually sensitive way of dealing with a very painful personal and social problem.

My studies of this topic became a book in 1992. Probably because this topic is such a "hot" one within American society, my book's suggestion that there may be, as discovered in Japan, an alternative way of dealing with legalized abortion but still in a spiritually sensitive and meaningful way gathered a fair amount of public attention in the USA – involving newspaper columns, radio and TV appearances, etc. And, in fact, it is the case that quite a few communities of American Buddhists have established sites and rites for what are now called "mizuko" even in English. What appears to be a growing sentiment even in America holds that, while we should not be callously indifferent to abortion (as if the fetus has no more value than an inanimate object), efforts to criminalize it remain ineffective and unjust. This whole matter, I was later pleased to discover, is very skillfully and sensitively discussed by Miho Ogino, a professor at Osaka University, in a book in Japanese. My book, *Liquid Life*, has now also been translated into Japanese and published in 2006 as *Mizuko: "Chūzetsu" o meguru Nihon bunka no teiryū*. The problem of abortion is certainly a serious one in modern societies such as our own, but I believe the religious dimension should not be ignored, even if we strive to keep it legal. And the "dialogue" among religions advocated by Eliade and our discipline can, I suggest, become concrete and useful to the wider population when we compare practices and ideas about such matters.

I should here mention that my attention to questions about the relationship between religion and ethics in Japan was greatly stimulated by a year (1985) that I spent at Tsukuba University studying the ethical thinking of Watsuji Tetsurō. I was fortunate to be sponsored by the Japan Foundation and to have my own research guided closely by the late Professor Yasuo Yuasa, Watsuji's last student and a scholar whose writings during the 1980s brought a new perspective on the importance of Watsuji as a philosopher. I have been much influenced by Watsuji's concept of ethics as the study of *aidagara* (relationality, betweenness). And I want to note that when I was studying at Tsukuba one of Yuasa's colleagues was our late friend and colleague Michio Araki. I had the privilege then and later to meet some of Araki's excellent graduate students.

My interest in religion and ethics subsequently drove me into territories I sometimes regret having ever entered. They are ones where the issues are very complicated and knowing exactly where to go is often difficult. One of these is the whole issue of brain death and organ transplants using the notion of brain death as a basis (*nōshi to zōki ishoku*). In some sense this issue is almost the opposite of the problem of abortion – at least in the sense that, although abortion debates were "hot" in the USA but initially almost non-existent in Japan, doing brain-death-based transplants had for decades been highly contested and widely debated in Japan, even though Americans, perhaps somewhat naïvely, assume that doing this type of modern medicine comes with no great religious or ethical problems. I have been working in and around this topic for more than a dozen years now, have accumulated and read a small library of books and articles in Japanese on the topic, and have completed a manuscript in English I hope to see published soon.

I confess that at the outset I was quite convinced that on this topic the Americans, accepting brain death as death and believing we have an obligation to show love to others by giving them our otherwise-useless organs, were right. Organ transplantation in America is presented to the public with a lot of rhetoric about love, about giving, about the uselessness of the corpse, and about this as a fine expression of the Jewish and Christian worldview. On the other hand, and perhaps because my college literature professor had showed its importance, I had long ago learned to give the benefit of the doubt to Japanese ideas and practices that I initially found to be perplexing or even objectionable. Snap judgments usually proved wrong – especially when made concerning such a well-read and sophisticated society.

Bit by bit I began to see the Japanese resistance to this particular form of biotechnology as ethically informed. Unlike the American tendency to look only at the good deed of the organ donor (referred to as his or her Christ-like *agapé* in the early literature on transplants), Japanese have looked at the mind and heart of the *potential recipient* and found worrisome what can be discovered there – namely, an intense desire that someone else die so that his or her organs can be "harvested" for that recipient's sake. Except for some rare and very sensitive American scholars working in this field, most ethicists, including those ready to look at perspectives from within religions, tend to ignore the terribly confused psychology and religio-moral sentiments of organ recipients. These ethicists assume that "counseling" can address recipients' concerns and focus solely on the goodness of donation and the ever-widening gap between the number of organ-desiring recipients and the number of available organs. And although the early advocates of transplantation had promised that organs would never, never! become commodities on the public market, we now find even in the USA those declaring in public that it might be a good idea to start selling and buying organs.

It interests me that, although the government of Japan during the spring of 2009 passed a law that made brain-death-based organ transplantation more easily available to a wider public, polls in Japan continue to show a fairly strong public concern about these procedures. It seems to me that any society that deems a "fresh" corpse – and maybe one that is so "fresh" that it is not yet even *fully* a corpse – to be valuable only for the "spare parts" that can be excised from it will be a society that, while able to present itself globally as having the latest in medical technology, may have thrown away what had in most societies throughout human history been the view that even a corpse is worthy of respect, not just something to be raided in a semi-cannibalistic fashion. My own study of this matter suggests that the American general public was from the very beginning somewhat deceived by transplantation promoters. They were never publicly upfront about the real condition – dead by definition but not empirically so – of the brain-dead person. They made sure that the public focused on the goodness, both ethical and spiritual, of a donor and never looked carefully at the morally debilitating desire – *yokubō* in Japanese – that a potential recipient has for another's organs. What I have found in what I read in Japanese is that our concern for the heart-as-pump (*shinzō*) ought not to blind us to what may be going on, maybe not for the good, in the heart-as-spiritual (*kokoro*) base of ourselves. I am, needless to say, very eager to see how these discussions proceed in both societies during the coming years.

One project was undertaken midway in my studies of religions, philosophies, and bioethics. It was a project that brought together scholars from Germany, Japan, and the United States for a conference at my own university, the University of Pennsylvania, for a few days in 2004. In the hope that a fearless look at some very disturbing episodes in the pasts of our respective nations might instruct us to be more prudent now in the adoption of new and easily touted biotechnologies, we explored how easily in the past some German ethicists rationalized the criminal medical research of the Nazi era, how Japanese and Americans tended to ignore or downplay what in the postwar era came to be known about the deeds of Unit 731 in Manchuria, and how American medics and politicians simply ignored what was patently unethical and even murderous in some medical experiments in their own country. Essays by important German and Japanese scholars were incorporated into a book jointly edited and published in 2007.

Today in America, in Japan, and elsewhere, people speak, often far too superficially, about "globalization" – as if that will happen automatically if our corporations go international and lots of people do lots of traveling. I am not myself convinced of that. I resist the idea that the world needs a homogenized culture, one that will be basically the same wherever you go. I hope we allow differing societies to retain their differing societal ways. But a development of the capacity to grasp why another society chooses to think and act differently from our own seems to be very important. And I think that Eliade was right to insist that religion and the variety of ways in which human beings respond spiritually to their world is central to this project. In his essay on the New Humanism he expressed the hope that the historian of religions would be at the very forefront of an emerging new level of cross-cultural dialogue. And dialogue, a dialogue not of abstractions but one that takes concrete historical situations and problems into its purview, is fundamental for the shaping of a more peaceful, sustainable world.

Readings

To read the complete 1945 letter written from Kyoto by Henry Zylstra to his wife, consult "A Letter from Japan," in his *Testament of Vision* (Grand Rapids, MI: Wm. B. Eerdmans, 1958), pp. 223–24. Mircea Eliade's "History of Religions and a New Humanism," which was featured so prominently in this essay for LaFleur's early attraction to the practice and promise of religious studies, was published by the University of Chicago Press in *History of Religions* 1(1) (Summer, 1961), pp. 1–8. LaFleur's early work on Saigyō, *Mirror for the Moon: A Selection of Poems by Saigyō (1112–1190)* (New York: New Directions Press, 1978), is significantly extended in *Awesome Nightfall: The Life, Times, and Poetry of Saigyō* (Boston: Wisdom Publications, 2003). *The Karma of Words: Buddhism and the Literary Arts in Medieval Japan* (Berkeley: University of California Press, 1983) opened new interdisciplinary ground, connected seminal literary figures to a broader medieval Buddhist worldview, and imaginatively explained diverse literary forms and Buddhist concepts in innovative and exciting ways that still exert influence today.

To read more about the ethical and spiritual dimensions of abortion in Japan, look to LaFleur's *Liquid Life: Abortion and Buddhism in Japan* (Princeton: Princeton University Press, 1992). This book is closest to the topic LaFleur had originally planned for this *Studying Buddhism in Practice* compilation, in part because of the enduring interest in this topic among diverse audiences from popular radio and television programs to Buddhist practitioners and non-Buddhists interested in a less polarizing discourse about abortion. To read more about the difficult bioethical issues surrounding organ transplant, consult Renée C. Fox and Judith P. Swazey's *Spare Parts: Organ Replacement in American Society* (Oxford: Oxford University Press, 1992). LaFleur, Gernot Böhme, and Susumu Shimazono were editors of *Dark Medicine: Rationalizing Unethical Medical Research* (Bloomington: Indiana University Press, 2007), which contains difficult but important discussions of history's lessons and the resulting critique by Japanese, German, and Jewish ethicists of biotechnology "advances" and their bioethical rationalizations. Some of LaFleur's other books are listed in the following section about the author. Although the subject matter of *Dark Medicine* can be challenging in the sense of readers' potential discomfort with unethical practices humans have inflicted upon each other, LaFleur's writing style throughout his career is unusually engaging.

LaFleur wanted his works to be accessible, and his poetic flair comes through in remarkably enjoyable reading. Rather than employing jargon designed to restrict his work to the domain of specialists, LaFleur wanted his works, including *Liquid Life*, to be read and engaged by generalist audiences as well as Japanese studies and Buddhism specialists. Moreover, he at times models the style we seek for this Studying Religions in Practice series by effectively using narrative vignettes that he then contextualizes to teach about Buddhism and the cultures of Buddhist countries. For example, I can still clearly recall when I first read his slim but excellent introductory text, *Buddhism: A Cultural Perspective* (Englewood Cliffs, NJ: Prentice-Hall, 1988). What stands out most clearly, even now, is the opening vignette, where a string of experiences in Thailand illustrate a very different orientation toward images of the Buddha which in turn sets up his explanation of cultural differences and various Buddhist developments as the tradition(s) spread through Asia. That book is one of a number of introductory texts that could be usefully paired with this compilation.

Author

William R. LaFleur was a distinguished professor of Japanese studies at the University of Pennsylvania from 1990 until the time of his unexpected death in February 2010. He earned his undergraduate degree from Calvin College, his master's degrees in comparative literature from the University of Michigan and in the history of religions from the University of Chicago, and his PhD at the University of Chicago, where he studied primarily with Joseph Kitagawa and Mircea Eliade. He held positions and trained graduate students at Princeton University and UCLA before joining the University of Pennsylvania (Penn) faculty. At Penn, he held the Joseph B. Glossberg Term Chair Professor of Humanities until 1998 and then became the E. Dale Saunders Professor in Japanese Studies. Although much of his earlier work concentrated on Buddhism and the literary arts in medieval Japan, the last two decades brought a shift to comparative ethics and especially bioethics as the focus of his writing, teaching, and public lecturing. In addition to his work in Japanese studies at Penn, he was a Senior Fellow at Penn's Center for Bioethics and commented at times on these matters in the public media.

He wrote, among other works, *The Karma of Words: Buddhism and the Literary Arts in Medieval Japan* (1983), his trailblazing interdisciplinary exploration; *Buddhism: A Cultural Perspective* (1988), an unusually nuanced introductory text; *Liquid Life: Abortion and Buddhism in Japan* (1992), his widely influential study that has even informed debates and rites for aborted fetuses beyond Japan; and *Awesome Nightfall: The Life, Times, and Poetry of Saigyō* (2003), a stimulating blend of insightful and sensitive translation in combination with illuminating analysis of the life and medieval context of the poet-monk. LaFleur also edited *Dōgen Studies* (Honolulu: University of Hawai'i Press, 1985), *Zen and Western Thought: Essays by Masao Abe* (Honolulu: University of Hawai'i Press, 1985), and co-edited the unflinching compilation, *Dark Medicine: Rationalizing Unethical Medical Research* (2007). We hope that some other of William LaFleur's nearly completed books, including his magnum opus on bioethics informed by Buddhist and Japanese cultural sensibilities as well as history's cautionary tales, will be published posthumously. In addition to the lasting influence of his scholarship, insights, and guidance, William LaFleur is dearly missed for his humor and humanity.

Index